Nie ... *rathustra*

CW01640560

Indiana Philosophical Guides

Titles in the series include:
Kant's *Critique of Pure Reason*
Douglas Burnham with Harvey Young

Derrida's *Of Grammatology*
Arthur Bradley

Heidegger's *Being and Time*
William Large

Plato's *Republic*
D. J. Sheppard

Spinoza's *Ethics*
Beth Lord

Descartes' *Meditations on First Philosophy*
Kurt Brandhorst

Husserl's *The Crisis of European Sciences and Transcendental Phenomenology*
Katrin Joost

Nietzsche's *Thus Spoke Zarathustra*
Douglas Burnham and Martin Jesinghausen

Nietzsche's
Thus Spoke Zarathustra

Douglas Burnham and Martin Jesinghausen

Indiana University Press
Bloomington and Indianapolis

This book is a publication of

Indiana University Press
601 North Morton Street
Bloomington, Indiana 47404-3797 USA

www.iupress.indiana.edu

Telephone orders	800-842-6796
Fax orders	812-855-7931
Orders by e-mail	iuporder@indiana.edu

First published in the United Kingdom by
Edinburgh University Press

© 2010 by Douglas Burnham and Martin Jesinghausen
All rights reserved

No part of this book may be reproduced or utilized in any form or by any means, electronic or mechanical, including photocopying and recording, or by any information storage and retrieval system, without permission in writing from the publisher. The Association of American University Presses' Resolution on Permissions constitutes the only exception to this prohibition.

Typeset in 11/13 pt. Monotype Baskerville by
Servis Filmsetting Ltd., Stockport, Cheshire

Manufactured in Great Britain

Cataloging information is available from the Library of Congress.

ISBN 978-0-253-35575-1 (cl.)
ISBN 978-0-253-22278-7 (pbk.)

1 2 3 4 5 15 14 13 12 11 10

Contents

Series Editor's Preface

To us, the principle of this series of books is clear and simple: what readers new to philosophical classics need first and foremost is help with *reading* these key texts. That is to say, help with the often antique or artificial style, the twists and turns of arguments on the page, as well as the vocabulary found in many philosophical works. New readers also need help with those first few daunting and disorienting sections of these books, the point of which are not at all obvious. The books in this series take you through each text step-by-step, explaining complex key terms and difficult passages which help to illustrate the way a philosopher thinks in prose.

We have designed each volume in the series to correspond to the way the texts are actually taught at universities around the world, and have included helpful guidance on writing university-level essays or examination answers. Designed to be read alongside the text, our aim is to enable you to *read* philosophical texts with confidence and perception. This will enable you to make your own judgements on the texts, and on the variety of opinions to be found concerning them. We want you to feel able to join the great dialogue of philosophy, rather than remain a well-informed eavesdropper.

Douglas Burnham

Acknowledgements

Much of the preparation and research for this book was undertaken in Nietzsche collections and libraries in Germany and Switzerland. Accordingly, we would like to thank Mr Erdman von Wilamowitz-Moellendorff; also the Klassik Stiftung, Nietzsche Kolleg and Nietzsche Haus, Weimar; and particularly Prof. Peter André Bloch and Dr Peter Villwock of the Stiftung Nietzsche Haus, Sils Maria, Upper Engadine, Switzerland. The picture of 'the Swiss Nietzsche' took on further, firmer contours thanks to Dr Alfred Heinimann, Ms Kathrin Engels, and Dr Jürg Amann. We would also like to thank the Research Fund of Staffordshire University which generously funded the archive visits. Thanks also to the British Society of Phenomenology, at whose annual conference in 2009 some of the ideas animating this commentary were given a first public airing. Finally, both authors would like to thank their colleagues friends and families for support, guidance and patience.

1. Introduction and Historical Context

Friedrich Nietzsche's life was nearly as unconventional as his writing. He was born in 1844 in Röcken, in the East of Germany. His father was a Lutheran minister, and died when Nietzsche was a child. Nietzsche, quite evidently, did not go into the ministry, to the disappointment of his family. Instead, he studied classics and philology – the historical study of language – and landed an appointment at the University of Basel (Switzerland) at the age of twenty-four.[1] He served as a medical volunteer in Bismarck's Franco-Prussian war of 1871, but was incapacitated early on (he contracted diphtheria and dysentery in the field). Also, a series of illnesses meant that he did less and less teaching until he was pensioned off early a decade later. He met with, and became part of the circle of admirers of, the composer Richard Wagner; like Wagner he was influenced by the philosophy of Arthur Schopenhauer. These two influences came together in his first book, *The Birth of Tragedy* (1872), which was simultaneously a study of the origins of Greek tragedy and a manifesto for Wagnerian music as saviour of German, and indeed European, culture. The book was not what his university and professional colleagues expected[2] – it was not scholarly philology nor, despite the presence of Schopenhauer, did it read like a conventional 'philosophical' book. In fact, no one was quite sure *what* it was. A minor controversy ensued, the result of which was that Nietzsche would not again be taken seriously in academic circles of his time (this is represented in *Zarathustra*, in Part II, Section 16). His later books sold modestly, some very badly.

This isolation from academic colleagues and from public recognition only grew worse. In the mid-1870s, Nietzsche's and Wagner's friendship disintegrated. Nietzsche's life became rather nomadic, and he lived in a series of rented rooms generally in Switzerland (in the summer months) or on the Mediterranean coast (in the winter); he also contemplated, though without much in the way of outcome, experimental forms of communal living: for example, an 'Academy of Free Spirits'. Thus the theme and narrative of wandering in *Zarathustra* is in part autobiographical. About the time he started writing *Thus Spoke Zarathustra* in the early 1880s, he met Lou Salomé, a Russian-born psychologist, poet and novelist; Salomé was also the author of one of the first books on Nietzsche. Nietzsche apparently proposed to Salomé and was rejected, and this too cast its shadow over the book he was writing. The first two parts of *Zarathustra* were published in 1883, the year of Wagner's death, and the third in 1884. The fourth part was printed privately and sent to a few of his friends in 1885. Immediately upon its completion, Nietzsche launched into a final few years of intense writing, publishing a number of now-famous books including *Beyond Good and Evil* (1886), *The Genealogy of Morality* (1887), and *Ecce Homo* (1888). In January 1889 in Turin he collapsed physically and above all mentally, and that was the end of his career. Fame began shortly after, though he was no longer able to appreciate it. He spent the rest of his life cared for first by his mother, at the family home in Naumburg, and later by his sister in a donated house in Weimar, Germany. By the time he died in 1900, Nietzsche was rapidly becoming one of the most widely read and deeply influential authors in Europe – and there was a growing 'Nietzsche cult'.

Thus Spoke Zarathustra is a difficult book for modern readers, and for a number of reasons. First and foremost, it is a complex literary text, rich with poetic passages; containing often obscure satire and parody; knitted together from allusions to hundreds of poets, philosophers, historical figures, events or places; containing sly but decidedly crude sexual humour; employing throughout a complex and evolving system of allegorical images; and all in the style of a mock-sacred text, complete with over-the-top prophetic bombast. In other words, it does not belong to any known genre; there are no pre-existing rules for how to read it. Secondly, it is not clear what we are supposed to *do* with it – beyond just deciphering it like a cryptic crossword puzzle. What would it mean to engage with this book, or to learn from it, or for it to affect us in some way? This problem is only exacerbated by the fact that it is a very personal book. Thirdly, there are a number of very suspicious or offensive sentiments in the text, especially about women (see especially Part I, Section 18). Finally, there is the infamy of Nietzsche and the celebration of his work by mid-twentieth-century fascism; this casts its shadow over his work, particularly *Zarathustra*.[3]

The Future and the Re-Imagined Past

The first thing a reader needs to understand about *Thus Spoke Zarathustra* is its relation to the *future*. It begins, curiously, with a rewriting of the past. Zarathustra is the Persian name of a religious figure who lived in what is now Iran about 1100 BC or perhaps earlier. The Greek name is 'Zoroaster' and from that comes the name of the Zoroastrian religion. Zarathustra, historically, is an important foundational figure in the history of religion, and also one of the first moral philosophers. Zoroastrian texts emphasise nature symbolism and the dualistic structure of the universe governed by the interplay of two main moral forces, the Wise Lord, or Ormazd, and the Evil Spirit, or Ahriman. For Nietzsche, the historical Zarathustra is as close as we can get to the origin of Middle Eastern and European religion, culture and morality. He represents a trace of early human thought, at the time (so Nietzsche imagines) of the turn from nomadic to settled agricultural societies. In brief, Zarathustra is the place where it all starts to go wrong. The way Nietzsche uses Zarathustra, however, contains no recognisable historical accuracy. He is no more 'real' than Virgil's shadow, Dante's guide in the *Divina Commedia*, or perhaps Jesus in the *New Testament* or Socrates in Plato's Dialogues. Thus, for example, Nietzsche does not have a problem with linking Zarathustra with Dionysus. Again, Zarathustra in Nietzsche's book finds himself already in a world of old religions, moral habits and indeed moral institutions. Nor is it a problem that this artificially historical Zarathustra expresses views about figures who lived 1,000 – indeed, 3,000! – years later. By not just offering a critique of Zarathustra, but re-imagining him as *beyond* good and evil, Nietzsche thereby sets off a kind of historical earthquake under every religion and morality that followed (that is, all of them: the *Old Testament*, Socrates and Plato, Jesus and so forth). In other words: Zarathustra is an allegory. An allegory of how the history of morality and religion could and should have been, and indeed can and will be *in the future*.[4]

Zarathustra as Nietzsche's Future

Thus Spoke Zarathustra is the first book of the later Nietzsche: it sketches out the future direction of his thought, and contains much of the material for his later projects, even though not all of it was used. Certainly, it is the first of his books that are constructed, from beginning to end, with the ideas of will to power and eternal recurrence at their centre.

In *Ecce Homo* Nietzsche gives an account of how he arrived at the two most obvious elements of *Zarathustra*: the notion of eternal recurrence and the figure of Zarathustra. The former apparently 'came to him' on a walk around lake Silvaplana near Sils Maria, Switzerland, in August 1881.[5] Of *Zarathustra* he claims that he was 'conquered' by the idea in 1882 on a walk amongst pine trees in the bay of Rapallo. Both accounts need to be qualified. Of the notion of eternal recurrence it could be argued that Nietzsche was thinking about it in one form or another as early as *The Birth of Tragedy*. There already he identified eternal return as the teaching of the Greek Dionysian Mysteries.[6] With their probable theme of regeneration and rebirth, the classical Mysteries were a regular subject of his lectures in Basel. The suddenness of revelation might refer more to Nietzsche recognising the significance of eternal recurrence as an integral part of his own thinking than to the fact that he 'discovered' it there and then by the lakeside. A similar story unfolds regarding the figure of Zarathustra. Nietzsche had in his possession the 1858 translation into German of Ralph Waldo Emerson's first two series of *Essays*, which is still in his personal reference library in Weimar.[7] This is one of Nietzsche's most cherished books, as the overabundance of reading traces (different styles of handwriting point to different periods of use), work notes, poem drafts, etc., demonstrates. It is also from Emerson's *Essays* that the initial idea for the Zarathustra project is most likely to have been derived (including the notion of the 'Overman': Emerson calls one of his essays '*Die Höhere Seele*', 'The Over-Soul', in the original).[8] On page 351 Nietzsche comments in the margin next to a sentence about Zoroaster: 'That's it!' ('*Das ist es!*'). Nietzsche and his contemporaries were acquainted with Zoroastrianism because some of the key historical texts were published and translated in the nineteenth century. Indeed, Nietzsche knew Hermann Brockhaus who put together an edition of the *Vendidad Sade* in 1850. The revelatory moment near Rapallo therefore may have been one where it became clear to Nietzsche what to do with this knowledge from Emerson and elsewhere – how to use Zarathustra as the central allegory of an allegorical narrative.

It is widely agreed that the text of *Thus spoke Zarathustra* works on four main philosophical ideas. They are listed below.

1. The 'will to power': this had been already introduced as a theoretical motif in *The Gay Science* (1881), but it is featured more prominently

here than elsewhere, and is never explicated in greater detail anywhere else in Nietzsche's published work. We will discuss this idea in detail in the commentary on Part I, Section 4. Suffice it to say that will to power would appear to be an ontological account of what life is, at bottom, which emphasises relationality, dynamism and situatedness. Nietzsche employs this idea in order to replace or redefine more traditional notions like soul, substance, intention, instinct and will (in an ordinary sense of that word). From out of the idea of will to power also come the notions of 'perspective' and 'interpretation'.

2. Platonism and Christianity: Nietzsche's critique of modernity is focused on his critiques of the continuing and often surreptitious influence of Platonism and Christian morality. The idea here is that these are not just ideas, but modes of human life – thus they cannot be analysed simply as ideas, but rather as cultural and ultimately *physiological* aspects of historical human life. These critiques, and to a lesser degree also his new methodology of critique ('genealogy'), are featured in *Zarathustra*. The project of re-evaluating moral values is one of the most consistently pursued and best developed themes of Nietzsche's philosophy.

3. 'Eternal recurrence': What we learn about eternal recurrence in *Zarathustra* is most of what there is in the published writings (there is a considerable body of additional comment in Nietzsche's notebooks[9] and in the last poetry, the *Dionysus Dithyrambs*). Introducing eternal recurrence in a paragraph is tougher even than explaining will to power – so difficult in fact that it takes Zarathustra half the book just to summon up the courage to try. Here we shall simply say that it is an ontology of time's cyclicality, and is seen as a kind of test or challenge of one's health, strength, honesty and nobility (see our discussion in Part III, Section 2).

4. The 'overhuman': The overhuman ties in especially with the utopian and futural dimensions of the text. However, Nietzsche does not pick up the overhuman in later work; instead we get similar notions under different names (the 'coming philosophers', for example, in *Beyond Good and Evil*). The overhuman, however, rather than being an independent *substantive* concept of the text, is a kind of sign-post (pointing up and forward, no doubt) for philosophy and for the human species, or even a methodological device. For these reasons, it is not surprising that it changes so much and goes by many different names. The overhuman is an allegory of that form of human life that has 'cleansed' itself, in body and spirit, of Platonism and Christianity, understood itself and the

world through the notion of will to power, and aligned itself right down to the living body both to the nature of life as will to power and to the thought of eternal recurrence.

Zarathustra, the Future and the Philosophy of History

Like all of Nietzsche's books, there is something of a manifesto about *Thus Spoke Zarathustra*. The question the book asks is: what does the future look like, and how can it be achieved? The starting point is that the overhuman is not accomplished yet, he remains an ideal, and this ideal is the 'gift' that Zarathustra is bringing to the rest of us. However, the figure of Zarathustra is only one device amongst many to draw us in. A kaleidoscope of techniques and devices is employed to open up the future as an ideal and as a moment – to Nietzsche it seems extremely near – of revolutionary change. Nietzsche thinks of this change of direction in history not so much as political than as *cultural* and indeed biological.

The future is being held back by contemporary forces; we require a critical assessment of what has gone wrong in the past to understand the present. This is where Platonism and Christianity come into play. Nietzsche thus still in a sense operates under the ancient motto (of Cicero): *historia magistra vitae* – history as life's teacher. In the end he is an heir to the legacy of German historical thought since Winckelmann, Herder and Hegel (the 'founding father' of modern source-based historiography, instigator of the German Historical School, the eminently influential Leopold von Ranke [1795–1886], went to the same school as Nietzsche), even though Nietzsche was fonder of the Swiss variety of contemporary historical thinking than the German; he detested the tendentious official historians of the Bismarck regime, such as Heinrich von Treitschke, but greatly admired Jacob Burckhardt in particular. However, Nietzsche's stance towards history is in the main a critical one;[10] he is constantly battling against much contemporary historical thinking which we can summarise under the category of 'historicism'. The historicist is a 'positivist' historian who reconstructs the past literally, factually, from 'sources'. He wants to capture the past 'as it has really happened' ('*wie es wirklich gewesen ist*': Ranke), rather than thinking about the impact the past has – and will have through his intervention! – on the future. Nietzsche sees this as a flawed, uncritical way of tackling history by means of a seemingly disinterested study of the past, but one that has a hidden agenda, especially when the Hegelian notion of absolute progress is still implied. In the second of the four essays of *Untimely Meditations*, Nietzsche's second publication, he delivers the outlines of a critique of historicist attitudes towards the past.[11] As the book of a philosophically minded historian, *Zarathustra* represents a step forward in Nietzsche's own historical thinking and methodology. Drawn from critique, in *Zarathustra* he provides us with a working alternative to historicist optimism: the theorem of eternal recurrence makes it possible, as we shall see (in the commentary on Part III, Section 2.2) to constitute the past without making concessions in any way to historicist approaches. Nietzsche is one of the first to have addressed the pitfalls of historicism, before it was later identified more widely (for example, by Walter Benjamin, the Frankfurt School and others) as one of the cardinal sins of nineteenth-century thought.

What makes Nietzsche desire the revolutionary moment of future change so urgently? In Nietzsche's view, man is a strange hybrid between biological organism and conscious 'free will'. His past history was one of suffering because these elements have not been successfully, and productively, integrated as they seemed to be in, for example, Greek mythology[12] and art. The two chief causes of this 'modern' and 'decadent' suffering are Platonism and Christianity – modern philosophy and morality. There we can see evidence that in Western culture human nature has become alienated from its natural base, and human faculties turned overspecialised and fragmented. In Nietzsche's view, Platonism and Christianity are linked. In the Preface to *Beyond Good and Evil*, he calls Christianity 'Platonism for the People': the Socratian questing for the perfection of knowledge has its equivalent in Christian striving for virtue. Under both systems humanity is made physically and spiritually sick through being conditioned to denigrate the natural basis of life. The 'cultured' humanity of Nietzsche's own time is either completely hollowed out (see Part II, 'On the Land of Culture') or completely solipsistically involved with itself: emptied of meaning, modern humans have lost all contact with life. There is something of the old Rousseauian formula still reverberating in Nietzsche's version of cultural anthropology, that man was born free and his entering into civilisation and progressing through history amounts to his enslaving. However, unlike Rousseau Nietzsche does not romanticise the 'original' state, and certainly does not advocate any kind of return to the past. Since Nietzsche was, as we shall see, influenced by evolutionary thought, the overhuman is a kind of evolutionary next stage. It follows that we moderns could no more return to some ancient way of living and thinking than a dolphin could go trotting about on the savannah.

The Text of *Zarathustra* as Vision of Future Writing

The future orientation of this book also manifests itself on the level of the writing. In this way, it can be argued, more than the protagonist(s) that feature in it (Zarathustra, Dionysus, the animals, the different other voices that sometimes take over), it is the text itself that is the main activist. Not a sentence goes by without at least one of four types of textual 'play'. These four are allusion, satire, symbol and allegory. In Nietzsche's hands, allusion and satire are closely linked. The text is alive with a multitude of references to literary, philosophical, musical, political and painterly objects of the past history of Western (and Eastern) art. At the same time it very often imitates or parodies the styles of these objects. Nietzsche is a master of hiding his sources: he is playing hide and seek here with the reader. Our commentary tries to pick up on some of these references and formal and stylistic intricacies, even though it is, of course, not possible to deal with them all. Translators generally pick out in footnotes the most important allusions; we here have identified a few others. Maybe you will spot still more! One of the difficulties of reading *Zarathustra* is that it is a visionary text that makes use of a network of symbols and a series of allegorical passages to realise its futuristic potential: it is deliberately condensed in its meaning. A single sentence stands in for the work of many pages. An added complication for the reader is that the text is constructed in more than one mode of symbolic condensation. We can distinguish between two main ones: on the one hand, there is the precision of a meticulously constructed system of images that fit together ever more tightly over the length of the writing, built from what we could call the text's leitmotifs, such as the camel, child, lion and many others. On the other hand, there are moments of poetic exaltation: for example, sections of seemingly disembodied voices inserted from time to time and speaking in a high lyrical tone from the inside of an unidentifiable subject, or emotional responses to situations or ideas. Everything has meaning; often more than one meaning.

Here, we argue that much of what appears to be straightforward symbolism in *Zarathustra* (for example, the sun) should actually be understood as allegorical, because of the changing contexts and variety of ways in which Nietzsche uses symbols as leitmotifs. Allegory is close to 'parable' as in the stories of the Bible, particularly the *New Testament*, and often instructs and uses personifications to get across a particular doctrine or moral message.[13] Nietzsche's use of allegory has greater complexity and flexibility compared to conventional literary symbolism. In allegory, an operation of artificial mapping has taken place. The literal meaning of the artistic ingredients and the 'hidden' background meaning with which they are invested are bound together.[14] There is a similar mapping in a symbol, but there the reference to meaning is more transparent, stable, less sensitive to the context, and simpler (for example, the Christian cross stands for holy trinity and crucifixion). By contrast, allegories are 'unorganic' or artificial, they develop across texts (syntagmatically) rather than immediately gesturing to a meaning outside. In Nietzsche's allegory, meaning has to be pieced together from the various, not always consistent and sometimes changing, elements that have been compiled into them. Thus, allegories bear on their sleeves the fact that they are the products of intellectual construction.[15] Allegorical writing wants to let the reader know that it is artificial. Nietzsche is trying here to represent a whole system of philosophical ideas by linking them together in allegorical form – and not just 'represent', but make the allegory part of the force of the writing that encourages transformation in the reader. Reading is thus one of what we could call 'practices of internalisation' by which the spiritual can reorganise the body. The most important and most complex allegory in the text is the figure of Zarathustra himself. Nietzsche wants us to remain aware that as a literary figure, and even as a historical figure, Zarathustra is a construct.

Zarathustra is thus in theme and form among the nineteenth century's most avant-garde books, and it exerted an important influence over the course of twentieth-century modernist literature. As original and revolutionary as it is, though, it did not emerge from a vacuum. Throughout the commentary we will draw attention to various precedents for the way in which the book is written, as well as what it has to say. One precedent needs to be mentioned up front: Richard Wagner. Wagner was the late nineteenth-century Germany's most famous and influential composer, and the young Nietzsche was one of his circle of admirers. Both Wagner and Nietzsche were heavily influenced by Schopenhauer's conception of music as the direct expression of the underlying will of the world. Nietzsche in fact fancied himself a bit of a composer and was indeed a talented amateur.[16] Knowing his limitations as a composer, Nietzsche sought to find a mode of poetic and narrative writing that would serve the same purpose, that could slice through layers of culture, language and habit in order to present the yearning of will.[17]

The task of attaining in musicalised writing what Wagner achieved in opera became especially urgent after the mid-1870s when Nietzsche came to two conclusions about Wagner: first, that far from being a revolutionary figure, he was yet another anti-Semitic puppet of Bismarck's new nationalist German state; and then, a few years later, that the religious imagery in *Parsifal* (Wagner's last opera) represented a capitulation to Christianity.[18] Nietzsche broke acrimoniously with Wagner; after that he had to go it alone. However, Nietzsche was (and forever remained)[19] an enthusiastic admirer of Wagner's opera *Tristan and Isolde*. In addition, he never lost his conviction in some of Wagner's aesthetic concepts, such as the above mentioned *Leitmotiv* or *Gesamtkunstwerk* ('all-inclusive work of art'), by which Wagner meant the total syn-aesthetic fusion of music, drama and poetry in opera:

> the great all-in-one work of art which must bring all the artistic media together, consuming each, as it were, in the interest of their common aim, i.e., the direct depiction, without concession, of perfect human nature – this great comprehensive work of art cannot be understood by the artist as a random achievement, but as the necessary collective achievement of men of the future.[20]

For more on this, see our note on Nietzsche, Music and Language, with the commentary on Part II, Section 17.

Zarathustra is the most impatient of all of Nietzsche's texts in its intensity of evoking a moment of revolutionary change. The text agonises over how close the possibilities are for human advancement, and it brings us again and again right up against this moment of transformation. One of the reasons for *Zarathustra's* fictionalised, allegorical account is that in this form the visionary intentions can be driven to the very limits of poetic intensity. Nietzsche thinks of this moment as one in which humanity is taking charge of itself for the first time in its history: finally we are taking 'fate into our own hands'. However, in the first three originally published parts, the text stops just short of realising the prophesied moment. In fact, Zarathustra, the book's prophetic hero, throughout only *foretells* but never *reaches* it himself. It is only in one short section towards the end, Part IV, Section 10, called 'At Midday', that the text succeeds in *pretending* that this utopian moment is really happening. There, the world is finally perfect – briefly. In a short sneak-preview of the future we are urged to jump across the divide and ahead in time to witness this moment: one of absolute identity of being, at one with itself in human experience. This moment too, however, dissolves into self-mockery.

About *Beyond Good and Evil* Nietzsche says that the 'book is in essence a *critique of modernity*, including modern science, modern art – even modern politics – along with indications of an opposite type who is as un-modern as possible, a noble affirmative type'(*Ecce Homo*, p. 135): the overhuman (by a different name) can there only be glimpsed as an 'indication'. All of Nietzsche's writings are built around this contrast between critique (of past and contemporary culture) and affirmation (of some future type of human being). Most of his writings foreground the critique and these are the most conventionally acceptable ones. Although little of Nietzsche's writing could be mistaken for conventional philosophical prose, these critical works are recognisably academic and follow the conventions of discursive argumentation more. They only provide 'indications' of something entirely different. However, Nietzsche's new innovative approach to writing philosophy, much more challenging to the reader, comes into its own when the positive, affirmative elements are more in the foreground. Particularly in his poetry and in *Thus Spoke Zarathustra*, Nietzsche believes he has accomplished a fragile form of unity between historical critique and supra-historical affirmation. In *Zarathustra*, the presentation of the affirmative type goes beyond that of a mere 'indication'. Here, the cultural critique leads directly into the new ideas and with them into a new form of symbolic expression. After *Zarathustra*, with *Beyond Good and Evil*, Nietzsche's writing returns again to the more 'traditional' style he had used throughout the 1870s. In Nietzsche's eyes, *Zarathustra* is unique, because it manages to urge upon its reader a prophecy of a future world that emerges seamlessly from the critique of the past and of the contemporary world.

Zarathustra and the Shape of Things to Come

The trailblazing *Thus Spoke Zarathustra* ends the nineteenth and begins the twentieth century – nearly two decades early. By this we mean that the text is ahead of its time, and indeed both as a philosophical work and as an extraordinary piece of experimental writing, it shapes and initiates the time that it is ahead of – exactly as Nietzsche thought, though not necessarily in the *ways* that he might have hoped. The reception history of the text is unfortunately characterised not only by the productive impulses it sent out, but also by considerable bafflement which led to severe misrepresentation. It is tempting to simplify the learning process the text wants to instigate by unravelling its tight form-content package and reducing its message to a few practically meaningful imperatives for political action. The text's specific use in the hands of the Nazis and Italian fascists is perhaps a less thorny problem than it is often made out to be: on the evidence of our reading of the decisive sections, especially Part I, Section 10, 'On Warriors and Warrior Peoples', it is out of the question to regard the text's use as a legitimising device in fascist propaganda as anything but blind misappropriation. This gross political misrepresentation of Nietzsche's aims and intentions has obstructed the realisation of the value of his work and generally overshadowed the history of its subsequent reception. After that it was harder to see Nietzsche's writings, particularly *Zarathustra*, as the paradigmatic, value-creating works that they are.

The following are some of the key areas of *Zarathustra's* impact. First, Zarathustra might be called the patron saint of the European Art Nouveau movement between 1890 and 1910. *The Birth of Tragedy* and *Zarathustra* seemed like manuals for new art and literary practice, and showed hitherto hidden powers at work in the human psyche and within the broad domain of cultural history. Both pointed beyond the demands and conventions of representation in nineteenth-century realism or naturalism. What was needed were new styles forged from the experience of an inner reality that no longer conformed to what was openly visible, well structured and ordered. From Munich to Brussels, Darmstadt to Vienna, Weimar to Paris, Zarathustra's presence can be felt in the new symbolist styles, often combining the youthful and prophetic with the monumental (the German term for Art Nouveau is *Jugendstil*: youth style), in writing, painting, musical composition and design. Hofmannsthal, Verhaeren, Schnitzler, Olbrich, George, Rilke, Count Kessler, Debussy, Musil, Simmel: these are some of the names who form part of the first wave of artists and writers on the threshold of the twentieth century who were greatly inspired by this book.[21]

Secondly, in addition to the above influences, which ushered in early modernism, *Zarathustra* 'foreshadows' many other developments in high modernist European culture[22] of the first half of the coming century. It opens up literary pathways into experimental twentieth-century writing in areas such as epiphany, stream-of-consciousness, montage, and 'making strange'. The book leads the way into psychological and literary investigations of inner inspirational states of mind. A key element of *Zarathustra's* notion of eternal recurrence – the physical experience of a momentary fulfilment of time as an elevation of the Self in an ecstatic body experience – is the theoretical blueprint for a new twentieth-century aesthetic philosophy.[23] Thus, for example, James Joyce's work-in-progress project, started in 1905 and centred on Stephen Dedalus, is based on insights into epiphany.[24] *Zarathustra*'s persistent use of 'stream-of-consciousness' discourse was not fully realised in European (and American) writing as a 'mainstream' technique before the 1920s, in Joyce's *Ulysses* and the works of, Woolf, Eliot, Proust, Faulkner and Dos Passos. The main principle of narrative organisation in *Zarathustra* is 'montage'. It is as if the whole of the text had been cut up and edited back together into a sequence of discontinuous segments. This is a technique essential to the requirements of film, and one that Bertolt Brecht used from 1918 onwards, the year of his first play, *Baal*, as a structuring device of what he later called 'Epic Theatre'. Another astonishing feature that links *Zarathustra* especially with Brecht is the idea of 'rendering strange' or *Verfremdung* which we can see being used extensively both in *Zarathustra*'s allegorical methodology and in Epic Theatre. This means to take persons or objects out of historical or conventional contexts, thereby making both the thing and the context stand out. As we have seen, this separation of context from phenomenon is the point of the figure of Zarathustra himself, who has the historicity of context removed from him.

Finally, *Zarathustra* has left a clearly marked trail in twentieth-century European cultural criticism and philosophy.[25] For example, Walter Benjamin's theory of allegory as developed in *The Origins of German Tragedy* follows on from Nietzsche even though Benjamin hesitates to acknowledge his inheritance. The same is to a certain extent true with regard to Critical Theory, particularly that of Theodor Wiesengrund-Adorno whose style of explication owes much to Nietzsche's and who is equally reticent about admitting his lineage.[26] More openly visible and acknowledged is the indebtedness to *Zarathustra* in the works of Freud and especially C. G. Jung, who himself traces back to *Zarathustra* his theory of archetypes and the collective unconscious.[27] (Jung's adaptation in turn has had an enormous influence on twentieth-century culture, traceable as diversely as in the works of the Warburg Circle, Eugene O'Neill, Arnold Toynbee, and David Lynch.) Philosophers such as

Martin Heidegger were fascinated by the way Nietzsche linked concepts of existence with time;[28] Nietzsche's wide-ranging critique of the philosophy of identity in favour of a philosophy of difference and relation is important for the French philosopher Gilles Deleuze;[29] Nietzsche's theories on history and power, and the relation to mental health, and his methodologies for an investigation of culture have been taken on board in French post-structural psychology and philosophy, most thoroughly by Michel Foucault,[30] and in *Anti-Oedipus* by Gilles Deleuze and Félix Guattari;[31] Nietzsche's textual experimentation and philosophy of language are important for Jacques Derrida;[32] the new conception he offers to hermeneutics is explored by the Italian philosopher Gianni Vattimo.[33]

About This Book

So, then, a new commentary. There have been others, and good ones,[34] but often these are highly sophisticated and thus perhaps not as helpful to a relatively new reader of Nietzsche, to someone who just needs some sense of direction. We are aware, however, that Nietzsche's book – more than any other perhaps in the history of philosophy – cannot simply be explicated. Even the ideal of a 'neutral' reading seems inappropriate. To say anything about *Zarathustra* is to interpret it. Thus we are 'pushing' a certain way of conceiving what Nietzsche is up to, one that is in certain respects novel, and we have sketched out the main lines of our interpretation above. We must also point out that our book is not intended to substitute for *Thus Spoke Zarathustra* itself. If you read the commentary *instead* of Nietzsche, it will not help you much, because so much of the job we have set ourselves here is about cross-referencing various images so as to construct these elaborate allegorical systems that we discussed above.

2. A Guide to the Text

Prologue

Section 1

Section 1 of the Prologue is a virtual reprint of the last section of the first edition of *The Gay Science*; the previous section of which was Nietzsche's first major statement on eternal recurrence. Here, this first section contains many of the key images in the book, which tend to come in pairs of images or concepts: sun and earth (here the cave), surface and depth, day and night, valleys and mountains, eagle and serpent. We will examine another of these pairings shortly: going over and going under. Zarathustra addresses the sun. The metaphor of sun, in opposition to darkness (here, darkness of the cave, of the underworld, of that which awaits illumination), is common in Nietzsche, from his first publications on. Of course, this is an old metaphor: we talk about 'enlightenment', 'seeing the truth', 'clear light of reason', or 'being in the dark' and so forth. Normally, it is epistemological in nature, concerning the acquisition of knowledge; here the emphasis is on the ethics of giving and receiving, and on the ontology of that which *must* give or must take. The sun is the 'overrich' star, burdened to overflowing with its illumination. It does not rest happy in itself, but its happiness is *relational*, and consists in giving (here, to Zarathustra and his eagle and serpent) who, in turn, bless it. Zarathustra says that, like the sun, he has become overburdened with wisdom and needs others to receive it; specifically, as we shall see, he needs the human to receive that the human might go over and under, sun-like, in reaching the overhuman. Among the most famous uses of the metaphors of sun, darkness and illumination are Plato's analogies of the sun and the cave.[1] In the latter, Plato compares ordinary human life with living in a dark cave, seeing only the shadows cast by a fire, and so unaware of what it is like outside the cave that these humans consider this viewing of shadows to be all of reality. In fact, it is doubly false: viewed is not only a shadow, but also a shadow of a deficient form of illumination (fire, instead of the sun). The aim of the philosopher is to leave the cave, acquire insight, and then descend again to try to 'enlighten' those still in the cave. The similarities with Zarathustra are striking: to acquire wisdom Zarathustra has indeed gone upwards (into the mountains), and then he will descend again. However, Zarathustra's wisdom was acquired not in and because of the sun, but in a cave. Zarathustra's wisdom is an elevated darkness, similar to the sun only in its overrichness (this image too is from Plato) and in the need to bestow. The sun is a friend or colleague to Zarathustra, something familiar (in the German the use of the familiar mode of address supports this), rather than a transcendent source of knowledge.

The passage (and the rest of the book) is full of word play on *untergehen* ('to go under'). The term has a number of meanings. Most straightforwardly, it means 'to descend or sink' including the setting of the sun. But it also means 'to be destroyed'. This becomes important later, insofar as the human in Zarathustra (and others) must destroy itself so that the overhuman can emerge. Thus, Nietzsche plays with the paradox that one must go 'under' in order to go 'over' like the sun in its perennial cycle; Zarathustra wants or needs to destroy himself as the wise *hermit*, he needs to move on from his years alone in the mountains. Here, we become aware of the parallel with Christ (if the going into the wilderness idea had not already done so). Christ is the God-become-man; Zarathustra is the elevated, wise hermit who 'goes down' among humans. However, there is an all-important difference. God's love of human beings which leads to the sacrifice of Christ that they might be saved is entirely different to Zarathustra's love of the human. For Zarathustra, the human is to be loved only insofar as it can 'go under' in order to 'go over', not insofar as it can be 'saved'. The complex and shifting inter-relationship between these two images is typical of the pairs of images discussed above. (On a *methodological* sense of 'going down', see *Beyond Good and Evil*, section 26.)

So, Zarathustra has developed himself to a point where he is overfull of wisdom and needs to bestow it. The need to bestow is not just because of the excess, as if Zarathustra would just burst if he did not get rid of some. If you give away wisdom you do not become less wise, after all. Rather, there is something about the nature of the wisdom itself – and especially something about the type of human being Zarathustra has become through acquiring such wisdom – that makes necessary the relationality that we discussed above, and thus makes it 'overfull'. The theme of 'bestowing' returns at the end of Part I, Section 22 'On the Bestowing Virtue'.

Section 2

The first person Zarathustra encounters is another hermit, a holy man. This is a point of transition: Zarathustra, having descended, is halfway to man; the holy man halfway to God. The holy man recognises him from ten years previously, but also sees that he has been transformed. Now Zarathustra brings fire and not ash, moves like a dancer, has become a child, is free of disgust – all of these are important ideas or images throughout the rest of the book. Zarathustra and the holy man are mirror images of each other. The holy man too has undergone a transformation. He went into the forest out of an excessive love of human beings, but now he only loves God; human beings are 'too incomplete' or 'too unfulfilled' (*zu unvollkommen*). From the religious point of view, human beings are either worthy of love and worth saving (the holy man's initial position) or unworthy because insufficiently god-like, and thus one should just stay away. (This holy man anticipates the 'voluntary beggar', one of the 'superior humans' in Part IV.) The holy man believes that his hermit life has given him a holy innocence like a bear or bird (although when Zarathustra offers a 'present' he is willing enough to be counted among the humans!); helping human beings could only mean relieving them of suffering. Zarathustra cannot agree with any of these sentiments. Humans are worthy of love only insofar as they are themselves the instrument by which the overhuman can be achieved.

Zarathustra says 'I love human beings', but then corrects himself or elaborates upon that with 'I bring human beings a present'. What is significant here is that, immediately after we get independent confirmation that Zarathustra has been transformed by his ten years in the cave, we discover that Zarathustra is *still developing*, his transformation incomplete. He is, in fact, making errors of judgement, and learning about the task he has set himself. The growth of Zarathustra makes this book into something akin to a novel (rather than, say, just a set of teachings) – specifically a *Bildungsroman* (a novel dramatising education or maturation) of a late eighteenth or nineteenth-century type. Moreover, the course of development carries enormous philosophical significance. Nietzsche substitutes a logical development of ideas with a narrative of the development of a form of life.

Notice in passing the reference to living in the sea. This is in part Nietzsche warding off misunderstanding of his own metaphor: there is nothing intrinsically valuable about the idea of physical 'height', of being in the mountains. The depths of the sea can also be a place of wisdom. Indeed, we have already observed that by residing in a mountain cave, Zarathustra's wisdom is elevated darkness. Zarathustra tends to use the image of height as either an image of development or striving for ideals ('ascent'), or of a state of nobility or health ('flying', 'looking down'); while the image of depth is an image of knowledge or insight, discovery of the nature of existence, or also self-discovery – and also destruction ('going under'). These 'directions' agree well with the symbolic meanings of eagle and serpent. Both depth and height are distinguished by being away from the *surface* (the flat lands, places of towns, cities, agriculture, commerce and industry); they are both places to which the surface denies any validity. Moreover, here the sea is a reference to evolutionary history: evolutionary theory suggested in the nineteenth–century that sea animals gradually evolved to live on land, to do so they had to create new limbs to bear their own weight. The evolutionary metaphors will be prominent in the next section, and generally Nietzsche's account of human psychology and development owes much (although often in bizarre ways) to nineteenth-century biology. While the holy man sees the life in the sea, borne up by the water, as ideal, and the move to dry land as a burden, Zarathustra gladly takes on this burden in the interests of promoting new developments in evolution. Again, they are mirror-images.

When the two part, Zarathustra to continue his 'going under' to the human, Zarathustra speaks 'to his heart'. This is a classical figure, meaning an inner wordless voice. However, it suggests also that Zarathustra is not one, but *many* (and later in the book we get various inner conversations between 'I' and 'me' or 'self' and 'soul', and indeed between Zarathustra and female personifications of virtues, wisdom, life and so forth). To his heart, then, he confesses surprise that the holy man has not heard that '*God is dead!*'. This infamous expression, which Nietzsche first used in his previous book (*The Gay Science*, Book IV), is subject to many interpretations. If, of course, we assume the expression means the same thing as it would mean if we said, for example, 'Nietzsche is dead', then the inference would be unavoidable that God once lived. This is not what Nietzsche means. God never was, if by that we mean as a kind of real and transcendent entity independent of the human. Instead, we must understand God as a function, or an effect, of a certain mode of human life. 'God is dead' means that something has changed in the human domain, such that the God-effect is no longer produced or at least is no longer fundamental or important. Nietzsche is thus referring, for example, to modern ethics or physics which appear to be able to discuss the value or nature of things without reference to God's will or God's goodness; still more he is referring to the phenomenon of nihilism (again affecting the nineteenth-century) which is the 'belief' in the utter valuelessness of all values and beliefs. (The holy man, in his words, reflects such God-less beliefs – though he does not recognise the fact.) Notice that the death of God is not an event in the ordinary sense of something that could be assigned a place or date. Rather, the death of God is an 'event' that could characterise the mode of life and thought of an exceptional human being at any historical juncture. It is just that in Nietzsche's nineteenth century the conditions are such that God-is-dead-ness is an epidemic, and thus also the conditions are right for a kind of revolution in thought and life. There are at least two philosophical problems associated with the theme 'God is dead'. The first is that of nihilism, mentioned above. In Nietzsche's thought, nihilism is a constant temptation, but one that must be overcome. The second problem is that the 'shadow' of God is still cast over everything: the conception of the human, of nature, of history and of value. This idea of 'shadow' is from *The Gay Science*, 109 and 125. In the latter of those sections, the 'madman' carries a lamp in the daytime (the allusion is to Diogenes of Sinope). The madman does this, Nietzsche implies, so as to illuminate those things that, even in the daytime, are still under the shadow of God. So, for example, in physics Nietzsche detects as still operative concepts whose only legitimacy is theological (see our discussion of Part I, Section 4). In *Zarathustra*, such ideas are explored in, for example, Part III, Section 8 and Part IV, Section 6. A thorough critique of concepts and values is required to 'de-deify' nature and our conception of the human.

Section 3

Zarathustra arrives at the first town, at the edge of the forest. A crowd in the market has come for a 'rope-dancer' (a tightrope walker, but the image of *dancing* is important).[2] He addresses them, entirely unsuccessfully. Again, from this first attempt to teach, he learns something, and his approach changes (in Prologue, Section 9). The speech that follows in Prologue, Section 3 is our first sustained instance of the style in which much of the book will be written. This is a highly imagistic language, in a series of relatively short verses or aphorisms. A storehouse of images is being built up which will be used repeatedly throughout the book, with a partially context-dependent meaning and with a gradual evolution of philosophical content. We discuss this style at greater length in Part I and in our note on Nietzsche, Music and Language (see Part II, Section 17). The speech in section 3 is the first part of a three-part teaching. The first part, here, concerns the overhuman and the 'great despising'; the second (Prologue, Section 4) concerns those who in some way are 'on the way' to, or preparing the way for, the overhuman; the third (Prologue, Section 5) concerns those 'last humans' that remain behind.

'I teach to you the overhuman (*Übermensch*).' This term was originally translated into English as 'superman', not in itself a bad translation; 'superman' thus entered the language, though rarely with authentic Nietzschean connotations. 'Over-' is to be preferred mainly because it echoes the going up/going under language pattern, also because it is entirely possible that Nietzsche was inspired by his reading of Emerson's *Essays*, which include the famous essay 'The Over-soul'. Moreover, '-human' is preferred first of all since unlike in English, there is nothing in the German term that implies or entails a gender, and, secondly, because Zarathustra is not speaking primarily of an individual or set of individuals, but of a transformation of the mode of existence of the human species. The biological/evolutionary language used here suggests that the overhuman is a real possibility of species development. However, Nietzsche at the end of this section speaks of the overhuman as a sea, lightning or madness that might in some way change the human. This suggests that the overhuman is less a biological type to be reached than an ideal of the leaving behind of types, of static evolutionary plateaus, in favour of a continual 'overcoming'. It is not just an evolutionary change, then, but a change in evolution – a change in how evolution functions on both an individual and group level (see Part I, Section 22.1: 'from genus across to over-genus').

Several important ideas are introduced in this section, beginning with the contrast between the overhuman as the 'sense of the earth' and those humans that preach 'over-earthly' hopes. Nietzsche's is a philosophy of immanence. If there is meaning or virtue, it is to be found within the domain of existing things and their realisation; it is not to be found either in a transcendent God (Christianity) or in an idea of the good or justice that is independent of existing things (Platonism), both of which create values out of the initial rejection or inversion of some other value, or the rejection of some aspect of existence. To despise the earth is to despise life – both Platonism and Christianity celebrate and long for death. The human, though, is a 'discord and hybrid' (*Zwiespalt* ['rift, conflict'] *und Zwitter* ['hybrid', but also suggesting hermaphroditism, raising for the first time the issue of gender in this book]) between 'plant and spectre', between the lowest, most material and passive form of life, and the most spiritual phenomenon. Zarathustra asks rhetorically 'Do I bid you become plant or spectre?', each requiring the elimination of the other. The implied answer is no, but Zarathustra *does* bid us transform that discord or hybridism into something productive. The greatest that 'you could experience' (where the 'you' is the human being in the crowd, but only if he or she undergoes a kind of conversion) is the 'hour of the great despising'. Such a great despising would be not to raise up one value through despising another (such as the over-earthly over the earth), but to realise that the latter (the earth) is not just another human value at all, not just more 'poverty and filth and wretched contentment'. It is a great despising of all that is human insofar as the human involves such arbitrary rejecting and artificial raising up. Zarathustra demands that the crowd he is addressing ask 'what good is my happiness?' Is it a value built on the rejection of something, a turning away from one part of existence in order to raise up another part (or something quite outside of the domain of existence), or does this happiness 'justify existence itself?'. The 'great despising' would herald the arrival of the overhuman as lightning, or as the 'innoculation' of madness. The latter idea is of an experience or defining moment that is, relative to conventional norms at any rate, mad – but also prepares one to endure a more profound or destructive madness to come. This madness to come comprises the idea of will to power and especially eternal recurrence (in Part III). (The madness also echoes the allusion to the madman with the lantern discussed above.) Before moving on, we should notice a few additional ideas or image patterns that are mentioned in this section, but which will be picked up and developed again shortly: shame, the lion, pity and miserliness.

Section 4

At the end of section 3, the crowd jokes that Zarathustra is speaking of the tightrope dancer, and the dancer begins his performance. Notice that Zarathustra does not look up at the dancer, but at the people, 'amazed'. Zarathustra uses the tightrope as a metaphor: the human is a rope, a dangerous 'going across'. This explains Zarathustra's love for the human in Prologue, Section 2: the human can be loved precisely as a going-over and going-under. What follows is an inversion of the Sermon on the Mount; instead of a series of 'Blessed are . . .' we have a series of 'I love him who . . .'. This puts Zarathustra in the place of God, of course, but at the end we realise that Zarathustra counts himself as one of the 'heralds'. That is to say, the only possibility for the human to love its own condition is as a herald of that which surpasses it. Thus the rhetorical paradox: the great despisers are the great reverers, love and despising merge. Notice that this entails a kind of redemption of notions of human practices: understanding, work, invention, virtue. These are instruments in the service of the 'arrow of yearning' for the overhuman, rather than instruments of human contentment. That is, one 'invents' (for example) in order to end the domain of the human, to squander oneself, not to preserve. We should evaluate cultural and indeed everyday activities as to their role in human overcoming. At stake is not an ethics, a set of principles about how to best live. Ethics (or morality) is the problem, not the solution – the reason why is the topic of much of Part I. Rather, these practices or virtues are introduced primarily insofar as they have an *ontological* meaning, as elements within a mode of existence that could overcome the human. See our discussion of Part III, Section 5.

Let us briefly mention five other things here. First, the notion of shame. Previously, the human was said to be shameful from the point of view of that which surpasses the human. Now we see one reason why: the dice have fallen in favour of the human. An evolutionary accident has given them a static dominion of the earth, an earth they then wish away; the human has no intrinsic value or meaning, it does not merit its dominion, it lacks 'right' (this theme is found in Part I, Sections 1 and 17, for example). Secondly, the idea of justifying the future and redeeming the past ties, in a way not yet clear, in with the notion of eternal recurrence. The present is the present day, the contemporary world of late modernity. It is not a place of achievement with respect to that past (see also Part III, Section 12.11), or a preservation in the face of the future (see Part III, Section 12.26). Zarathustra's/Nietzsche's critical energies are most fiercely directed at this contemporary world, and the 'great despising' of this present will indeed cause one to perish, to 'go under', in order to 'go over' to the overhuman. As we shall see shortly, Nietzsche does attach significance to the 'moment' – but this is moment as epiphany, not in the sense of the present day or the contemporary. Thirdly, we have the notion of 'overfull' again, from Prologue, Section 1. To forget oneself is to lose identity in a quasi-mystical state, as our translator notes. It is also, though, to forget to care for or preserve oneself: it is to squander oneself or 'go under'. Moreover, when Nietzsche writes 'all things are in him', he is referring again to the idea of the moment as a kind of epiphany involving insight into time and history as a whole, and thus also a moment in which one could effect revolutionary change. We will discuss such ideas in Part III, Section 2.

Fourthly, the notion of a 'free spirit' shows up here, a phrase Nietzsche uses often, throughout his career (see Part II of *Beyond Good and Evil* and especially section 44). Freedom in the phrase 'free spirit' here seems to mean, as a first approximation: freedom *from* any idea of the despising of the body (that is, independence from such cultural forces, for example as embodied in Christian morality) and thus freedom *to be* the 'entrails of his heart'. The point is Kantian, in structure at least: one is only free if one is capable of both giving *and obeying* the law that one gives (see Part III, Sections 12.4 and 12.9). Notice that spirit and mind are functions of body. This will become clearer in Part I, Section 4, 'On the Despisers of the Body'. Fifthly, the image of lightning returns at the end of the section. The lightning will flash from the 'dark cloud' which is 'over' the human (or, in section 7, which is the current state of the human). Lightning is of course an electrical discharge of energy built up in the turbulence of clouds. This idea of the human as a long build-up of energy returns in the next section as the 'chaos within'. (And see the frequent images of explosion, discharge or release in all of Nietzsche's work, paticularly *The Gay Science* and *Beyond Good and Evil*.)

Section 5

Zarathustra is frustrated at his failure to communicate thus far. He surmises that 'culture' – something these people are proud of – makes them too proud to listen to talk of despising. By 'culture' here is meant, broadly, the higher and more spiritual products of distinctively human activity, which express but also reinforce the values of a group or the human generally. Culture thus means morality, philosophical and scientific ideas, religion, art, governments, and so forth. Culture thus serves to preserve. On the idea of preservation of the human species, see *The*

Gay Science, section 1. There, Nietzsche argues for a largely unconscious economy of human life that requires both the 'good' of the herd as well as 'evil' (see *GS*, section 318, and our discussion of Part I, Section 15, 'On the Thousand Goals and One').

Zarathustra's first reflections lead naturally to a discussion of the 'last human', as ineradicable as the 'ground flea' (a less accurate, but to us more meaningful translation might be 'cockroach'). The last human is a stage of human 'development', but one that completely freezes all development.[3] 'We have invented happiness', having given up all that is hard or dangerous, say the last humans. And they 'blink' – this is an image of stupefaction, or a tic signalling inner degeneration, it is also an image of the present (*Augenblink* in German means 'moment'), all that is left when the past is all known and the future is controlled. 'No herdsmen and one herd!' introduces Nietzsche's famous notion of the 'herd' – the vast, undifferentiated mass of humanity; it is also a political notion critical of a democratic age. However, Zarathustra insists that the humans in the crowd still have the 'chaos within', capable of producing the 'dancing star', and are still capable of the 'arrow of yearning' (see our discussion of Part III, Section 1). The last human is a warning, meant to appeal to the crowd's pride. However, as before, Zarathustra's words are taken in a sense opposite to their intent: the crowd want to be these contented last humans. Zarathustra concludes that he fails because he is speaking to the crowd as to goatherds. This means either that the humans in the crowd are too sophisticated for such straightforward tactics, or that they are already the last human.

Sections 6–7

The previous section was the end of Zarathustra's first series of teachings; what follows is a sustained allegorical narrative. Again, this will be typical of the rest of the book: a series of short speeches, poems or songs from Zarathustra, and passages of narrative concerning Zarathustra's travels through symbolically-charged geography. The narrative here concerns the death of the rope-dancer, and Zarathustra's response. The rope-dancer falls from the rope when a devilish jester (*Possenreißer* – the defining emphasis is on the playing of pranks, rather than other forms of foolishness) jumps right over him on the rope. Importantly, there is no suggestion that the dancer is killed by the jester's jest, rather, he 'loses his head and the rope': he kills himself from the shame of being bettered at his profession. Zarathustra tells the dancer that his life and death were not meaningless since he 'made danger his calling'. The jester here is symbolic of the necessary or intrinsic vulnerability of those who attempt the dangerous across to the overhuman. The vulnerability is intrinsic both because the ideal of lightness, always beyond one, is a burden without compassion, and because the dangerous across is necessarily also a 'going under' (see 'where the strong are weak', Part III, Section 12.19). However, the theme of the jester is returned to and developed regularly in the text (see the rest of the Prologue; Part I, Section 3; and Part III, Section 12.4). Zarathustra chooses to honour the rope-dancer's life by burying him. But is this an act of honouring, or an act of pity?

The brief section 7 consists of Zarathustra's reflection on the events and on his failure to communicate. The 'catch of fish' is a reference to the image of Jesus as a fisherman. Human existence (notice he does not just say 'human lives' – he is not referring to existentially anxious individuals or even to this or that specific historical community) remains without meaning; a jester can deliver it to its fate. The image of the jester becomes more complex: not only an image of vulnerability now, the jester (one who plays pranks or jokes) is now a metaphor for contingency or meaninglessness. It is not only the greatest dangers and most noble adversaries (or the devil) that bring down a human as he crosses to the overhuman; in its aimlessness, human existence can be derailed even by a foolish joke, a random bit of bad luck, and nothing more. The human is still without meaning, and therefore also the jester is without meaning (here the Prologue refers forward to the idea of a redemption of contingency, developed in Part II, Section 20 and Part III, Section 1).

Section 8

On the way out of the town, Zarathustra encounters the jester in person. The jester tells Zarathustra that he was lucky to be thought of as a fool, to have 'abased' himself by tending and carrying the dead rope-dancer, because the townspeople would otherwise have considered him a danger. Again, the image of the jester becomes more complicated: being foolish is now a disguise or a form of self-defence. The jester warns him to leave town, or meet the same fate as the rope-dancer; the jester here stands for the reactive wrath of the townspeople, the embodiment of their will to preservation. The gravediggers – representing those who deal with the dead figuratively, such as historians, or scholars of dead concepts – also see Zarathustra and mock him. The dead rope-dancer is too 'unclean' for them – he is a failed transgressor, after all, and an exception rather than a rule – and they reckon Zarathustra will not succeed in stealing the Devil's mouthful. The gravediggers 'put their heads together', an image reminiscent of the last humans huddling for warmth, but also a phrase that means to work on an intellectual project collectively.

The image of the thief returns in this section. Zarathustra is accused of stealing the Devil's meal; and his hunger 'waylays' him. That Zarathustra should think about food while carrying a dead man (and listening to wolves' howls) shows how little we should expect 'normal' responses from him. It also, however, indicates how far Zarathustra has allowed himself to stray from his body (the entrails); he is guilty of starving the body just as he described in section 3. This hunger is thus the beginning of a new insight for him, which culminates in the next section. There follows a curious short scene where Zarathustra requests food from yet another hermit. The hermit lives there because it is a wicked place for the hungry, as if it is his calling to refresh his soul in that way. Nor does it matter that Zarathustra's companion is dead: he must take what is offered. This is a parody of creating a new law or value, and then following it inflexibly; it is also an image of a (rather bad-tempered) bestowing that refuses to indulge itself in pity. This hermit, like the rope-dancer, is a miniature portrait of what Zarathustra will call the 'superior humans' in the final part of the book: those who accept (at least some of or perhaps a distorted version of) Zarathustra's teachings and prepare for the overhuman – and yet also have some all-too-human limitation. Notice that while all is dark, Zarathustra knows the way; but when dawn breaks 'he could no longer see any path'. This is the second sign that he is coming to a new realisation.

Section 9

Zarathustra awakens after dawn and also after 'forenoon' – that is, he awakens at high noon. But, he says, 'a light has dawned for me' and this has happened between dawn and dawn. In other words, this truth came to him before he slept (at the level of perception or bodily affect), but only at noon did his ability to reflect upon it and conceptualise catch up with that new truth. As with his hunger, Zarathustra (as the conscious, spiritual being) is trying to catch up with the truths that his body – in the broadest sense – already knows. The task of higher forms of humanity is not to return to the animal, nor depart entirely from the animal, but to realign the spiritual being with the animal body. For differing reasons, the dawn and the noon (together with twilight and midnight) are important throughout the book as moments of transition and realisation. Zarathustra decides that he will speak no more to the people *en masse*, nor to the dead (Nietzsche slyly implies that these might be the same category). Instead 'companions I need and living ones', these companions will not just listen and learn from Zarathustra, but will themselves be fellow destroyers (of old values and systems of value; they are 'despisers of good and evil'), harvesters (the image is akin to the dark cloud in which is contained a build-up of energy that might flash as lightning; it should also remind us of the redeemers of the past in Prologue, Section 4), 'celebrants' (in the sense of a harvest celebration, which is also of course a praising of the earth) and creators ('who inscribe new values on new tablets'). Thus the subtitle of the whole work: *a book for everyone and nobody*. The book is available to anyone who can read – moreover, it is not technical or deliberately obscure – and yet the audience capable of understanding it, and indeed of transforming themselves through that understanding, may not *yet* exist.[4] The section concludes with Zarathustra using the same complex verb phrase ('*hinwegspringen über*' – 'to spring over and away') that was used in connection with the jester. Is Zarathustra also the jester? The question is closely related to the question we asked of section 6 concerning pity. Zarathustra must become willing to leap over and leave behind, without pity, those who go under even in the attempt to go across. His bestowing of wisdom must not lead him to be a 'crutch' for those who follow him (see Part I, Section 6, 'On the Pale Criminal'). He must become the serious prankster, the one that gives to human under-going the meaning that is the sense of the earth. Since the next section ends 'Thus began Zarathustra's going under', we realise that he does not exempt himself from this leaping over. (The figure of the jester returns in Part I, Section 3; also, the test of pity will return, at the end of Part IV.)

Section 10

Zarathustra becomes aware that his animal companions have found him. This reappearance stamps its approval upon Zarathustra's new plans. Notice that the eagle sweeps in wide 'circles' and the snake is 'coiled like a ring'; this is the symbolism of eternal recurrence (a key idea of Part III), although neither we nor Zarathustra could be aware of the significance of this yet. Only the reader of Nietzsche's *The Gay Science* could be aware of it; this is a kind of dramatic irony. Zarathustra proceeds to chide himself: he can never be clever 'from the ground up' like the serpent. The animals are often used as symbols of pure or simple virtues, abilities or drives (thus also the camel and lion in the next section). The human, though, is a 'discord' or 'hybrid' between 'plant and spectre' (Prologue, Section 3). Humans tend not to be pure, not to have just one virtue, or not to persist with it. If, then, his cleverness should fail him (as it inevitably will, and already has) then may his pride fail him too, lest he die from shame like the rope-dancer.

The Prologue has given Zarathustra not only a new plan of action – to seek disciples, not large-scale conversions – but it has revealed him as not exempted from the process of development that he names 'overhuman'. We do not meet Zarathustra fully formed, so to speak. Finally, the Prologue has given Zarathustra a methodology: he cannot speak directly to the people, banging on kettledrums (Prologue, Section 5). Perhaps he must 'stammer'. This is either a reference to Moses or Demosthenes. However, in retrospect we see in the earlier reference to stammering a light-hearted description of an indirect form of communication, one that lacks a good, clear, straightforward style, that progresses by repetitions, diversions and going backwards, and is characterised by fragmentation, allegory and, above all, poetry.[5] Zarathustra's other prototype for such communication is of course the jester, who communicates through jokes or pranks (inversions, surprises, exaggerations, nonsense, puns and other wordplay, irony and parody), who appears most foolish when he is most serious, and *vice versa.* (Nietzsche no doubt has one or more of Shakespeare's fools in mind.)

Part I

Section 1, 'On the Three Transformations', and a Note on Spirit

A Note on Spirit

This is one of the most famous sections of the book, probably because it seems to offer an overall view on Nietzsche's philosophy of overhuman development, and because it appears to do so in straightforward symbolism (that is, there appears to be a clear, one-to-one mapping of images onto ideas). We are presented with three different stages of the spirit and three different behaviours. What does Nietzsche mean by 'spirit'? He uses it in at least two ways: first, as 'your' name (that is, the common, human designation) for reason, for the mind in its more abstract, self-conscious, and (apparently) more free thoughts (see Part I, Section 4). This first meaning references particularly Judeo-Christian thought for which the spirit is the soul, in opposition to the body. The second, preferred meaning cuts right across the distinction between body and mind or soul. Nietzsche famously writes in Part II that 'Spirit is the life that cuts into life' (Part II, Section 8).[6]

Spirit is a mode of the living body, specifically of those drives that have become dominant among the system of drives that make up life. Indeed, they have become so dominant that, in the case of spirit, *therefore* they can come into (or force themselves into) consciousness as our sense of who we are, and we can think about this manifestation and formulate it as a normative principle, perhaps even an abstract principle, for ourselves. This principle, duty, or the underlying sense of direction of spirit – especially insofar as these form a mode of life – Nietzsche has been calling 'virtue'. In this coming to consciousness the underlying drive is likely to be sublimated, in a broadly Freudian sense (Nietzsche uses 'spiritualised' in just this sense, for example, in *Twilight of the Idols*, 'Morality as Anti-Nature', section 3). That is, the drive finds an outlet in an intellectual, cultural or social fashion. In spiritualisation, will to power might come to appear disguised, reversed and turned against itself; spiritualisation can be dishonest. Freud thought that such spiritualisation happens to make the drive conventionally acceptable; more important for Nietzsche is that will to power can realise itself as spirit (as law, institution or virtue perhaps) and in that way moulds groups into new modes of human life.[7] This latter idea is what Zarathustra calls the 'bestowing virtue' in section 22. Thus the passage in Prologue, Section 3: 'I love him who . . . wants to be wholly the spirit of his virtue'. In brief, spirit is a way of thinking about the living body's relationship to, and manifestation in, thought and 'character'. Ultimately this means the will to power's objectification of itself as thought and character. For, will to power is Nietzsche's characterisation of the metaphysical nature of all living, and perhaps also non-living, things (for the idea of will to power, see our note on Part I, Section 4).

Since we are talking about terminology, it is worth mentioning that Zarathustra also employs the concept of 'heart', often in conjunction with 'spirit' (for example, Part I, Section 21 and Part II, Section 7). In such cases, although not everywhere, we take 'heart' to mean the dominant will to power insofar as that manifests as the immediate expressivity of the body as pathos or affect: one's inner emotional life and desires. (Sometimes, too, Nietzsche uses the words 'spirit' or 'heart' in a broader, more conventional sense, just meaning the self, its preoccupations and its intimacy, as in the first sentence of the Prologue, or in the frequent addresses of Zarathustra to his 'heart'.)

* * * *

Notice that the first stage of the spirit is *already* a transformation ('the spirit becomes a camel') – Zarathustra is already no longer talking to 'ordinary' humans in the market place. The camel is a beast of burden, not in the negative sense of a mere slave, but in the positive sense of that which is capable of great strength of will: the spirit of the camel 'kneels down . . . and would be well laden' and 'presses on into the desert'. For example, such spirit exercises its strength in annulling its pride, remaining always opposed to the victorious (the popular, the in-fashion, or what is considered true), working at intellectual problems that do not admit of quick, easy or safe answers, if any answers at all, and so forth. How is the development of the overhuman furthered by this self-burdening? Nietzsche has given us one, complex, reason thus far: those that stand in the way of the overhuman (the last humans) naturally shun what is heavy, hard or difficult, in order to preserve themselves like the cockroach. The difficult path is one of self-overcoming, it is akin to a purification of one's drives through the elimination of the natural, but comfortable, impulses (see *Twilight of the Idols*, 'Skirmishes of an Untimely Man', section 41). This self-fashioning is not, like a repression, simply a covering over of one's nature (and thus becoming in some way 'artificial'), but a change in one's human nature. A strong drive that has become dominant in this way could not want anything but the manifestation of its strength. The path of heaviness leads into the desert and precisely there is the place of the *second* transformation. The desert is the symbol of both the difficulty of the camel's burden, and the fact that this path takes it far from the human. It is also of course a reference to the various retreats into the desert in the *Old* and *New Testaments*, particularly Matthew 4 and Luke 4. (Thus it is also an image of the South and the East – leaving behind European culture.) The camel thus prepares for, or is the condition for, the second transformation.

The lion becomes lord in the desert, makes the desert its own, by defeating the dragon named 'Thou shalt'. The diction of this last phrase should of course remind us of *Old Testament* commandments, the model for all absolute moral rules. The dragon thus represents both the accumulated values that one's historical period has inherited and internalised, and also the jealousy of these values, forbidding any further independent willing. The camel 'renounces' (in so far as it turns from and seeks to eliminate contentment) and is 'reverent'. The reverence is for the 'heroes' that provide its burden, on whose behalf it exercises its newly found strength. These might well be the very 'Thou shalt's' of the dragon, since moral rules are often difficult and require the dismantling of drives or habits that lead towards self-satisfaction or contentment (recall also the description of the despisers of life in Prologue, Section 3). That is why 'to seize the right to new values' is the most terrifying thing for such a spirit. The camel is not (yet) free. The dragon is not the *desert's* 'ultimate Lord', but the *spirit's*.

But only the child can create new values, for the child does not just eliminate what has gone before ('sacred Nay even to duty') but – by being a forgetting and an innocent new beginning – offers a 'sacred Yea-saying'. The lion is free and independent will, but is a virtue without content (so to speak), without meaning, purely negative. However, the child 'wills *its own* will'; the forward direction or 'virtue' of the spirit-child does not have some 'Thou shalt' as its content, but its willing is its own content. This is a beautifully concise first description of the will to power. In its victory, the spirit-lion thus loses even the already-impoverished 'world' that is the desert. Let us permit ourselves a crude gloss here: the 'world' here means that sense of being somewhere meaningful or intelligible. This meaning or intelligibility is given us (as we shall see) by will to power in the form of our virtues and other spiritualisations. The world shows up for us to the extent that it assists virtue or stands in its way. The destruction of a virtue is the destruction of a world.The spirit-child attains '*its own* world'. The idea of creating a world alludes to the very beginning of the *Old Testament*; what we are getting is a symbolic creation.

In Prologue, Section 2, the holy hermit called Zarathustra a child, and yet we also saw that Zarathustra's own development as philosopher and teacher is incomplete. Zarathustra is not speaking of the three transformations from a position at their conclusion (if there is one at all), but as a fellow traveller. Since there are three stages in a book that was originally known as having three parts (the fourth part was only circulated among Nietzsche's friends), it is tempting to see a correlation. Although, to be sure, Zarathustra and his teachings undergo transformations in these three parts, these are not easily mapped onto the categories described here. Moreover, it is also tempting to see these transformations as sequential stages – like a series of promotions to higher military rank – leading to the overhuman as to an end. But the heavy burden carried by the camel, and the negation required of the lion, are never simply past. Thus, it may be better to think of the three transformations as discussing the methodology of transformation, which would need to be repeated in the perpetual process of overcoming, rather than as stages.

Section 2, 'On the Professorial Chairs of Virtue', and a Note on Nietzsche and Satire

A Note on Nietzsche and Satire

Whenever the text homes in critically on issues close to contemporary culture, the writing takes on a satirical tone. There are many moments of satire in Part I, and Part II is even more focused on Nietzsche's contemporaries; then, in Part IV the satire becomes particularly personal and biting. Satire works by ridiculing its subject and exaggerating its negative features, often through distortion (enlargement of insubstantial detail/reduction of major features, cf. *Gulliver's Travels*), gross parody, or rendering its subject absurd. The world described in satire often stands 'on its head' (*verkehrte Welt*, 'world the wrong way round'). The satire in *Zarathustra* follows in the footsteps of a long tradition of European satire going back to Lucilius, the Roman originator of the genre, and Juvenal; and in modern times to Cervantes, Swift, Sterne and Lichtenberg. More recent figures of importance were two German Romantic writers: Jean Paul Friedrich Richter (called Jean Paul, 1763–1825), and Friedrich Klingemann (1777–1831), who in 1804 under the pseudonym Bonaventura published the satirical novel *Night Vigils* (*Nachtwachen*). In the 1830s and 40s satirical *Zeitkritik* blossomed (in a movement of young radicals including Karl Gutzkow, Heinrich Heine, Ludwig Börne and Georg Büchner). Satirical critique became a widespread feature of political and literary protest against German politics and culture. Here, a frequent seminal image is that of the figure of 'the German Michael' (*der Deutsche Michel*), an emblem of German national character (like the English bulldog). He is frequently depicted as an overgrown baby, or obese, juvenile idiot, dozing and oblivious.[8] As an allegorical main prop, he often wears a sleeping cap with a pointed top ending in a pom-pom dangling on a piece of string – a dullard's version of the *Sans-culottes*, the radical poor in the hot phase of the French Revolution. The works of these radical critics were banned by the authorities, and some of them went into exile to escape prosecution. This political commentary in satirical form carried on into the *Vormärz*, the period leading up to the events of 1848. Nietzsche's satire in *Zarathustra* and elsewhere is constructed on models of this kind of *Zeitsatire*, also to be found in the works of the more 'respectable' figure of the novelist and dramatist Karl Immermann. Immermann's notion of 'epigonalism' – as outlined in his novel *The Epigones*, latecomers born in a mediocre age[9] who cannot compare themselves with the best of their predecessors – has also found entry into Nietzsche's thought world (see, for example, Part II, Section 14, 'On the Land of Culture').[10]

* * * *

There are strong echoes of Bonaventura's satirical novel in *Zarathustra*, and specifically here in this section. There, the night-watchman on his lonely post with all of mankind asleep around him in the deserted city sees the world like nobody else can. Zarathustra is such a vigil-keeping visionary of the night. The likes of Zarathustra, the night-watchman, are in this section called 'shameless' by the prototype of a modern professor of ethics, who wants to stay awake through his work during the day so that he can sleep soundly at night. (In his 'chair': he is already sitting down.) The satire of this section presents the professor as a kind of philosophical night-cap wearer, set in his ways, unambitious, incapable of opening up to the unknown – a *Michel* of the mind. The routine of virtue is set up as a daytime activity, inflated and absurd, and solely for the purpose of staying awake so that the ensuing sleep will numb the fear of night. The true experience of day and night is avoided in an act of man-made and highly artificial psychological engineering. This artificiality of purpose-driven rationality impacts on the content of what is being taught. Virtue is merely defined negatively here. The number forty of the four groups of ethical tasks prescribed (self-overcoming, self-reconciling, discovery of truths, and laughing and being cheerful) reminds us of the forty days of moral testing Jesus underwent when fasting in the desert. Nietzsche thus alludes to Christian morality, but the principles as they are invoked and strangely formalised are devoid of true Christian ethical substance. Thus, for instance, the Ten Commandments are rendered absurd by the examples given: 'Shall I covet my neighbour's maidservant?' With these principles we are presented with a watered-down modern academic version of Judeo-Christian ethics that has replaced the fierceness of moral justice in the original Commandments, and their historical authenticity as expressions of the way of life of a people (see Part I, Section 15). Thus philosophy propagates a type of ethics that preserves the status quo, and indeed prevents the raising of any important, difficult or dangerous questions. The pale criminal in section 6 and the young man of section 8 are far more advanced on their way towards overhumanity. The section ends with an evocation of the revolutionary guillotine: the heads of the likes of the professor 'shall drop off'.

Notice, in this section of Part I of the book entitled 'Zarathustra's speeches', the main bulk is delivered not by Zarathustra, but by the professor. Zarathustra's learning is emphasised in this way. For ears attuned to the nonsense of modernity, this is what professors of ethics sound like. Critique of conventional university philosophy is Nietzsche's starting point for the elaboration on the meaning of the transformations of the spirit, and the shape of a new understanding of ethics. Strict oppositions as a founding mode of thought need shedding altogether: good and evil, just like waking and sleeping, do not exist except as one through the other. States of mind and time need to be experienced as parts of a flowing continuum (on this point, see our discussion of Part I, Section 16, and the first few sections of *Beyond Good and Evil*). Zarathustra's conception of the health of the human is to be based on the living experience in the natural body, for there *is* a 'sense to life': the 'sense of the earth'.

Section 3, 'On Believers in a World Behind'

'*Hinterweltler*' is a derogative phrase for one who lives in the back waters, the provinces, thus a yokel, a redneck. So, the title is, really, 'On the Back-worlders', or perhaps 'Back-worldsmen' to create a pun on 'backwoodsmen'. Thus, Nietzsche applies *Hinterwelter* to brand metaphysicians and theologians as out-of-touch rednecks. We should not forget that the first 'believer' (if we could call him that) we encountered was a hermit. Zarathustra confesses that he too once believed in another, hidden world behind this one; but not the domain of a loving and perfect creator, but rather a 'divinely discontented' creator who creates an imperfect world as a drunken distraction. The point here is that even should one be convinced by the existence of a creator who in some way occupies an ontologically transcendent domain (for example, is of a world behind this world, is eternal), it by no means follows that this creator is good (traditional problem of evil). Soon, though, Zarathustra 'carried his ashes to the mountain' and overcame himself as a sufferer; he realised that this positing of a tortured God was a creation of the human.

Belief in another world, then, is a product of a suffering, despairing, unhealthy and exhausted human existence, that no longer wants to will and that 'wants to attain the ultimate in a single leap' because 'the stars' are too far. (Notice the link back to the jester of the Prologue: the jester would like to overcome, perhaps, but only if it is *easy*. See also Part III, Section 12.4.) A belief in a creating God is created so that the human can abdicate its will and its body (that is, the material, immanent nature of its being) and join a domain of redemption and happiness. But it is the body (in its sickness) and the earth (the broad domain of immanence) that created this other domain. More even that this, Zarathustra suggests that 'this most honest Being, the I' (on which Zarathustra will elaborate in the next section) still talks of body and earth, and still *wants* body and earth, even as it 'poetizes and raves and flutters with broken wings'. To put it differently, belief in a world behind is another mode of human life doing what life always does and must do: finding a way to live, including even the 'leap of death'. In other words, it is will to power yet again. Notice that the 'god-similar' want to be believed in and themselves preach. The sickness and the belief in God is not something that happens primarily to individual humans. Rather, it is a social and cultural phenomenon, complete with institutions (the church), cultural activity and production (preaching), and a set of values ('doubt is a sin'). Thus, Zarathustra is 'gentle' with the sick: 'may they become convalescents' (as Zarathustra himself did in the past, and will have to again in the future; see Part III, Section 13). Zarathustra entreats 'my brothers' to listen to the body in its health, for it speaks of the 'sense of the earth'.

Section 4, 'On the Despisers of the Body', and a Note on Will to Power

The succinctness of this section is in inverse proportion to its significance. It contains the outline of Nietzsche's philosophical psychology. This is the initial argument: quite unlike children who can be educated about the body because they are instinctively and naively aware that body and soul *co-exist*, there is nothing that can be done for the despisers of the body, Christians, Idealists, Puritans, who simply reject the body. The overman *knows*, however, that all sensual and spiritual aspects of human life are functions of the body: 'soul is merely a word for something about the body'. What follows is like a diagram in prose of the structure of the individual psyche with the body as physiological root of psychological functions.

As a creative, dynamic, biological organism, the body is the manifestation of the will to power in individual human beings. It is a 'great reason, a manifold with one sense'. 'Manifold' is one of Kant's key notions, meaning the disparate field of various sensations internal and external which (for Kant) are subject to synthesis in an act of understanding, such that there can be thought properly speaking and consciousness. Nietzsche's wording suggests that this 'manifold' *already* has a sense running through it, long before the 'small reason' or the 'I' perform a synthetic act, even if elements of that manifold seem to be diametrically opposed (like 'war and peace', 'herd and herdsman'). It employs as a 'tool' the 'spirit' ('small reason' – this is a use of spirit in the more conventional sense; see our discussion on Part I, Section 1). The activities of senses and spirit need to be understood as bodily functions, as 'tools and toys' of the body, not ends in themselves (respectively, naive empiricism and naive rationalism). In Nietzsche's holistic physiological model, spirit is the product of 'the creating body' that has 'created spirit for itself as a hand of its will.' Nietzsche uses the term 'I', and like in Freud (1856–1939) this is the consciousness-driven sense of individual self-identity. However, the bodily agent Nietzsche calls 'Self' is placed over and above this I (or ego). The Self causes, governs and coordinates all psychological activity in the individual, including that of the I – much to the chagrin of the proud ego, that has, like the senses and spirit, long deemed itself independent of the Self.[11] (Compare *The Gay Science*, section 11 with its 'ridiculous overestimation' of consciousness.) The body 'does I' – 'I' is not a thing (for example, a soul) but a function or activity of the body. Even in the despisers of the body it is the Self that speaks, albeit there a Self 'that wants to die and turn away from life'.[12] This is important for the understanding of the rift within certain humans (described in some of the following sections, for example 6 and 8) where the protagonists have not yet learned to overcome their self-destructive streak, their despising, which they need to leave behind as a precondition for the overhuman.

A Note on Will to Power

However, what the Self 'wants the most' is 'to create beyond itself'. In order to understand this idea, we need to understand Nietzsche's conception of the will to power. The exact status of the idea of will to power is (deliberately, it would seem) unclear in Nietzsche: is it a metaphysical claim about the nature of reality – and within that, about only living things, or all things – or a thought-experiment, or an account of the way that appearances function? Here, for convenience, we will initially treat it as a broad metaphysical claim: being is will to power.[13] All 'things' exist as the desire for power-over some other 'thing', or the desire to express, intensify or magnify themselves as power-over. Power-over is experienced as an affect, as the feeling of power (see *The Gay Science*, 13, 118, and *Beyond Good and Evil*, sections 22, 36). Nietzsche's most immediate example of this is consumption and digestion. Nietzsche seems to be envisaging something like a micro-organism that is all stomach, whose only function is to surround and incorporate other living things. Not only have we innumerable images of foods, meals, nausea or well-being but 'the spirit is a stomach' (see Part III, Sections 12, 16). In a manner less straightforwardly egoistic, this image of incorporation leads all the way up to the notion of the comprehensive soul of the future philosopher who constructs a new form of humanity from the fragments of the past and present (see Part III, Section 7, and *Beyond Good and Evil*, section 259).

As a theory, the will to power is intended also to rectify several faults that Nietzsche sees in recent scientific thought, especially evolutionary biology, psychology, or physics (such as atomism). Nietzsche argues that such broadly mechanistic accounts illegitimately (1) create a fixed substance behind all action (something that is already there and can act or be acted upon; for example, a species or individual member of a species, the atom, an instinct, and so forth); (2) abstract cause from effect in the formulation of 'laws' of physics, as if there could exist one without the other; and (3) pretend that a *descriptive* quantification of cause and effect is actually some kind of *explanation* of what links them together; (4) study as real merely ideal and abstract cases where variables can be 'controlled'; (5) propose taxonomies of things and then assume these are essences of things and not fluid approximations. The will to power is a theory intended to rectify these faults.

Substance is not, Nietzsche argues, a fundamental notion, but an effect of the will to power, another of its tools or toys, a temporary 'objectification' of the will, which simplifies (that is, 'falsifies') nature in order the better to exercise power (for example, to make something into a 'possession'; see *The Gay Science*, section 14). Likewise, the will to power does not abstract cause from effect, because it is originally relational, existing as the relation of power-over or over-powered (thus the idea of relationality that we discovered in the first section of the Prologue). It follows from the above, Nietzsche believes, that the will to power could never be in-itself, and power relations are always absolutely particular, rendering quite dangerous any abstraction or formalisation (we will discuss later the idea of *perspectivism*; see Part III, Section 10). To briefly mention the other faults: the will to power is not a description that something happens, but an explanatory account of why; as entirely relational, as are its 'variables', it is impossible to isolate 'one' will to power;[14] and will to power is dynamic (it is the becoming of things), meaning it cannot be isolated in time, either, as this or that individual or type. We should note here that these errors are in some way *necessary*. Their necessity is ultimately biological: a human who did not falsify appearances in this way would be at a severe evolutionary disadvantage. Substance and the apparatus of cause and effect are intellectual errors that mistake similarity and continuity for identity and general law – the world thereby becomes *on average* a place where human life can thrive (see *The Gay Science* 110–12 and 121). To align oneself to the will to power – which is how we have been describing the metaphysical nature of the overhuman – is dangerous for this reason if no other.

Now life (here, the living body or the Self) is a form of will to power whose power relations additionally fold back on themselves. Thus, not only does a living being seek power over other living beings (for example, in competition for food, shelter, sex – and, at the level of spirit, for ideas, or political and social power) but also power over *itself*. That is, it seeks to 'create' from out of itself a new form of life that will exist as a higher or more intense expression of power-over. This new form might be physiological in nature (thus literally a new variety or species), psychological (new habits, practices), or spiritual (new ideas, political forms, technologies, works of art, and so forth). The will to power is thus the dynamic behind evolution on all levels. This need to advance to higher, more powerful, more complete forms is, for Nietzsche, a fundamental characterisation of life. The overhuman, then, would have to be that new 'form' of humanity that is 'from the ground up' aligned to the will to power. Such alignment would mean that it understands and affirms this constant development (even though that necessarily means individual or collective 'going under'); moreover, that it understands and affirms that as integrated within existence as a whole, characterised by becoming and, as we shall see, eternal recurrence.

Significantly, though, this advancing is not happening on behalf of individuals, but rather through individuals on behalf of human life itself, and ultimately on behalf of life as such. There is thus a distinct Dionysian element here: the individual Self as an objectification of the will aims at going beyond itself into merging with the general will of nature. Through self-overcoming, the Self seeks to align the individual human being with the general will of nature. We should point out that among the simplifications that Nietzsche indulges here is the implication that the body or Self is 'one sense', a single commander behind the diversity of the manifold, and thus is in a one-to-one correspondence with manifestations of will to power. However, more often he talks of the self as a battleground of drives (of opposed or competing manifestations) – as indeed in the very next section with its 'conflict among your virtues' (this was also the substance of our discussion of the camel-transformation in section 1. On this idea, see *Beyond Good and Evil*, section 19.) To designate this notion, we will here often talk of the body as a 'system of drives'.

****

We have here the outline of Nietzsche's psychology in its basic principles, which we can call a radically 'materialist' one in its emphatic body-orientation.[15] This section is important in laying the foundations of the concept of the overhuman whose task it is to learn to understand and to internalise this holistic psychological model based on the supremacy of the living body. In general, much of this anticipates later twentieth-century psychological theory: thus it is possible to read this as an early manifesto of *both* neural science (where psychology is understood primarily in terms of the nervous system and brain organisation and chemistry) and psychosomatic approaches (where physiological symptoms can be induced by psychological states). Nietzsche's conception thoroughly integrates physiology and psychology. We can perhaps also bring it into proximity with psychological positions such as Deleuze and Guattari's in *Anti Oedipus*[16] or even Wilhem Reich's[17] in *Function of the Orgasm* where the idea of the body is of equally central importance.

Section 5, 'On Enjoying and Suffering the Passions'

The title of this section (*Von den Freuden- und Leidenschaften*) is a difficult one although the elements are simple enough. *Freuden* means 'joy'; *Leiden* means 'suffering'; *Leidenschaften* means 'the passions'. The simplest translation would be 'On Joy and Suffering'; Parkes in the Oxford edition tries to capture something of Nietzsche's implied meaning. To understand this, we should start nearly halfway through the section with 'At one time you had passions and called them evil'. Traditionally, the notion of passion has two interlaced meanings: first, it is an emotion, desire or interest that is *passive*, it takes temporary control of me, perhaps from outside of me (thus 'the passion of Christ' – the abasement and crucifixion that Christ allowed to be done to him). Secondly, the passions are associated with the body (for example, lust). For these twin reasons, the passions were associated with vice and with evil. Nietzsche's new idea is that 'You set your highest goal in the heart of these passions: then they became your virtues and sources of joy'. (We discussed the meaning of the concept of 'virtue' under Part I, Section 1.) The point is that passion was always a kind of suffering (in both German and English, the words, or at least their meanings, are closely linked), whereas a passion of joy would be an oxymoron. Thus *Leidenschaften* is a common German word; but *Freudenschaften* is not (it may even be a Nietzschean neologism). Nietzsche's section title is trying to capture this all-important transformation of the human spirit, from the point where passion is only a passive suffering to the point where passion now becomes a joyful and active virtue (see *Twilight of the Idols*, 'Morality as Anti-Nature', section 1).

The first third of the passage reinforces this: 'If you have a virtue, and it is your virtue . . .'. In other words, 'your virtue' would be a virtue that does not come to you (as a duty, perhaps) from outside, demanding a passive response from the Self. As soon as it is named, though, it becomes something shared in the cultural space of language – and culture is *always* normative, for or against, as the expression of the dominant will to power of a group. A people share a language because they share a mode of life, thus have a common experience of a common world, and common language for discussing matters of mutual value (see the account at *Beyond Good and Evil*, section 268, and also our note on Nietzsche, Music and Language, with the commentary on Part II, Section 17). Again, 'stammering' is a methodological shorthand for the type of writing Nietzsche is developing which does not immediately resort to abstract concepts and already shared meanings. (Notice also the personification of the virtue as a woman and a lover; such devices are common in this book and we will return to their significance.)

This transformation is important because, as the overcoming of a previous conception of virtue and passion, it is a key progression towards the going-under of the human. Thus, it is worth noting, the 'you' to whom, but mainly *of* whom, Zarathustra speaks here is, for the first time, no longer the ordinary human of the market place. He is speaking to disciples. Of course, suffering – both in the sense of that which is painful, and in the sense of that which is out of control – has not gone away. But it is the virtues themselves, in their struggle (each virtue 'wants your whole spirit'), that are this 'evil'. Through this jealous struggle some virtues – and, Zarathustra suggests, thereby also the human mode of existence itself – can perish, which is precisely also how we understood the function of the spirit-camel transformation in Part I, Section 1.

Section 6, 'On the Pale Criminal'[18]

This is the first in a series of sections illustrating the deficiencies and perils of certain types of 'transitional man'; by this we mean human beings who are at the camel or lion stage of the spirit, or who perhaps just exhibit certain features that, like the pieces of a jigsaw puzzle, Zarathustra can assemble. The portrayal of the figure of the pale criminal is one of the most fascinating passages of the book and at the same time one of its darkest. There are close parallels between Nietzsche's conceptions of this figure and the portrait of the murderer Raskolnikov in Dostoyevsky's (1821–81) novel *Crime and Punishment* (1866) – all the more astonishing because Nietzsche only started reading Dostoyevsky after 1886 (in French translation). The pale criminal commits crimes because his ego wills him to despise: this is the criminal as nihilist. At the same time he is aware that 'my I is something that is to be overcome: my I is for me the great despising of the human' – that is, the great despising of the current state of human life, or some particular mode of human life, and thus the will to surpass it. This is Zarathustra's reading of the pale criminal's inner conflict which is the starting point for this speech on crime, guilt, justice and morality. The section points forward to the treatment of crime as a phenomenon of social deviancy and the means, motivations and meaning of punishment in *Genealogy of Morality* (1887).[19]

The pale criminal might appear to be at the lion stage of spirit transformation, waging war against 'Thou shalt', but he is acting from revenge ('he wants to hurt with that which hurts him') and thus it is his destiny not to 'create freedom'. There is a paradox opening up here: the pale criminal would have to affirm his crime in order to overcome it, but he is caught in a cycle of revenge built on rejection, and it is thus impossible to affirm. In this insoluble conflict, 'there is no redemption for one who suffers from himself so much, unless it be a quick death.' Thus the judges who condemn the pale criminal to death should look upon their judgement as a compassionate act, not one of juridical revenge, because death is the only way to release the pale criminal from his unbearable inner conflict. The criminal is guilty not on the level of thoughts, but through his deed, and through the image of his deed in its aftermath. Between these does not roll the 'wheel of grounds', meaning that these three do not explain one another (as a causal sequence) but rather that all three are manifestations of the will to power. Because of the image of the deed, he suffers from a guilty conscience: this is what makes him pale. In this way the criminal is guilty twice, first through his deed, and second through its image, which he can *neither* overcome as merely an exception, an aberration (in which case he would be 'reformed'), *nor* overcome by willing it as life-affirming virtue (shaking his head, rejecting the judge's authority and values, and thereby perhaps breaking the cycle of revenge, rather than nodding). This is 'madness after the deed'. Since it is the judges who have the power to condemn the criminal, it is they who will remain and can thus contribute in clearing the way for the overhuman. This is why they are the main addressees of the speech that forms this section.

There is, however, a link between the pale criminal and the judges: both are comparable on the level of despising. Potentially the judges can be as life-denying in their thoughts as the criminals they condemn, if their motivation is hatred and revenge (they wish his humiliation: 'the beast has nodded'). By freeing society of human beings that desperately want to overcome themselves but whose sickness is such that their actions are merely momentary (only an exception) or cannot be affirmed as virtue, the judges have an active role to play in inaugurating the age of the overhuman. But the judges also need to be aware of another dimension of the criminal's spirit distorting his deed: this is on the level of motivation for it. Nietzsche calls this the madness 'before the deed'. The criminal case presented by Zarathustra is that of a robbery and murder. In this case, Zarathustra argues, there is the likelihood of the robbery being carried out as a disguise of the true motive of the crime which is primeval blood-lust, the mad 'joy of the knife'. The criminal's spirit, his 'meagre reason', seeks for a socially acceptable justification for the primeval barbaric madness, so he takes watch and wallet too. 'What is the point of blood?' Robbery is the culturally 'acceptable' face of pre-cultural killing instinct. The point Zarathustra is making here is that true crime is anti-social and ultimately Dionysian in nature (compare *Beyond*

Good and Evil, section 229). This question arises as a consequence of the perpetrator's immersion in a social context determined by the logic of instrumental reason. His mental illness which, as we already know, stems from being haunted by the image of the deed, is exacerbated by the fact that he feels guilt also about the madness of its motivation, because it is inexplicable to him and to the judges.[20]

For Nietzsche, the criminal provides a particularly good case study to demonstrate two insights: first, in the criminal can be shown the suffering of humanity from the pressures of civilisation, for, dysfunctional forms of social behaviour are inevitable as long as the human race has only an imperfect understanding of, and is incapable of reconciling itself to, the pre-civilised core of its biological nature. In criminal transgression biology revenges itself on civilisation; in guilt, civilisation revenges back (thus the image of 'ball of wild snakes').[21] Secondly, in the criminal Nietzsche can demonstrate the cultural history of guilt as a dysfunctional (Freud would say: neurotic) form of negative psychological motivation based on the socially determined rejection of primeval human impulses. You hurt others with what makes you ill (that is, biology revenges itself in precisely the ways that civilisation had sought to repress it) and your transgression is expressed in the historically produced parameters of your own time. Zarathustra illustrates this with an example from the Middle Ages where 'doubting' and 'will to self' were branded evil; the pale criminals of that era were heretics and witches and, suffering as such, 'wanted to inflict suffering'.

Zarathustra now interrupts himself with a sarcastic flourish directed at the judges. He rails against the complacency of the 'good' judges, who, he suspects, in reality could never understand what he is explaining to them here because they are not 'mad' enough. The pale criminal is sick because he does not understand his own madness. The judges are useless, because they are not sufficiently mad in the first place to understand the pale criminal, let alone themselves: by this Zarathustra means that they are not sufficiently driven by 'truth or loyalty or justice'. They are therefore inferior to the pale criminal who at least has the courage to transgress and through transgression 'perish', whereas the judges, like the professor of ethics in section 2, only 'have their virtue in order to live long, and in wretched contentment'. Zarathustra ends this speech by pointing out how its recipients are meant to utilise it, couched in Swiss mountain metaphor: the torrent (perhaps of criminal and judiciary madness or revenge) will flush those away who come too close to it, but with Zarathustra as a railing to hold on we can safely examine it. But, assistance with living, and above all assistance in crossing the torrent, we have to facilitate ourselves.

Section 7, 'On Reading and Writing'

This section is the most disparate section yet, covering a great deal of ground in brief aphorisms, all loosely collated under the heading. Thus it exemplifies its most famous aphorism, which is *about* aphorisms. Moreover, as quickly becomes apparent, it is not so much about reading and writing as *particular* forms of cultural activity or production, which might be ends in themselves. Rather, after the first few sentences, the problematic is much more general: what the human being must become like such that, among other things, a certain kind of reading or writing is possible. Zarathustra's pedagogic intent is to bring about such human beings by first encouraging such readers. 'Of all that is written, I love only that which one writes with one's own blood': blood, of course, as ink, literally putting oneself into the writing. But more importantly blood is the image of the living body and its dominant drives (the spirit) insofar as they either make possible, or impossible, certain *communities* that can communicate about what is important to life. Accordingly, not just the writer but the reader too needs to be able to read with blood. The 'learned by heart' means to internalise beyond simply the meanings of the words. Given that consciousness is not the 'centre' of the self, making new knowledge or ideas count – bringing them to the point where they affect one's development – means to internalise or incorporate them as a kind of acquired 'instinct' (see *The Gay Science*, Section 11). Other kinds of readers – the 'Idlers' – are ruining both writing and thinking. Again, this is a quick critical slap at lowest-common-denominator democratic ideas of education, journalism or free public libraries, which make of reading and writing something akin to huddling together for warmth.

The mention of 'aphorisms' is of course an allusion to the style of writing Nietzsche has been developing, and which is exemplified in precisely this section. This disparate, aphoristic writing is deliberately difficult, but not so much on a sentence-by-sentence level. Nietzsche's writing here is perfectly clearly etched, taking each aphorism on its own. Each summit, taken on its own, is manageable – or appears to be, since Nietzsche's images are serial, stitched in across the whole book, and therein lies the problem. The aphorisms stride or dance from summit to summit, but one summit could only ever be fully intelligible as a step on the dance. This creates a challenge to readers. The point of Nietzsche's/Zarathustra's communication then is not so much to describe something, but to aid the realisation of a change in the reader; writing is an act towards the overhuman (see our discussion of Part III, Section 9). The challenge to the reader, accordingly, is not just an interpretative challenge. The argument has to be that only in conjunction with a change in the order of one's drives at the level of the body could a reader understand Zarathustra. Moreover, the former change might be precipitated, aided or furthered by newly acquired wisdom or understanding, to be sure. Nevertheless, readers must already be capable of self-transformation; they must already be to some extent disciples even before meeting Zarathustra.

The image of the 'summit' leads Zarathustra to expand on the theme of elevation. Elevation here partly signifies remoteness from human norms (thus we have already seen various hermits), hardship or danger (the image of the desert), overcoming and growth, and of course spiritual insight (Zarathustra's ten years in the mountains). Elevation here also means the capacity to laugh, to take things lightly: 'Not with wrath but with laughter does one kill'. Laughter signals a kind of disengagement from 'normal' affective responses or the struggle for or against. We laugh at things that do not concern us, and are not worth our zeal or wrath – that which has already in our person been overcome.[22] (The phrase 'what does that matter to me' is common in the book.) Thus, laughter, mocking and making-light-of is also a writing strategy, as Zarathustra employs it in Part I, Sections 2, 3 and 9 for example. However, laughing and being 'uplifted' at the same time is rare; in such laughter there must be both understanding and joyful acceptance. By contrast, many fools laugh at things they simply do not understand (for example, the misunderstanding laughter of the crowds in the Prologue). Likewise, many wise men become too solemn, unable to look down and laugh upon their discoveries. ('Spirit of gravity' is an alternative, and highly appealing, translation – unfortunately it is less accurate.) Throughout the book we will observe in Zarathustra's progress a back-and-forth relation between, on the one hand, solemnity and the anguish brought about through insight, and on the other, an overcoming of it with laughter and dance.

Finally, we have yet another female personification, this time 'Wisdom', who loves us only as 'courageous, untroubled, mocking, violent', a 'warrior'. We will see the personification of Wisdom again, especially in connection with a sexually charged, allegorical *ménage à trois* with the figure of 'Life' (Part II, Section 10). The key idea in these personifications is that the relationship between virtues or other dimensions of personality can be modelled on the relation of the sexes: quarrels, reconciliations, sexual desire and pregnancy are all images in the book. The last of these is perhaps the most important, addressing the question of how it is possible that a relationship between drives – a situation that characterises all life – could be productive of new forms of life.

Section 8, 'On the Tree on the Mountainside'

This section leads on from section 6 and makes some reference to the Prologue, particularly the tightrope walker. The young man is another example of a human being crushed under the realisation that he is ready for 'overcoming' without finding the means within him to achieve it. The young man shares with the pale criminal the quarrel between wanting to grow over himself on the one hand and life-denying despising on the other, which leads both figures into a neurotic stalemate. But there is a difference between them. The criminal is a lost cause, 'a heap of sickness' and revenge. The young man's case, however, is not altogether that hopeless; he has some understanding of his conflict, or rather, Zarathustra helps him to achieve it. Zarathustra is his psychoanalyst. This is why Zarathustra is getting close to him; it is worthwhile for the young man to be mentored. Later on in the section Zarathustra honours (and humours) him by even walking with him (how great an honour this is can be gleaned from section 22, where Zarathustra leaves his disciples behind to walk alone). Here now there is for the first time in the text real contact with a disciple who might further the cause of human life and growth. Though the leading metaphor of the parable is again borrowed from the world of Swiss mountain scenery, in tone and atmosphere the passage has a feel of *Chinoiserie*. It brings to mind Brecht's didactic experiments of Epic Theatre with its key element of 'rendering strange' as a means to further understanding, as practised for instance in *The Caucasian Chalk Circle*[23]or the *Lehrstücke* ('Teaching Plays').

Zarathustra compares the young man's situation to that of an isolated tree on a mountainside high up overlooking the valley (a scene that could have occurred near the lookout point of Marmoré above Sils Maria). These are the three levels of comparison between tree and man on the level of parable: first, both are 'bent and tortured' by elemental forces of nature beyond their control; both react to this by wanting to grow taller and stronger. The will to power in life seeks to transform its objectification so as to increase its feeling of power; it can only do this if it meets resistance or opposition and thus encounters danger. Zarathustra frequently praises the 'best enemy' (and see *The Gay Science*, section 19, – which includes even the image of the tree). Secondly, the man is like the tree when he wants to achieve greater heights of accomplishment: like the tree growing taller he needs to put out deeper roots into the dark and 'into evil'. This has two meanings: it means that free spirits will be threatened from *within* by new types of temptations or vices (inappropriate despising, envy); it also means that the advancement of life must necessarily come at the cost of those values held by other forms of life, and thus be threatened from *without* by those who call themselves good. Thirdly, tree and man want to grow so tall as to outgrow everything else around them and are 'perhaps waiting for the first lightning'. Solitude is one of the main conditions for going beyond oneself. With this allegorical image we are entering the sphere of mythology, and at the same time also that of modern science, namely of electrical atmospheric phenomena. As an awe-inspiring natural phenomenon (the sublime) and as a metaphor for spontaneous natural animation, lightning is one of Romantic literature's (particularly the Gothic variety's) favourite metaphors (*Hyperion*, *The Ancient Mariner*, *Frankenstein*). A mode of life must go under in order to transform. The allegory suggests an advancing moment of Dionysian apotheosis of nature where the world becomes one with itself, and new forms will emerge. But the young man is too troubled to see the euphoric positive meaning in Zarathustra's image: he can only think of his envy of all that grows, and envisage his own destruction. He breaks down and weeps. Zarathustra has to take him away to calm him.

In a way, therefore, Zarathustra's instruction via parable has failed here: The young man keeps misinterpreting the meaning of the parable. This should be compared with the question of reading and writing in the previous section. Zarathustra here does what he seemed to claim he would not do in that previous section: he strips his speech of much of its allegorical props, aphoristic discontinuity and poetic 'stammering'. The young man is still 'a prisoner plotting his own freedom'; he has yet to purify himself to struggle free. And Zarathustra entreats the young man, for the sake of his own love and hope, not to throw his love and hope away. The speech ends with Zarathustra introducing the important notion of the 'noble' man as opposed to the merely 'good'. The professor of virtue and perhaps the complacent judges are 'good'. They regurgitate 'what is old', and want 'that the old be preserved', whereas 'the noble man wants to create what is new and a new virtue'. Thus the noble man is a revolutionary. But even the noble man cannot afford to rest on his laurels, because even he can easily throw away the 'highest hope', which is aspiring to the overhuman. He can be tempted away from growth by mere negativity, and redefine his noble spirit and virtue as lust. Zarathustra deemed the young man worthy to be addressed in this way. There is hope yet for his sickness to be cured – or else Zarathustra is guilty of a second crime of pity (the first being for the dead rope-dancer). We must not miss these moments where Nietzsche is poking fun at his own prophet and mouthpiece; nor should we miss the fact that such self-mockery is *also* part of the pedagogic strategy of Nietzsche/Zarathustra.

Section 9, 'On the Preachers of Death'

This section is a taxonomy of the preachers of death. Within this family, there are three basic genera: the religious, the pessimists and the industrious. The first genus was already introduced in Prologue, Section 3; the pessimists are exemplified in Schopenhauer (by whom Nietzsche was heavily influenced in his early work), for whom the basic character of life was endless and fruitless striving and suffering. Schopenhauer appears later as the 'soothsayer'. The industrious appear at the end of the passage, and refer to the modern European citizens Nietzsche sees around him ('even you'). The industrious engage in 'furious labour' but only in order to create or afford 'what is fast, and new, and strange'; this is a flight from one momentary present to the next, without a proper sense of future or past or the meaning of existence, all of which amounts to, Zarathustra implies, a continuous longing for death.[24] (We will discuss these ideas further in 'On the Flies in the Market-Place'.) This description should be compared with that of the last humans in Prologue, Section 5. The joke here is that all three should be considered part of the same family: 'it is the same to me – as long as they pass on to it quickly!' Since all values are functions of underlying life, the function of life here is to rid the earth of the 'superfluous', which probably includes the preachers themselves.

Section 10, 'On War and Warrior-Peoples'

This section and the next look at the problem of crossing over from an angle of the social collective. The 'political Nietzsche' comes into view here. This section could be interpreted as a deep and disturbing bow to German militarism and fascism – except that it is in fact a *critique* of the German character. The Germans are, at best and for the foreseeable future, merely camels. Since the 1870s, and after his experience in the Franco-Prussian war, Nietzsche had been developing an account of 'the good European'. By this he means a modern outlook that rejects all nationalisms as idiotic romanticism, and instead sees the future of European civilisation in the same frame as he sees the future of humanity. This 'good' future lies only in the experimental devising of a new, comprehensive, pan-European form of culture, and ultimately, of humanity (see, for example, *Beyond Good and Evil*, section 254).

Zarathustra's human world is a hierarchically arranged one in which the different types of humanity develop according to their intrinsic psychological characteristics (see our note on Nietzsche and Social Taxonomy, with the commentary on Part II, Section 6). This applies to humans as individuals and as social or national collectives. They will all, in their different ways, contribute to bringing about the future of the overhuman, even if they are filthy camel drivers and well poisoners, like the rabble in Part II, Section 6. 'War' is a concept and an activity that features more highly in Zarathustra's system of values than 'peace' because existence as will to power is essentially struggle. Here 'war' is meant both literally and figuratively. Literally, in that Nietzsche has in mind the rampant German militarism which was the main ingredient in the engineering of German national unification in 1871.[25] Nietzsche makes Zarathustra his mouthpiece here for an ironically disguised, tauntingly patronising diatribe against the German war-people. Writing *Zararthustra* in perennially neutral Switzerland, he is looking across to Germany from a distance, psychologically as well as geographically. Zarathustra's haughty tone is confirmation of this. This literal meaning of war is complemented by the more important metaphorical meaning: this is indicated by 'you shall wage your war – and for your own thoughts' (compare *The Gay Science*, section 283; essential and continual change are just two ways Nietzsche is indebted to Heraclitus).

Zarathustra says that he is also this people's 'best enemy', a notion further developed in section 14, 'On the Friend'. As such, he is entitled now to 'tell you the truth'. When he later in the speech says that 'you shall seek your enemy', Zarathustra also implies that they seek him out as their 'best enemy', a reflection on the treatment the prophet Nietzsche received in his own country. What follows is a programme to educate the German people to manage the transition from a people of blindly obeying ant-like soldiers (their current state, 'I see many soldiers: I should like to see many warriors!') to a people of warriors. The first lesson that needs to be learned is for them not to be ashamed of hatred and envy, since they will never be 'great enough' to overcome them. Hatred is the appreciation of one's enemy (later in the section distinguished from despising the enemy, which would lead into the cycle of revenge); envy is the recognition of the nobility and height of others (see Part I, Section 8). In other words, understood correctly, these are positive traits and even virtues – for warriors, at any rate. Next, since they cannot be 'saints of understanding', they can aim to be 'at least . . . its warriors'. It is a hard-hitting insult in the German direction when Zarathustra/Nietzsche argues that the Germans do not possess the capability to deal adequately with their illustrious heritage of philosophical Enlightenment. Besides, they are also too ugly to join the community of transformers; Nietzsche says that there is not much they can do about being ugly, apart from putting 'the sublime around you, the mantle of the ugly': a brilliant piece of biting, aesthetic criticism in the style of *Zeitsatire*.

Section 11, 'On the New Idol'

The section is a critique of the modern, pluralist state. Zarathustra contrasts it upfront with both a 'people' and a 'herd'. Of peoples, we will learn more in Part I, Section 15. Nietzsche's rather infamous use of the term 'herd' was introduced in Prologue Section 5. Since the term is used there for the 'last humans', but here for something that has been replaced by the state, clearly Zarathustra's point is not straightforwardly historical. These three terms are not periods in the development of the human, primarily, but three ways of characterising the social ontology of human groups.

Zarathustra's account of the state has four key features. First, the state lies: it pretends to be a people, but uses a mish-mash of 'all the tongues of good and evil'. That is to say, it does not have a historically and physiologically rooted set of defining values, but accepts them all (the pluralist state) or perhaps manufactures an artificial set from the thin air of reason (we could call this the Enlightened state, and the artificial set of virtues was lampooned in Part I, Section 2), but all the while claiming that this is the will of a people. This is part of what Nietzsche has in mind later in the passage in talking about the 'theft' of 'culture'. Secondly, whether pluralist or enlightened, since these values do not flow from an actual form of life, they signify sickness and the will to death. Similarly, the state exists to marshal and 'devour' the far-too-many, those who are sick of life and who sicken life. Thus, the phenomenon of newspapers is said to be an effect of the inability of the superfluous to be a properly functioning, living organism. Thirdly, it is not just the all-too-many with which the state concerns itself. In order to 'sun itself in the sunshine of good consciences' and thereby to 'bait' the far-too-many, it bribes even those humans of a higher order, the 'great souls'. Nietzsche has in mind the manner in which the German nationalism of Bismarck sought legitimation by becoming a patron of the arts, luring Richard Wagner (whom, like Schopenhauer, Nietzsche had once idolised but later largely rejected) into the service of the state. He is also claiming that the new state may be secular, but this secularity is just another guise of the preachers of death, who formerly appeared as religion. This seduction of the great souls is another part of the state's theft of culture. Fourthly, the state is characterised by a hunger for a specific type of power: political power over others, by no means unrelated to the accumulation of wealth. (As a consequence, a 'moderate poverty' is a route to freedom: for to have possessions is to be a part of the system of nimble apes clambering over one another for the throne. See also Part III, Section 6.)

Again, though, Zarathustra tells us that all is not lost: 'free still for great souls a free life stands'. As in Prologue, Section 5 ('you still have chaos within you'), the critique of modern culture or politics is not a pessimistic or nihilistic one. Indeed, in the Prologue it was suggested that it is precisely the 'dark cloud' of the human that creates the condition for the overhuman. Far from being a cause for despair, it is *necessary* that there be herds, states, preachers of death and last humans, for through them the human will go under. These phenomena are necessary, but the individual humans are not, they are superfluous. Only where the state ceases (either in the sense that there is no state, or in the sense of the 'great soul' having escaped the clutches of the state, to the 'vacant' seats of the earth) does the song begin of the one who is necessary – 'necessary' in the sense of being required for the sense of the earth to realise itself as the overhuman. Notice that we no longer have a rainbow 'to' the overhuman, but rather a rainbow 'of' the overhuman. The overhuman is not a destination, it is a continual process of overcoming the human, again and again.

Section 12, 'On the Flies in the Market-Place'

This section is pretty much self-explanatory. The speech is addressed to the disciples, who by now know that it will be their task to uncover their inner nobility, revalue all values, overcome the temptation of nihilism and generate new values. What is their relationship to contemporary mass society? Here, such society is signalled by the market-place, a place of artificial gathering, anonymous economic exchange and exchanges of news or other information, noisy display and the squalor that breeds flies. Zarathustra divides the humans in the market-place into two broad categories: the (little) people – imaged here as biting insects – and the 'great men': play-actors or jesters, who make a great deal of 'noise' (that is, those who the 'flies' consider to be great; on their 'noise', see Part II, Section 18). The allegorical image of vermin animals plaguing the 'free spirit' is frequently used in the book. Both categories are characterised by a need for revenge (the blood motif) and petty envy. The play-actors, the cultural, political or artistic movers and shakers in the market-place, attract the masses ('people') and worldly values ('fame'), have spirit but no 'conscience of the spirit'. That is, their mode of life as an objectification of will to power is dominant enough to enter consciousness as principle, duty or virtue, and to give them social or political influence – but wavers in its content and feels no compulsion not to wander. Their values and virtues consist of whatever is found to convince others; they are consummate actors but rotten human beings. (In an age of newspapers and popular culture, we are not that far from opinion polls, soundbites and focus groups.) Despite this wavering content, their values still present themselves as 'unconditional' –that is, presented as valid regardless of circumstance. Thus, they demand 'Yea' or 'Nay'. The higher and noble human is a living reminder to all such people of their falseness; thus, 'you are the bad conscience for your neighbours'. Flee into solitude, Zarathustra counsels. The market-place, meaning the values of capitalism, work or industry, is everywhere (see section 9). Philosophy and self-growth require something like *leisure*, a time available for reflection (see Nietzsche's fine image of thinking 'with a watch in hand, as one eats lunch with an eye on the financial pages' in *The Gay Science*, section 329; and the discussion of city spaces in section 280; see also *Beyond Good and Evil*, section 58).[26] This market-mentality is not just a 'lifestyle', though – something that could be changed like a set of clothes – but is, rather, the expression in institutions, virtues and habits of the mode of life of modern Europeans (and Americans).

Section 13, 'On Chastity'

This is one of the most overtly psychological sections of the book. Now, it is often the case that when Nietzsche says 'one' he also says 'two' (as in

Prologue, Section 9 and Part I, Section 11); there is clearly an important role for the lover, spouse or friend. At the time of writing the first two parts of Zarathustra, Nietzsche is deeply infatuated with Lou Salomé, with whom he hoped to make up such a two. But it is not a question of numbers (the relationship with Lou Salomé was briefly a three, and *ménage à trois* is a rather persistent image throughout the book), rather, it is a question of the health or productivity of the relationship and its suitability to the system of drives that is the Self. These are the key points of this section. The contrast Zarathustra is after is between 'lust' or 'sensuality', on the one hand, and 'innocence of the senses' on the other. The former hides even in inappropriate chastity, for example looking out of the coldness of the spirit. The latter term may be meant in both its superficial meaning of reason or mind (in which case Zarathustra means that 'lust' occupies even the intellectual life which might otherwise appear to be abstracted from the body), and also the preferred, technical meaning (from Part I, Section 1) of the will to power insofar as it forces itself to the level of explicit consciousness, self-identity or principle of virtue (in which case Zarathustra means that inappropriate chastity might be the disaster that inhabits and awaits a great soul). Lust may also appear disguised as pity, suggesting that the virtue of pity is actually a way of possessing or gaining power over. It is the forcing of the virtue, or the feeling that sensuality is 'filthy', that robs the senses of their innocence. The beasts are not ashamed of sex, and there may be humans like this too (see also the treatment of the sensual in Part III, Section 10). Still others, 'chaste from the ground up', do not possess this virtue insofar as they seek to avoid a vice; rather, chastity 'came to us and not we to it' (compare the final lines of the section with Part I, section 5: 'this bird has built its nest with me').

The 'innocence of the senses' may not be equivalent to, but is certainly a condition of love, which is one key way in which Zarathustra describes either the propriety or fertility of one's desire for overcoming, and also relationships with others that are productive with respect to overcoming. (See, for example, Part I, Section 17, 'the lover wants to create'.) This section is the first of a series of consecutive sections up to section 20, all of which discuss some form of love (though it is often disguised).

Section 14, 'On the Friend'

This section is important as a complement to sections 12 and 13. The prospective overhuman must seek solitude. This does not mean, however, that he needs to be lonely; friendship is a mode of proper solitude: 'are you pure air and solitude . . . for your friend?'[27] Nietzsche symbolises the multi-layered ensemble of psychological functions within the Self (cf. section 4) and the struggle for dominance and purification, by a duality within the ego: in his solitude Zarathustra divides in 'I and Me'. (Elsewhere we have 'Self' and 'Soul' or 'Self' and 'Heart'.) He is having 'deep' conversations with himself which tend to get out of hand; these are the struggles for reform of the drives but these struggles 'are always too zealous'. The image of the 'Tree on the Mountainside' is re-evoked: solitariness plunges the transforming seeker into 'too many depths'. The solitary is faced by nihilism, self-destruction or a betrayal of his nobility (which is what the young man in 'Tree on the Mountainside' is warned about). There is thus a temptation to seek the wrong kind of friend, who would be used to provide mere comfort and as an evasion of struggle. A true friend is needed 'for his height' – our belief in him betrays what we want to believe in ourselves; this allows the 'zealous' struggle to remain focused on its ideal. Thus, as Nietzsche writes in *The Gay Science*, a Self and friend have a 'shared higher thirst for an ideal' (section 14). We suggest that the growth of the individual being is dependent upon the community of friends. The ability to enter into friendships is in itself already a highly developed state: slaves cannot find a friend, and tyrants cannot have any, so that the ability in a human being to find a friend points to the potential in him for self-overcoming. What is needed as a precondition for friendship is compassion of a specific type: this compassion manages to divine whether the friend wants compassion. For, perhaps 'he loves in you the unbroken eye and the glance of eternity'. A friend insinuates himself (by guessing and keeping silent) into the friend's soul more than openly invading it. 'At least be my enemy' is the preliminary stage of asking someone for their friendship, because it requires the same kind of respect for the other. The previously mentioned notion of the friend as best enemy is developed further here; when striving against a friend 'you should be closest to him in your heart'.

The speech ends with a reflection on difference in gender attitudes towards friendship, a passage that anticipates section 18 ('On Old and Young Little Women') and requires the same kind of disclaimer: reading Zarathustra/Nietzsche on women is fraught with difficulty for the reader more than a century later. Women, it is argued here, fall from one extreme into the other, oscillating between love and hate, or socialising (ruminating cows, particularly unfunny – and see Part IV, Section

8). The mediating activity of friendship, and its respectful distance, women have not yet learned to embrace. Zarathustra finally ponders whether men are any more suited to friendship than women. The fact that it is conceded that men are also mostly herd animals of a different sort ('comradeship') and incapable of friendship qualifies the statement regarding women and friendship, but does not altogether disperse its unpleasant aftertaste.

Section 15, 'On the Thousand Goals and One', and a Note on Nietzsche and Evolution

A Note on Nietzsche and Evolution

All of Nietzsche's work profiles the fight for realisation of humanity caught up in forces located on the intersection between biology and culture. Thus it contributes to solving a problem left behind by Darwin's original theory outlined in *The Origin of Species* (1859), namely whether the laws of biological development are applicable also in the sphere of human history and culture. The existence of consciousness in the human species and the social and culture-building faculties of human beings necessitate a special investigation of this sphere which is both analogous to nature in the wider sense but also to an extent independent from it. Darwin himself addressed the problem of cultural evolution in 1871 in *The Descent of Man, and Selection in Relation to Sex*, which discusses – amongst a number of related issues – the applicability of evolution in the social realm. This leads to a whole new European movement of social theory in the 1880s and 1890s: 'Social Darwinism'.[28] *Zarathustra*, with the prominence given in it to the theorem of the will to power, should be read as contributing in this area. However, none of Nietzsche's work can be claimed as having fed in any significant way the more unsavoury offshoot of Social Darwinism that later gives prominence to notions of race and eugenics.[29] Nietzsche's central question is not whether, but in which ways the natural laws of evolution apply in the cultural realm, and what it takes for mankind to acknowledge and realise this revolutionising information. It is not clear whether Nietzsche read Darwin's work directly (the first German translation appeared in 1860). There is no doubt, however, that Nietzsche read books such as Friedrich Albert Lange's *Geschichte des Materialismus und Kritik seiner Bedeutung in der Gegenwart* (*History of Materialism and Critique of its Significance for the Present*), published in 1866. There, the attempt is made to transpose Darwin's biological notion of struggle into the social realm. Nietzsche had a copy of the book in his personal library.

There is also present in the background here a peculiar German variety of evolutionary thinking which precedes Anglo-Saxon attempts by more than half a century. A German strand of *Entwicklungsdenken*, or evolutionary theory, originates in the 1770s as part of the so-called *Sturm-und-Drang* movement. Such theory encompassed aspects of art criticism and human and cultural anthropology as well as earth science and the physiological study of geographical environments, single-handedly breaking new ground in all these areas. There is considerable evidence, moreover, that Darwin was aware of these ideas.[30] It is within this context that Nietzsche uses the notions of development and drive.[31]

* * * *

Section 15 is Zarathustra's account of the nature of a 'people'. A people is defined, we shall say, as a group with a homogeneous, successful (in their sphere) and broadly healthy mode of life. The most evident feature, though, is a set of values ('good and evil') that are enshrined in cultural activities and institutions (for example, religions or laws). It is by way of these values that a people 'maintains' or 'preserves' that life and thus also that 'health'. (We can now understand the section title's allusion to the *Arabian Nights*: the framing story is about preservation relative to the forces of destruction, and eventually about coming to an accommodation, a proper marriage, with those forces.) The 'good' are those things that are required for preservation, and the more rare or difficult to obtain, the more 'good'; evil are those things that threaten. These values reflect their overcomings or will to power – that is to say, they express this very mode of life and the history by which it became homogenous, successful and so forth. Within 'mode of life' Zarathustra includes a people plus 'land and sky and neighbour' – in other words, a people is a mode of life that has grown into a particular geographical, climactic and historical situation. It is a historical, biological and ecological system. Its values belong to it alone, they are inexplicable to other peoples (here, the 'neighbours'; thus the 'lie' of the pluralist state in Part I, Section 11). Its 'goal' or 'hope' would be continual self-overcoming towards more complete realisation of these values. A people cannot maintain itself simply if the individuals within it remain alive, regardless of circumstances (it cannot exist enslaved, for example), nor can it relax just because a landscape or neighbour has been tamed (it wants enemies not peace: Part I, Sections 10 and 14). For these would not be the exercise of virtue that is the expression of the will to power defining that people. To maintain or preserve can only mean to *continue* pursuing the highest goals – thus, in *Beyond Good and Evil* Nietzsche argues that self-preservation on the part of an individual organism or collective is actually a *derivative* effect; it is just one way in which the will to power seeks to exercise and enjoy its feeling of power (*Beyond Good and Evil*, section 13). Thus the repetition in this section of 'hard': that is laudable that struggles most to further a people's goals. Notice also the duality of 'the love that wants to rule, and the love that wants to obey', both the destructive/creative moment (ruling) and the preserving moment (obey) are essential to the overall process of the health and advancement of life (see our discussion of Part III, Section 12). Of course, this duality is generally characterised by Nietzsche as masculine and feminine. We see this most clearly in Part I, Section 18 or Part III, 12.23; and also in that virtue (will to power manifest as a particular mode of living) is imagined as a woman in Part I, Section 5, or again as the woman-child relation in Part II, Section 5.

Halfway through the passage, Zarathustra identifies four peoples in particular by naming their highest values through which they made themselves 'great'. The first three are pretty obviously the Greeks, Persians and Jews. The fourth one is less clear. Is it a reference to the Romans, or the Germans? The ambiguity is probably deliberate, and this is signalled by the appeal not to existing achievements but to a future 'pregnant and heavy with great hopes'. The ambiguity forces a German readership to confront the dangerous and creative problem of their own identity as a people and their relationship with the ancient world, and to do so quite separately from the nationalism and militarism of the new German state which is clearly one of the targets in Part I section 11.

Values result from a people's acts of evaluating or, ultimately, creating. Existence would be 'hollow' and without value were it not for such acts. What are these acts? They are identical with a people's historical task of overcoming itself so as to attain a successful mode of life. Creativity is defined as the invention or singling out of that which furthers a mode of life (an activity, state, idea, institution or resource – see *Twilight if the Idols*, 'Skirmishes of an Untimely Man', section 39). But a still higher creativity would be the invention of a new mode of life ('Change of values – that means a change of creators'). It is this higher creativity that Zarathustra envisages at the end of the section: 'there is lacking the one goal'. Such higher creativity would repeat the 1,000 original acts of creativity, but would do so on behalf of humanity as a whole, creating the overhuman. (Thus the notion of a 'chosen people' at the end of Part I, Section 22.2.) Creators were peoples, originally, and the individual creator is only a recent creation. Creation happened then pre-consciously or instinctively; this is in accord with the analysis of human cultures in Nietzsche's first book, *The Birth of Tragedy*. More recently, in several contexts of 'peoples', the human individual has become central as the bearer of political or economic rights and moral responsibilities, and singled out by law as the agent responsible for all actions. But this individual is a creative achievement that somehow aids the continual self-overcoming of a people. Nietzsche is clearly not an individualist, if by that we mean that the value and meaning of life begin and end with an individual's acts of evaluating or bestowing meaning. The individual exists only because life wants him or her to exist, as a function or instrument – as Zarathustra puts it at the end of Part I, Section 7, 'now a God dances through me'. Zarathustra names the function: the 'going under' of the herd. This conception of the individual is explained more clearly in *The Gay Science*, section 23. There, he writes that the individual emerges as a function of a culture (or a people) that has passed its sell-by date, so to speak, and needs to develop; once development has happened, the individual as such may again submerge, now redundant with respect to human life. The sudden use of the term 'herd' reminds us that, despite the enthusiastic language Zarathustra has been using in this section – marvelling at the acts of creativity that produced great peoples – 'people' has been a concept negatively evaluated since the Prologue as something dangerous to Zarathustra's task. From the perspective of human life as a whole, a people is a barrier. The creative function that had been the domain of peoples must now pass to those whose creativity means the overcoming of the human. (See *Beyond Good and Evil*, section 262, both for the account of a people and their virtues, and for the moments of transition in a state of volatility.) This also means that the latter will bear the title of 'evil' – and also 'godless', 'mad', 'barbarians' or what have you (see *The Gay Science*, section 76, for a particularly clear exposition). The new goal that is the overhuman marks the end of the age of peoples (although, again, not necessarily the inauguration of an age of 'individuals'!). This will become clearer in Part I, Section 17.

With these ideas comes a valuable set of distinctions. For example, the distinction between human life as such or as a whole (life that as system of anonymous will to power exceeds any individual and even any people) and life as a particular mode of living (will to power realised as a people – or subtype within a people, such as its priests or soldiers, or in exceptional cases even a single individual – with its values and celebrated virtues). The preservation of the latter might in some way harm the preservation of the former (see, for example, the apocalyptic beginning of Part II, Section 14). Similarly, we should distinguish between health as such (the health of human life as a whole, which, as all life, must grow and develop in order to exist at all) and the health of a particular mode of human life (the health of its suitability to its environment, history, and which maintains itself through its values or virtues). The latter 'health' may – especially in the ends to which it goes to preserve itself and destroy its 'evil' – actually be a sickness from the point of view of the former, insofar as it closes down or postpones the possibilities of human growth. Finally, we might distinguish between a narrow sense of 'preservation' (maintaining a form) and the preservation of life as such (which would include the destruction of form in the interest of new form). We have seen many examples of such distinctions at work, the clearest is probably the 'last human' in the Prologue. We will discuss the idea of perspective in the context of Part III, Section 10.

Section 16, 'On the Love of One's Neighbour'

This section follows on from sections 12 and 14. In section 12 (and in section 2, 'The Professional Chairs') the concept of neighbourhood was introduced. Section 14 profiled friendship as the most intimate bond between human beings, and also the social nucleus of overhumanity. In contrast, here now the negative context is further explored: inappropriate inter-personal relations. The speech puns on the compound German noun '*Nächstenliebe*' ('love of the neighbour') which Nietzsche turns into '*Fernstenliebe*' ('love of the farthest'). The Christian principle of the love of one's neighbour (for example, from the *New Testament*, 'Thou shalt love thy neighbour as thyself': Matthew 22: 39) is turned on its head and replaced with an imperative suited to induce the overhuman: to love those who are furthest away and the 'spectre' of 'what is to come'.

Nietzsche attacks Christian utilitarianism and philanthropy as hypocrisy: love of the neighbour amounts to 'bad love of yourself', and to escapism from the Self into the Other. This notion of 'bad love' means two inter-connected things: either 'bad' modifies 'love' (a reactive or unhealthy form of self-love), or else it negates it (self-loathing). The former case is closely related to pity, where the ostensible 'love' for the other is actually an attempt to gain power by diminishing or producing shame. We saw the latter in, for example, those that reactively hate the body, this life and this world. The love of the neighbour then is a 'virtue' meant to reflect well onto the self ('gild yourself with his error' – thus also the religious and indeed legal metaphor of 'witness'). 'Reactive' means that values are manifest not as a striving for overcoming but as stubborn preservation and, moreover, are formed not just as a response to but as an *inversion* of others, in an attempt to annul or sidestep the powerful: here, the inversion of the 'honest' spiritualisation of will to power as love of life. (See our note on Reactive Will to Power, with the commentary on Part III, Section 11.) Notice Zarathustra's nice description of such 'dishonesty': 'he who talks contrary to what he does not know'. In this type of social transference, the projection mechanism from Self into Other and back again that we saw succeeding in friendship goes wrong. The neighbour is a greater enemy than the friend turned enemy: it is the mediocre, average nature of grey modern man, a great hindrance for inducing the cultural and evolutionary revolution.

Zarathustra provides some anthropological explanation for this piece of counselling: 'the Thou is older than the I . . .' The moral rule of love of thy neighbour is derived from an ancient stage in human civilisation preceding the development of the historically later stage of individuality (see the previous section). The moral rule thus stems from a historical period where the social bond of the neighbourhood collective provides human shelter through absorbing single human beings. The neighbourhood-sphere is a primeval form of the market-place of section 12, 'On the flies in the Market-place'. Here its festivals are singled out again for critique, which Zarathustra abhors because they are populated with self-important artistes throwing their weight around (Wagner) and with shallow crowds following them as their role models. In contrast, the philosophy of the overhuman recognises that the individual stage of human culture is an instrument of life's further development, and should be understood as such – thus 'the I' should be pronounced holy as a temporary instrument of the overcoming of the human. 'Love of the farthest' implies love not for human beings as they are but for their possibilities of growth, for 'causes and spectres'. The neighbourly festivals are to be replaced by the society of the friend as a continual 'festival of the earth' (see also the 'ass festival' in Part IV, Section 18 which, in a way that only seems paradoxical, is both an example of such a new festival and *also* a parody of festivals). Notice that the friend that one 'creates' (earlier in the section) is now the 'creating' friend (see also Zarathustra's comment in Part I, Section 8). This signals not so much a reciprocity, as if Self and friend just help each other out; rather, as we will learn in the next section, creation is always transformation. So, to create the friend means also to transform the Self into the being capable of recognising and being worthy of friends; it means also to compassionately interpret the other as friend (to be his 'solitude' as section 14 put it); and to love the Self-friend dyad as nothing other than a love of the overhuman. For this reason the friend 'has a complete world to bestow'. (See our brief discussion of the concept of 'world' in the commentary on Part I, Section 1.)

The end of the passage gives the briefest of Dionysian visions; the world in rings is reminiscent of Dante's cosmos in the *Divina Commedia*. For the friend, in whom we glimpse the overhuman future, the world rolls apart (this is the destructive moment, the view into the depths, the danger of nihilism) and together (the creation of new values, the recognition of possibilities within the human that project beyond the human). And moreover, it rolls *as* the becoming of values and of purposive interpretations. Here, in a stunningly condensed form, is the essence of Nietzsche's mature philosophy, comprising (1) a methodology of analysis, (2) the stages of the growth of the spirit, (3) a cosmogonic model of planetary destruction and reconstruction (the imagery looks forward to the notion of eternal recurrence), and (4) also the principle behind historical evolution of moral values. That apparent opposites such as good and evil, or purpose and chance, are not foundations – that is, not ahistorical or transcendent principles – but rather develop surreptitiously from one another is Nietzsche's basic principle for understanding the nature and function of values, purposes and other associated cultural forms (see *Beyond Good and Evil*, section 2ff). A few years later, in *On the Genealogy of Morals*, Nietzsche invents the famous term 'genealogy' for the philosophical practice of discovering and describing the historical genesis and inter-relation of apparently opposite evaluations in a complex series of active and reactive creative episodes.

Section 17, 'On the Way of the Creator'

This section is a series of closely related meditations on the subject of what it means to be a creator, in the sense of 'creator' found in, for example, Part I, Sections 1 or 15. The first, preparatory theme is isolation as a way to oneself. Isolation we have seen many times before, from

Zarathustra's ten years in the mountains, to the camel pressing into the desert (Part I, Section 1), to the advice to flee the market-place (Part I, Section 12). And we also know that solitude is not incompatible with a certain form of friendship and perhaps also love. So what is new here is the idea of a 'way to yourself'. (This idea of becoming who you are is a frequent motif in the book. See especially Part IV, Section 1.) As we have seen, the individual as such is by no means *already* in isolation, for it may be that the individual was created to serve the needs of a people. It hardly matters if a people is said to have 'one conscience', or whether it is said to be made up of individuals with 'one conscience'. Conscience here designates value insofar as it has and is felt to have normative force. Thus, individualism is not the key idea here, isolation is. Isolation – whether this happens in a cave in the mountains or in the middle of a city among friends – means that one must isolate oneself from the herd even in one's conscience; one must undergo the 'agony' of annihilating this conscience within oneself, in order to rediscover the core of what is healthy and noble in the self. However, many who do throw off the yoke also 'threw off their last shred of worth'. There are those who are valuable not only to others, to the bulk of humanity, and perhaps even to the project of overcoming the human only insofar as they do *not* isolate themselves from the conscience of the people; and there are those whose individuality is in the service of lust or ambition ('the cunning I, the loveless' as this is described in Part I, Section 15). Who is it then that has the 'right' to such isolation?: the 'self-propelling wheel', which echoes the description of the spirit-child in Part I, Section 1; in other words, the one that is not merely an annihilator, but also a creator. What you are free from does not matter, what you are free for – being free for the expression and pursuit of your new 'ruling thought' – is what gives you this right (again, the Kantian conception of freedom as giving the law to oneself).

But he or she that is 'today' a creator will still face trials: 'one day solitude will make you weary'. The trial is of nihilism: even your creation will seem false and without value. Likewise, the creator will face trials externally. 'You compel many to relearn about you' (see, for example, the poem that ends *Beyond Good and Evil*). The greatest danger in any self-overcoming is from the self. Again, the conscience that 'you' had in common with the people is not a foreign influence coming from outside, but it is you, right down into the body. Even should this conscience be overcome, still there are the 'seven devils' of yourself that await. The list of these 'devils' is offered by Zarathustra here without much elaboration.

The list contains what must be for the moment empty and meaningless symbolic figures. However, there is some resemblance between this list and the cast of characters Zarathustra meets elsewhere (the 'witch', perhaps, already in the next section), and especially the series of 'superior humans' that Zarathustra encounters in Part IV.

Curiously, the 'dangers' discussed in this passage are seen primarily negatively, as trials or warnings. There are two more positive variations on the idea which should be added. The first is most notably found in Nietzsche's famous aphorism: '*From life's school of war.* – What doesn't kill me makes me stronger' (*Twilight of the Idols*, 'Arrows and Epigrams', section 8). The idea is that adverse conditions not only test one, but also provide a kind of discipline and thus the opportunity for a gathering of strength or the production of higher forms. An example would be arbitrary constraints on artistic practices that, far from being opposed to the possibility of art, are in fact its condition (see *Beyond Good and Evil*, section 188). Second, the necessity of struggle, war and overcoming to any process of growth is a theme we have encountered several times already (see 'On the Tree on the Mountainside' among others). Accordingly, the full account of the way of the creator would have to include as well the ideas expressed in Nietzsche's famous exhortation to 'live dangerously' (*The Gay Science*, section 283). Will to power exists relationally as differences of power and the feeling of those differences; without these differences and the consequent struggle among them, there could be no enhancement in the feeling of power and thus no organic development (even bestowal is a struggle in this sense – see Part I, Section 22; Part II, Section 9; and Part IV, Section 8). To stay safe is to be like the last humans, and preserve a specific mode of life at the expense of the greater health of the human. It is also the case, though, that not all struggles are valuable to life: rather than stay and swat flies, one should simply leave the market-place (similarly, see Part II, Section 4). For example, to seek power over the weak is demeaning; to seek power where there is only stubborn disease risks infection. Nietzsche often talks of 'self-control' (for example, *Twilight of the Idols*, 'Skirmishes of an Untimely Man', section 49) – the ability *not* to react to just any stimulus – but this is distinguished from the Stoics insofar as it does not amount to a retreat from the world.

Section 18, 'On Old and Young Little Women'

Like the end of section 14, 'On the Friend', this section presents problems to the twenty-first-century reader because it utilises late nineteenth-century stereotypes of gender and plays with them without critically destroying them. Many critics have lamented the unpalatable clichés of male domination.[32] Others hold that the symbolic system Nietzsche constructs is both subtler and less value-laden than it first appears. What is certain is that Nietzsche's rather perverse sense of humour has its field day particularly in this area. The present section has more elements of buffoonery than any of the previous.

Zarathustra is presented here as a shifty-looking rogue scuttling along to a *tête-à-tête* (as becomes clear from the end of the section). Unusually, we have a narrator other than Zarathustra or any other protagonist of Zarathustra's narrative, and it is an unknown, authorial voice (like the voice from heaven in Goethe's *Faust*, for example). This voice enquires of Zarathustra where he is going so sneakily at twilight and what he is 'hiding so carefully under his cloak'. Zarathustra, caught in the act (or right before it, to be precise), stops to justify himself. He recounts a discussion with 'a little old woman'.[33] Note that the woman has not spoken to him as a person, but to his soul, similar to Zarathustra's addresses to his 'heart'. This certainly distinguishes the old woman from any other character. What follows is a short speech as a 'story within a story' that not only explains Zarathustra's philosophy of the sexes but also what he is wearing under his cloak and where he is going. The old woman asks him to talk to her about women. At the end of his speech to her the shoe is on the other foot and the old woman instructs Zarathustra in some truths about young 'little' women. The complications created by these narrative devices (a strange narrator, Zarathustra's embarrassment, the fact that his wisdom is compromised by him turning into the unwitting recipient of truth, and the circular development of the 'bottom-heavy' plot that ends with a punchline) are all subservient to creating doubt about Zarathustra, now all of a sudden not so much wise teacher of overhumanity but an 'unreliable narrator' who has something to hide. The form of narrative irony thus also throws doubt over the chauvinistic and stereotyped content of his core speech, which is made to sound pompous and self-serving. It is possible to see the whole litany of clichés for what they are: *deliberate* clichés, because the text yields a reading that the whole of this speech is the product of a male mind thinking with his genitalia. Zarathustra is not preparing for overhumanity all the time; he is also 'only too human'! And it is women who make him lose his composure. He is portrayed here as being out of his depth and the reason is that he is 'going to women'.

The old woman holds the truth about women. She replies to Zarathustra's harangue with a sarcastic riposte ('Many charming things has Zarathustra said . . . does not know women well'). She reprimands him by cutting through the whole list with the sentence: 'with woman no thing is impossible'. This is a hugely significant statement, echoing as it does Luke 1: 37, which portrays the angel Gabriel saying to Mary, 'with God no thing will prove impossible'. Truths have been 'conceived', despite Zarathustra's little 'knowledge' (like the Virgin Mary) and the woman's age (like Elizabeth) – but this miracle originates with *woman*, not man. Finally she presents him with a 'little truth' which leaves the reader with the riddle of what it actually is that Zarathustra carries under his cloak. There are a number of possibilities, all of them amusing. First, the translator suggesting that this could be a reference to Phaedrus hiding a scroll under his cloak containing a 'speech about love', draws our attention to a passage in Plato's *Phaedrus* (which, it should be noted, is a dialogue famous for its critique of the nature of writing in its vulnerability to misinterpretation). The voice of irony from the mysterious intervening narrator suggests three teasing possibilities: a treasure, 'a child that has been born to you' (particularly deflating, because of the subsequent sexist cliché of women as birthing machines), or loot from a robbery, since Zarathustra has been siding so openly with evil-doers. The old woman holds the key to solving the riddle of what is going on under Zarathustra's cloak. She gives him 'as thanks' for his failure of a speech 'a little truth' ('"I am certainly old enough for it"'): '"You are going to women? Then don't forget the whip"'.

This section is part of an extended multimedia in-joke that goes beyond the mere text of *Zarathustra*. The whole passage needs to be located in the context of Nietzsche's relationship, or rather lack thereof, with Lou Salomé. Instead of marrying her, in the summer of 1882 he travelled around Europe with her and his friend Paul Rée, in an odd *ménage à trois* of 'free spirits'. At that time, on Nietzsche's wish, the three of them hired a professional photographer and posed for a photograph which shows the following scenario: centre-stage depicts a little wooden cart facing right. Salomé kneels in the cart on the left, brandishing a whip, the two men are standing on the right, with Nietzsche looking out of the picture to the right into the high distance. The whole scene is one of joking role-play, suggesting that the group is resting for a moment and that the woman will whip them back into submission at the yoke. The most common reading of the 'truth' is that, 'take the whip because you will have to use it for disciplining or control purposes'. Now a contrary reading suggests itself. The eminent Swiss Nietzsche biographer Curt Paul Janz suggests that the advice means that 'she, "woman", has the whip; that is what men need to bear in mind'.[34] If Zarathustra therefore was not carrying a whip (since woman has it), what is the 'little truth' that Zarathustra is carrying under his cloak? The riddle is solved by process of elimination: Zarathustra, going to women, is hiding an erection. As an account of real, inter-personal sexual relations, that self-mocking joke is as far as it goes.

So, a comic episode – but beyond that what is its philosophical significance? There are two important ideas. The first is put poorly here: the biology of human sexes cannot simply be transcended in psychology or culture. Men and women are biologically different and thus could not but be different spiritually also. '[W]ho has fully grasped how *strange to each other man and woman are*?', Zarathustra asks us rhetorically in Part III, Section 10. Not that this difference should be translated into social or political inequality (see, for example, Part I, Section 20), but equally there may be impulses to forms of equality that would mask the difference. The second idea is more carefully put: the social and sexual comedy of the section is a metaphor for the problem of human overcoming. We have already suggested that a central element of Nietzsche's psychological analysis of the human is the internal relationship of masculine and feminine drives (see our discussion of section 15). The old woman talks to Zarathustra's soul – she is *part of* Zarathustra, a metaphor for an aspect of human psychology. This section, then, concerns the struggle (perhaps the whip is *mutual*) and impossibility of any mutual understanding (indicated by masculine Zarathustra's offensive speech) of these competing drives. The social comedy is a sign both of this essential struggle, and, more importantly, that Zarathustra has not yet been able to make this struggle *productive*. Not with the masculine on its own, but rather only when the masculine gives itself over to the feminine aspects of the total economy of the healthy human organism is 'no thing impossible' (see also the symbolic drama of Part III, Section 14). With the feminine aspect of the living organism comes the possibility of pregnancy and birth – literally but more importantly symbolic: preservation of life in the mode of *creativity*. This 'metaphysical' interpretation of the symbolism of gender also allows us to reread and redeem Zarathustra's clichés earlier. (However, it does not redeem the sexually-distracted Zarathustra who said these clichés about biological woman rather than the symbolic feminine, nor the sexually repressed Nietzsche who thought they were funny.) We will be developing further this interpretation of the gendering of drives as the commentary proceeds; see especially the commentary on Part III, Sections 14 and 15.

Section 19, 'On the Bite of the Adder'

This is the first time in the book that the 'disciples' are explicitly mentioned (although it is possible we are meant to read Part I, Section 8 in this way); and significantly this mention falls only a couple of sections prior to Zarathustra's departure from them. The disciples are not a cast of characters (and ultimately narrators and interpreters) as they are in the *New Testament* and in Plato's dialogues. Here, they simply represent the other side of a teaching activity, and have no further definition than that. Zarathustra offers his disciples an allegorical story (with religious imagery: serpent and figs; see Genesis chapter 3) and an interpretation of it. Continuing with the broad theme of love, here we have the love of one's enemy. The relation to the enemy is either mutually productive of overcoming, or it is merely petty and mutually demeaning (this is also the message of Part I, Section 10). The relation to the enemy is here generally a playful inversion or distortion of the Christian ideal of turning the other cheek. 'Enemy' is given a range of meanings, from a personal opponent (perhaps an intellectual adversary), to a criminal as an enemy of the people. Accordingly, love of the enemy ranges from 'join in a little with the cursing' to a conception of justice as love and higher compassion, which recognises the law's constitutive responsibility for transgression and would will its going under as law. The discussion of justice in a broadly criminal sense rapidly metamorphoses into the topic of the economic or social justice of distribution ('to each his own'). Zarathustra's 'philanthropy', his love of and gift to the human, is, as we have seen, the bestowing of his wisdom (Prologue, Section 1) which serves neither the people in general nor Zarathustra, but serves the overhuman.

Section 20, 'On Children and Marriage'

In contrast to the distorted definitions given by Zarathustra in section 18 of the relationship between the sexes, this section redefines it in terms of a responsible union in marriage entered into with a view to furthering the development of the human towards overhumanity. Here both men and women are presented as equal in their aspiration for moral responsibility and mutual 'reverence', as a precondition for good marriage. Zarathustra argues that the partners in marriage have to be morally prepared for it, as both 'the victor, the self-compeller, commander of the senses, master of virtues'. In the light of the previous sections this is fairly self-explanatory: marriage as the sum (in the child) greater than its parts – 'the will of two to create the one that is more than those who created it'. The second half of the section deals with mismatched and failing marriages. Of interest is the discussion of love as an ingredient of good marriage. As such, love needs to sympathise 'with suffering and disguised gods', whereas 'for the most part two animals find each other out' (the animal imagery is thus used differently here than in section 13). This extends the idea of 'reverence' mentioned previously, but is also a mutual yearning for the overcoming of the human. Love in marriage then joins friendship (section 14) as a mode of real social relation, the meaning of which is not personal or private, but rather a productive part of the historical development of life itself. As such, love becomes 'a rapturous allegory' (the personal as symbol of the continual striving of life) that lights 'your way to higher paths'.

Section 21, 'On Free Death'

This section suitably follows the previous section, with its treatment of the child as a 'living monument', the 'duality' that is the married couple having an impression upon the future. One's death should be such a monument, a festival (celebrating the life, its achievements, and the continuing impact of those achievements). Just as the meaning of human life is or should be the 'sense of the earth', so likewise should the meaning of death. One's death should be considered as part of the task and strategy of overcoming the human: 'Whoever has a goal and an heir wants death at the right time for his goal and heir'. To die too soon, or too late, signals a death that is not free because it is the end of a life that has not liberated itself from the various evaluation-dogmas that inhabited its conscience, a life that, in short, was not consummate with life. The section includes a taxonomy of deaths, including a set of variations on the metaphor of ripeness: never ripening, ripening too early, going rotten, hanging on the branch too long (Zarathustra wishes for a 'storm' of 'preachers of *quick* death'). Zarathustra explicitly and, of course, anachronistically discusses the life of Jesus, lamenting that he died too young before he had spent sufficient time in the wilderness to have 'learned to live and learned to love the earth', and especially lamenting the 'catastrophe' that resulted from the propagation of his immaturity. 'Noble enough was he to retract', Zarathustra affirms (one should compare this brief discussion of Jesus with that in *The Antichrist*).

The section ends curiously. After praising death 'at the right time', Zarathustra begs forgiveness for lingering 'a little longer on earth'. Is he in danger, then, of being like the rope-makers? Or does he sense that the 'living monument' of his disciples is not yet ready? The tension of this ambiguity animates the next section, wherein Zarathustra takes his leave.

Section 22, 'On the Bestowing Virtue'

Part I has explored the basis of what, often enough, *looks* like a new morality. This has been shaped by a critique of an old set of moralities that have proved to be no longer adequate, because they are based upon a model of man that has been superseded by new (scientific, psychological) insights into his make-up. The old morality was based on a rejection of the human body and a theory that placed it under the control of artificially and metaphysically detached psychological capacities (senses, spirit), all validated by some transcendent principle. The rejection of body is the key instance of a more general rejection of the nature of life as will to power. The ensuing period of moral values, particularly in its Christian variety as dichotomy between good and evil, reflects and perpetuates this mind/body misunderstanding. Although it must be regarded as historically necessary, such a system of values represents and preserves a particular mode of life completely out of alignment with life. Such a system is equated with morality as such – that is, Nietzsche often seems to define the 'moral' as any system of value understood as foundational and universal rather than perspectival. (See our note on Perspectivism, with the commentary on Part III, Section 10.) Thus, as we have noted before, Zarathustra's new philosophy should be seen as beyond the moral.

Zarathustra's new insights begin with the locating of all psychological drives, and their coordination, regulation and calibration, in the living body. If there is 'good' or 'virtue', it should therefore be a new type of mental and, of course, physical health based on acceptance of the supremacy of the body and, beyond any one body, the supremacy of life and will to power. The groundbreaking, revolutionary claim of Zarathustra/Nietzsche is that the alignment of the constituent elements of the self under the aegis of the living body (thus, alignment to will to power) amounts to an evolutionary completion or 'perfection' of humanity – although, to be sure, not in a new, static species-form that would then tenaciously hold onto life come what may, but rather in a form of life that has no essential form except its continued healthy striving for new form. Also, in this 'completion', the human has arisen to a full understanding of his unique and previously misunderstood position as 'spiritual animal', and insofar as this spirit is consummate to the will to power – and not a self-denial of it – the overhuman represents the pinnacle of life. This is a position which the death of God and Darwin's evolutionary theory had stripped it of. It is a restoration, but on entirely different grounds. Nature and the human are at one in the overhuman; she or he is nature through and through, spiritualised, and in individual human form.

The section consists of three short and highly compressed subsections that could be entitled Zarathustra's epiphanies of the overhuman. Additionally, we have anticipations of the notion of eternal recurrence, and further work on the new language of philosophy, a life-long concern of Nietzsche's (see Part I, Section 7 and note on Nietzsche, Music and Language, with the commentary on Part II, Section 17). The three speeches of this section conclude Zarathustra's first period of 'going down' amongst men and are his leaving present for his disciples. Speech 1 expounds the idea of creating new values; Speech 2 explains the need for overhuman value-willing to be anchored within the material world of nature and of anchoring it historically; Speech 3 reflects on the relationship between Zarathustra and his disciples, between teaching and learning.

Speech 1

This speech contains two key ideas. First, Zarathustra explains the nature of bestowing, which has been a theme of the book since the first section of the Prologue. Bestowing is a virtue – this means it is a defining activity of the spirit, expressive of a dominant will to power. Specifically, insofar as spirit has been transformed so as to be aligned with the nature of life, it will recognise a new type of 'selfishness' that accumulates (the feeling of overabundance) only in order to bestow. Its selfishness is identical with its position as a kind of channel through which the resources of humanity, wisdom and history are directed towards the overhuman. That is, it will seek to further the healthy interests of life beyond its own contingent individuality. As such, it is the 'highest virtue'. An existence that has recognised its relational nature and its belongingness to the historical and cultural development of human life must bestow. What is bestowed, though, may be new values to replace the old (together with an understanding of the necessity of their being temporary), or, like Zarathustra, wisdom as 'the sense of the earth'. Thus the bestowing virtue is radically different from the virtues of the past, not a tool for biological survival and generated from fear of being, necessity of regulating social life, or laziness of convention (see the professor of ethics in Part I, Section 2. There is a nice discussion of such bestowing in *Beyond Good and Evil*, section 260, which also has the virtue of being located in a more general context.)

The parting gift of the golden staff to Zarathustra from his disciples sets the scene: it is an allegory of eternal recurrence, the snake coiled around the sun, reminiscent of the Dionysian vision of the recreation of the world in section 16. But its symbolic qualities do not end there. Zarathustra explains how this bestowing works by comparing it to gold, and specifically the gold standard in monetary value creation (a similar idea occurs in Marx's *Capital*).[35] Through its symbolic propensities, gold links morality and economics, although this idea is not developed here in any detail. (The analysis of the relationship between monetary value and exchange, on the one hand, and the development of moral attitudes, on the other, is an important part of *The Genealogy of Morality*.)[36] The important realisation is that gold, even though it sets value, is in itself 'of no use' – it stands outside all instrumental value (all value to a mode of life).[37] Rather, it is 'luminous and mild in its lustre' and thus the model of bestowal. The bestowing virtue gives value to other, specific virtues insofar as they are an enhancement of the health of life as such.

Also, though, gold is able to 'make peace between moon and sun'. This beautiful lyrical idea refers forward to the image of the moon as pale and cold, abstract and disinterested reflection (this symbolic meaning only becomes clear in Part II, Section 15). We should put this together with the image of golden illuminated water in Prologue, Section 1. Gold represents the possibility of a secondary reflection (of the sun, of insight into the nature of things) which is not moonlike, but itself is 'like the glance of the one who bestows'. Gold then is *the allegory of allegory*, or more generally, the allegory of philosophy as allegory. Philosophical allegory functions, that is, by being the very activity of bestowing, by being a form of language use that, like the bestowing virtue, has aligned itself with will to power such that its meaning, purpose and validity consists entirely of its encouragement of the elevation and advancement of the listener. An allegory is 'true' if and only if it *works*. (See our discussion of Part I, Section 7 and Part III, Section 9.) The disciples, like Zarathustra, seek this virtue that they might accumulate 'all things toward' them, only that all things may flow back out as gifts of love (for the overhuman).

Zarathustra makes it clear where the new bestowing type of virtue originates. An alignment of psychological agents in the self under the supremacy of the living body is needed, the opposite of modes of selfishness that are mere 'degeneration'. In the bestowing human the senses (the most immediate contact with the world or with ourselves, which language would seek to communicate) fly upward, seeking a sensible encounter with higher states and above all the feeling of the enhancement of power through self-overcoming towards new, healthier and more powerful modes of life. This must also involve an overcoming of the despising of the body which sees the senses as the lowest form of spirit. 'Virtues' Zarathustra calls allegories of such bodily elevation. That is, a virtue is the spiritualisation (the allegorical 'herald') of the *movement* of bodily elevation. The language of virtue cannot be a direct naming, because then it is caught up in a people's language, which has as its function precisely *stopping* such movement (see Part I, Section 5). Even the virtues of a people are not directly named, but allegories of a bodily elevation that *once happened*. Zarathustra's disciples must give up having knowledge of virtue by way of a taxonomy of its names; rather he or she must learn to interpret and use allegory. This involves penetrating the layers of psychological and cultural history by which a form of life spiritualises itself as a virtue. New virtues will be no different, except that they will be understood as such, and will represent an alignment to will to power rather than a fleeing from it. When the psycho-physiological alignment is reached in the Self, human beings turn into 'willers of one will'. This makes it clear again that Zarathustra is not seeking individuals in any recognisable sense of that term; if the individual has value, it is only so that it too can go under in becoming the 'willers of one will'. Through the body they are at one with themselves, with what Zarathustra will shortly call 'the chosen people', and with nature and the yearning of all nature, which is will to power (see the image of becoming 'whole' in Speech 3).

Zarathustra calls 'this new virtue' 'power' (that is, will to power). All virtues are will to power, of course. They are a 'ruling thought', but are not necessarily a golden sun – that is, not necessarily bestowing. Only a virtue that is an allegory of the enhancement of human life must also be a bestowing virtue – its selfishness will consist of wishing to be the instrument of advancing life. Moreover, only around such a virtue will curl 'a clever soul' (serpent of knowledge). The curling of the snake is an image of proximity and alignment to will to power,[38] and in that proximity and alignment lies also its wisdom, a secondary and allegorical reflection that is not distant and cold.

Speech 2

We do not know the impact of the previous speech on his disciples, but we are informed by the omniscient narrator that Zarathustra's 'voice was transformed'. In this second speech Zarathustra reinforces some ideas, for example, that there needs to be a correspondence between the bestowing activities of the disciples and 'the earth' whose sense Zarathustra bids his disciples to serve. This earth is not nature in its opposition to human beings and their culture. Zarathustra's materialism is again emphasised: the cultural revolution as completion of the evolutionary project of humanity is not an act of abstract spiritual renewal, but is happening in the theatre of this world we live in: 'a site of convalescence shall the earth yet become'. Next, the notion of history of morality is introduced: a history of delusion and mistakes based on flying from the earth (among other things, this means seeking transcendent founding principles) and despising the body. As again the creation of new virtues will be, so the creation of the old virtues was 'experiments' which a later and higher perspective judges to have been mistakes or to have become liabilities. These delusions are not just 'ideas', but have inscribed themselves into our bodies. We carry in our body 'not only the reason of millennia – but also their madness'. All this 'breaks out in us'. In other words, however metaphysical and moral mistakes begin, they become hegemonic by creating a form of human life that internalises these mistakes, that reorients and organises the drives so that spirit can express itself in no other way. For example, in *The Gay Science*, Nietzsche discusses how the idea of human equality has become a part of the modern mode of life, even for those who intellectually might oppose it (section 18). Also, Nietzsche was rather fond of the eighteenth-and nineteenth-century biological idea of 'atavism' – see, for example, *The Gay Science*, section 10. A genealogical analysis is required to uncover the hidden history of a value. It follows that self-overcoming is literally a physiological process, and many of the most dangerous enemies are within: 'Dangerous it is to be an heir'

Zarathustra here explicates the fascinating notion of history as a theatre of psycho-physiological events, much applied and followed-up in twentieth-century theories of culture from Freud to French post-structuralism. We can fortify ourselves against such suffering from history and heal ourselves 'through knowing', by means of which 'the body purifies itself; experimenting with knowing, it elevates itself'. In other words, just as spirit is a mode of expression of the body and its drives, so a modification of the spirit (coming to know, understand, or have insight) might reciprocally serve the realignment of the body along the path of the will to power (this is a psychosomatic notion). This would happen insofar as new knowledge or new ideas are internalised or incorporated into the system of the drives of the body, insofar as a new 'instinct' is acquired (see *The Gay Science*, section 11) that could then in turn spiritualise itself as a new virtue. This knowing is not just intellectual; it is an exploration of possibilities ('a thousand paths'), a sensual wakefulness that is contrasted to mere observation (Part II, Section 15), and an experimenting (the trying-out of modes of life). These are all sets of actions that attempt to create new everyday practices, social and cultural forms, and thus virtues. Thus, for example, we have seen Zarathustra advise on the practices of solitude, friendship and marriage which, when properly carried through with understanding, can be experiments that promote the development of the human. It is important to note this great trust in knowledge (broadly speaking). Despite the mystique that surrounds notions such as will to power, overcoming, bodily elevation and eternal recurrence, they are grounded and counterbalanced in a core of something like Enlightenment inquisitiveness. Speech 2 ends with an invocation of a 'chosen people' – chosen not by God this time, but by themselves, who function through the new or reformed social practices, and who with 'one will' strive for the overhuman.

Speech 3

The main thrust of Zarathustra's argument here is that his coming down from the mountains to be amongst his fellow human beings is also a 'going down' in the sense of redundancy after the fulfilment of his mission. In the advancement of life everything goes under, even those elements that are strongest, healthiest and contribute most. Bestowing must ultimately be destruction. In stark contrast to Jesus who wants his disciples to remain loyal to him, Zarathustra positively demands that his own disciples deny him, because, as he has already said in section 6, he cannot be their 'crutch'. They have to probe what he has taught them ('perhaps he has deceived you'). They must realise in practice (through 'experiments') what they have learned from him ('find yourselves' – not an entreating to individualism but rather to internalisation, the reformation of one's constellation of drives so as to align them to the life that one already is). Finally, they must unlearn their reverence for him ('What does Zarathustra matter?'; indeed, those who come after will even be 'ashamed' of him) and direct it to the overhuman (see also *The Gay Science*, section 303): all sound advice that should form part of any enlightened pedagogy. Only when they have 'denied' him will he return to them.

Nietzsche writes, at *The Gay Science*, section 286, 'These are hopes [that is, for new forms of humanity] . . . I can only remind – more I cannot do!'. In other words, unless the reader has already experienced certain yearnings and seen themselves and the human in a certain light, unless that is they are *capable* of transformation, then nothing Nietzsche says or does will make a difference. Here in *Zarathustra*, what the disciples do *now* is the test of this (and see Part II, Section 1 and Part III, Section 8). The first part ends with the vision of 'the great midday' as the world-historical mid-point of humanity between beasthood and overhumanity. Midday is a point of transition, but because it is also when the sun is highest, then the 'shadows' are both shortest and closest. 'Shadows' has two meanings, both as that which must be or remains to be overcome (shortest), and as image of the ideal (closest). At the great midday, when it is realised that all gods are dead (shortest shadows) – and realised not just intellectually, but with all its implications at the level of the body –, the epoch of the overhuman can begin.

Part II

Section 1, 'The Child With the Mirror'

Zarathustra returns to the mountains for 'months and years', impatiently waiting. The child in the dream is the future of Zarathustra's teaching, and thus Zarathustra's own 'child' (notice the images of pregnancy throughout), after Zarathustra's 'wild wisdom' gives birth. The child is also the last stage of the transformation from the spirit-lion, a transition that looks more difficult and terrible as this part continues (the idea of eternal recurrence will start to trouble Zarathustra in Part II and complete itself at length in Part III). The metaphor of the mirror serves two purposes: Part II will reflect on and deepen the teaching of Part I, while also representing the image of Zarathustra that is being, or will be, disseminated. His teaching is being distorted and mocked (as at the beginning of Part II, Section 3); however, Zarathustra does not arise pained or anxious about this, but with an 'imminent happiness'. The dawn of morning image repeats the moment from the Prologue when Zarathustra addresses the sun and resolves to 'go under'. Here, the idea is not that Zarathustra will simply correct the distortions, or repeat his teaching, but rather that a new phase of teaching is about to begin ('New ways I walk now . . .'); this newness was already suggested in the final section of the previous part.

Notice that his love 'overflows in torrents . . . towards rising and setting'; there are many possible interpretations of this image, but most striking is the idea of Zarathustra on a watershed. That is, the geographical place where the direction of flow of water switches from one side to the other; metaphorically, then, a moment of chance, incalculability, decision or creativity. The watershed image is used even more clearly in Part III, Section 16.1: 'a high ridge between two seas'. This idea of a point of sudden change or emergence is echoed later in the passage in the notion of 'tension'.[39] All of these images will be gathered in the conception of the 'moment' in Part III, Section 2. At the end of the passage we have Wisdom personified again as a woman (see Part I, Section 7).

Section 2, 'Upon the Isles of the Blest'

The 'Isles of the Blessed' or 'Fortunate Islands' are a reference to Greek (and possibly Nordic) mythology. There they feature as a paradise-like resting place for retired heroes allocated by the Gods. As a title of Zarathustra's speech they signal a place of solitude (or the special communities Zarathustra has been discussing) in which human growth can realise itself away from the human; and perhaps also a metaphor for the world as a whole as the playground for the overhuman after the Gods have been banished from it. Zarathustra is the harsh north wind that shakes not mere apples, but the luscious, ripe figs (representing his teachings) from the trees of paradisical knowledge. The image combines the forbidden apple of Eden with the means Adam and Eve found of hiding their shame (fig leaves). So, it is the image of wisdom not only without shame but *with* sensual pleasure. This is the Book of Genesis re-written by the Greeks, not to tell the story of the banishment of the human race from paradise, but to clarify the conditions for its re-entry back into it. Part I mostly dwelt in an abstract space of a supra-historical critique. The rural and urban vignettes of the case studies were generally set in a faux-archaising atmosphere that had the effect of creating timeless, allegorical situations. In Part II now, history and historical time play an increasingly important role. With the title of section 2, we are now entering the civilised climes of Ancient Mediterranean and Northern cultures; and Nietzsche's critique of European culture becomes more focused. Curiously, the further we advance in the text, the more Zarathustra turns into a phantasmagorical hybrid, invented as a legitimising device for allegorical narrative. Increasingly he reveals himself to be what we could call 'a narrative *deus ex machina*', engineered for narrative and allegorical effect.

This section is given over to the dismantling of the doctrine of divine creation of the world and replacing it with the insight that 'God is a supposition'. From this follows that man needs to stop willing and thinking the unwillable and inconceivable, and instead align his will and thought to the immanent nature of the real. This immanence is figuratively represented here by the fullness and ripeness of autumn. Moreover, the view of the 'distant seas' (an image of the world as an immanent whole, and of distant, connected horizons in time) does not invite one to say 'God' – that is, this view is not 'sublime', transcending us in magnitude or power, the symbol of a creating God. Rather, contemplating the seas is now 'beautiful'. They symbolise an immanent world of which we have become an integral part. The contemplation should remind us of the overhuman as the bringing to fruition of the human. In this beauty, the world is complete in itself. The overhuman is humanly possible; it can build on precedent, on the experience of past humanity. Thus the overhuman inherits and continues the past history of human achievement, including especially those like Zarathustra and his disciples who refashion themselves in order to further that possibility: 'verily, through a hundred souls I have gone my way'.

God is a needless, additional 'supposition' and moreover, not 'thinkable'. The notion is similar to analyses found in Descartes and Kant, and before them in a long tradition of negative theology. The transcendence and eternalness of God with respect to the world renders Him (or at least the idea of Him) in some way unthinkable – not an idea we could have created, argues Descartes; not cognisable and unavailable to any knowledge, argues Kant. The idea of God is thus a kind of negative image or shadow. Zarathustra seems to use this to stress the limitations of human capacities, as other philosophers have; but this is not the chief point. Rather, he is pointing to the absurdity of will, thought or sense reaching beyond the immanence of world. It is not, then, so much that human capacities are limited, as that they belong to the world, and it to them. Thus the human becomes the yardstick for creation: 'your reason, your image, your will, your love'. The overhuman takes shape in an age of understanding where the 'unwillable' and the 'unthinkable' have been abandoned – this is not just an abandonment of belief in God, but a revolution that reaches 'through to the end' of all human capacities and their meaning. Zarathustra reveals his heart: '*if* there were Gods, how could I stand not to be a God! *Therefore* there are no Gods.' How could a will exist which permitted the existence of something *necessarily* beyond its power? Will to power is essentially relational; God would be something exceeding all relations; therefore 'there are no Gods'. The radicalism of his own conclusion brings Zarathustra to a position ('it draws me') where he can see the enormity of the delusional supposition that there be a God. Theological speculations conceiving of principles describing God as 'the One and Plenum [a term that here means 'space entirely filled with matter'] and Unmoved and Complete and Permanent' run counter to the principles that have emerged from an understanding of nature and not just Nietzsche's own understanding. He is talking about themes from nineteenth-century physics and biology: multiplicity and dispersion (thermodynamics), attraction and repulsion of bodies in empty space (mechanics and cosmology), developmental dynamism of natural processes (evolutionary biology), and transience of developmental stages (the controversy about transitional evolutionary forms, already alluded to in Prologue, Section 2). Zarathustra summarises the theistic stage of human civilisation by calling it a 'turning sickness'.

Nietzsche concurs with Plato's critique of poets in the *Republic* where they are branded as necessarily peddling dangerous untruths, and has Zarathustra reprimand them for having helped to back up the absurd theistic principle of permanence. (Of course, his concurring with Plato is ironic, since the reasons they have for these apparently similar views are completely opposed. The discussion of poets resumes in section 17.) 'All permanence – that is mere allegory!' With this sentence the Plato reference is immediately followed by one to Goethe's *Chorus Mysticus* at the end of *Faust Part II* – again ironic because Goethe's text reads the opposite: 'All impermanence – that is a mere allegory!' The poetry of the overhuman requires the finest of allegories that tell 'of time and becoming'; they need to be in praise and justification 'of all impermanence'. Despite its closing lines, Goethe's pagan philosophy of *Faust II* is thus admitted into the gallery of ancestral influences that have gone into Nietzsche's text. (On allegory see our discussion in Part I, Section 22, our note on Nietzsche, Music and Language, with the commentary on Part II, Section 17, and Chapter 1 'The Text . . .'.)

The speech moves towards Zarathustra re-emphasising the principles of human creating as introduced in Part I, Section 22. Through creating man finds redemption from suffering, but the precondition for creating must have been 'suffering and much transformation'. There is much of the past in us in the form of drives, systems of belief, habits, virtues or vices; we must give birth to ourselves. The child image returns, but with an important variation: the human creator must himself 'be the child that is newly born, he must also be the birth giver and the pain of the birth giver'. The human creator is envisaged here as a child that carries the whole cycle of birth inside of him (this links in with contemporary evolutionary thought about the relationship between ontogeny and phylogeny of the species). This also throws an interesting light on the gender debate that is being led in *Zarathustra*. It is suggested here that masculine and feminine elements come together and need to be realised together in the transition towards overhumanity. See our discussion of Part IV, Section 19.

The passage ends with a reflection on the liberating effect of creating as an intrinsic human activity. When it is dependent on understanding nature, willing will set humanity free, because then human will coincides with the will of nature. It is humanity itself that is the object of human creating: the 'blind' process of evolution of life has, in human beings, created a species that can self-fashion. A modification of spirit is a modification of body, thus 'in understanding too I feel only my will's joy . . .' (and see Part I, Section 22.2). If this self-fashioning were healthy, meaning aligned to the nature of life as will to power, then the 'can' self-fashion becomes 'must': 'the hammer is driven to the stone'. Zarathustra illustrates this with the example of the hammer releasing the sculpted image of beauty hewn from a raw piece of rock. In this way, Zarathustra demonstrates what was meant in the demand above that the finest allegories should be of 'time and becoming'. He uses a simile reminiscent of one frequently employed by Michelangelo[40], who describes artistic creation by means of the same neo-platonic allegory: ideas, shades of things, are inbuilt in the raw material of nature; they have to be released into phenomenal existence through the hard toil of the creating artist. Nietzsche had used a very similar analogy in *The Gay Science*, section 215, which also adds the observation that merely having the ideal is insufficient if it does not express honestly the underlying physiology of the 'stone'. The reference to Michelangelo becomes complete with the words 'shadow' and 'perfect'. Michelangelo said that 'the true work of art is but a shadow of the divine perfection'. But in this case the shadow is not an image of anything other than what in fact lies within the stone, a perfection immanent to humanity and nature, awaiting progressive release by the hammer, and thus Zarathustra can say: 'what are the Gods to me now!'. We should note that the word 'perfection' suggests that the overhuman is a fixed state, 'stillest', the evolutionary completion of the human and indeed of nature – but in a section that has made so much of the notion of impermanence, that would be a mistake. The overhuman as perfect is an ideal of becoming, a 'state' of endless, destructive and joyfully creative striving. The notion of eternal recurrence, as employed at the end of Part III and in Part IV, will help us to understand how the notion of stillness is compatible with Dionysian becoming (see especially Part IV, Section 19). The ugly and the beautiful are thus in relation, and this relation preoccupies much of Nietzsche's thinking. On the one hand, the persistent object of critique, the disease and horror of life in human form, static, fragmented and ineradicable; on the other, the euphoria and ecstasy of creation, noble achievement, prophetic vision, and insight into the world as an immanent whole.

As we are following the text, a striking feature of Nietzsche's new philosophy has begun to emerge: it could be called 'a post-Darwinian form of humanism'. As the example of references to Goethe and Michelangelo in this section showed, Zarathustra's thinking is well schooled in the modern tradition of humanist thinking. The Renaissance notion of 'man as the centre and measure of all things' as it features in all the important philosophical and artistic works of that period (from Dante to Erasmus) can still be seen behind Zarathustra's teachings – albeit in a modified form, for what is 'measure' for Nietzsche is not the human as such in its current form but the underlying will to power, and the possibilities of the enhancement of power in new forms of humanity. Similarly, as critic of morality, Zarathustra bears features from the French tradition of Diderot and Voltaire. The emphasis on pedagogic theory in the teaching of the overhuman (the child stage as precondition) is a reference to Luke 18: 17, but we can also hear echoes of Rousseau's

Émile (1762). The core demand of Zarathustra to introduce a new stage in the human evolutionary project through 'understanding' reactivates the old Enlightenment principle of *sapere aude* (dare to know), a motto for free thinking from Horace (65 BC–8 BC) to Kant and Schiller, and which is behind the French Enlightenment project in the *Encyclopaedie* (1751–72). This is a Humanism now based broadly on the findings of evolutionary theory and Nietzsche's own 'discovery' of the will to power (see 'from genus to over-genus': Part I, Section 22).

Section 3, 'On Those Who Pity'

The human being is the animal with red cheeks. (Zarathustra will get no argument from the *Old Testament*, since shame was the outcome of original sin.) Animals, with their 'innocent' senses (Part I, Section 13), do not experience shame. Shame is something like the consciousness of inadequacy, of failing to live up to one's values or achieve one's goals. (See also the discussion of figs, knowledge and innocence in Part II, Section 2.) To incite or even notice such shame is itself shameful. If the sufferer receives pity, it is a public acknowledgement of failure or deficiency. Thus, pitying is only productive of more suffering, both directly and indirectly through revenge. From that follows the secondary shame of the one who pities, for creating suffering like that is just petty and in pitying, the creator will have failed to be a creator. If (and perhaps Zarathustra means: like the beasts) we 'learn to enjoy ourselves better', we will also plan and produce less suffering. Beyond the not implausible *psychological* point about human dignity and its frailties, this passage carries a philosophical message: the way of creation is above pitying because its love is not for the human that suffers but for the overhuman that might be achieved by the overcoming of the human. Suffering then is not something to be pitied, and the sufferer is not to be helped to *preserve* himself. To be sure, the pitying, helping response is natural and generally not without merit, but in the moment of his or her 'great love', the creator must be 'hard' and 'hold on to one's heart'; thus, 'Myself I will sacrifice to my love, *and my neighbour like me*'. Even your help for your friend will not, like pity, seek to preserve that friend in his or her suffering but rather aid him or her towards the joy of overcoming (see *The Gay Science*, section 338).

Section 4, 'On the Priests'

The majority of the case studies in Part I featured individuals (or individuals representing types) in various stages of development relative to the emergence of the overhuman. In contrast, Part II widens out the perspective more into the study of social or political groupings. Zarathustra is gradually drawing for us a picture of modernity as he (or rather Nietzsche) sees it. The text is structuring itself in terms of repetition with variation[41] – the findings of the earlier sections are expanded upon and taken further and deeper. For instance, the section under discussion here corresponds in this way with section 4 of Part I, 'The Despisers of the Body'. It takes that section's thesis and gives it a new airing with respect to a historically more specific target for critique. In this pattern an 'upward spiralling' of argument is created that makes the text curve like rings around the core of the 'ruling thought'. The text thus fulfils the allegory of the staff in which the snake coils itself around the sun (see Part I, Section 22.1).

The 'despisers' of Part I, Section 4 are now the Christian priests. A caste of infectiously sick people, they are 'evil enemies' whom Zarathustra does not love, even though he wrestles with the pain of his sorrow for them. There are several things to notice here. First, Zarathustra would pass by – some struggles would not promote the cause of the overhuman. Secondly, the importance of the notion of vengeance: 'nothing is more vengeful than their humility' and they besmirch 'whoever attacks them'. This echoes the idea concerning pity and revenge which we saw in the previous section. Thirdly, they are prisoners of their own making as the Redeemer whom they have created 'has cast them into bondage'. Someone needs to 'redeem them from their Redeemer', an ironic reference to the final words in Wagner's last opera *Parsifal.* Fourthly, we should also note the description of the psychological projection mechanism of the priests that made them call God 'whatever contradicted and hurt them' (see Part I, Section 6) and that they 'knew no other way to love their God than by nailing the human being on the cross'. Neither of these, in itself, Zarathustra despises, for, the love of the overhuman also contradicts and hurts the human (thus, 'there was much of the heroic' in these priests). However, a transcendent God, in the form now of the 'redeemer', demands condemnation of the body, shame, and a desire for death. Again, the God they have created is an instrument of their self-loathing and of their suffering.

Fifthly, only when the sky looks in again through the ruined ceilings and 'down onto grass and red poppies on the walls' will Zarathustra 'turn his heart' to churches again. The religious instinct – an instinct for celebrating and loving what lies beyond one's narrow individuality as the sense of the earth – is not the problem here. The problem is when this 'beyond' becomes a *transcendent* projection of one's disease ('ashamed before the clear sky'), rather than an immanent ideal of health. (See the similar discussion in *Beyond Good and Evil*, section 53.) Finally, the images of nakedness and beauty are of considerable interest. Nakedness recalls the paradisical state, before shame, before the despising of the body (see Part II, Section 2). Beauty in particular has become a frequent leitmotif in Part II, and we will see it again in the first sentences of the very next section; Zarathustra's treatment of the notion of beauty will culminate in section 13, where we will discuss it much more fully.

Section 5, 'On the Virtuous'

This is an important section in that it develops in more detail Zarathustra's account of virtue (it is also an echo of Part I, Section 5). This is pursued largely by way of three overlapping contrasts. First, there is the philosophical contrast of Zarathustra's account with alternatives from the history of philosophy. The traditional accounts of virtue alluded to are: virtue as yielding a reward in Heaven, as being its own reward, as founded on fear of punishment, virtue as social regulation ('police'), as being disinterested or objective (not being selfish), as being virtuous only because of consequences, or as according with principles of duty, so that a virtuous action is independent of consequences. Secondly, there is a taxonomy (one of the book's most extensive) of human types and their 'virtue'. Notable in this taxonomy is the type whose virtue is the expression of their hatred of life and self: 'What I am not, that, that to me is God and virtue!', echoing the priests of the previous section. We should hear in this also an echo of the 'unthinkability' or negative image of God as discussed in Part II, Section 2. Thirdly, the section is complicated still further in that it is an address to 'you virtuous ones', who are the object of a quite different critique. The virtuous ones are those who are 'too cleanly' for the 'words' associated with, or that define virtue in, Zarathustra's taxonomy (see Part I, Section 5). But these words have nevertheless penetrated 'into the ground of your souls'. That is to say, the dishonest modes of virtue have been internalised and stand in the way of the virtuous ones being able to understand their own virtue and to disassociate themselves from the former (the point is akin to 'Dangerous it is to be an heir' in Part I, Section 22.2, or Part III, Section 12.6: the old idol-priest dwells 'in us ourselves').

We have provisionally defined virtue as the spirit's sublimated sense of direction for its willing: that is, the dominant will to power insofar as that will expresses itself as principles for living and valued activities in a mode of life (See Part I, Sections 1, 5 and 22). Here, the emphasis is placed on the future: virtue is virtue not insofar as it returns to the Self as some kind of payment (for example, an afterlife in heaven), nor is it even its 'own reward'. The reference is to Aristotle's distinction between activities with exterior ends or with ends-in-themselves, at the beginning of *Nichomachean Ethics*. Zarathustra rejects both as models. Rather, virtue lives on into the future the way the mother is in the child, or the light of a star, even if a dying star, carries on without end (both striking and beautiful images). That is to say, virtue is virtue insofar as it helps to create the overhuman, but not as an after-effect or as an accidental by-product; rather, the virtue is the continuous or unbroken expression of the 'love' of the Self into the future. In that sense, virtue is 'selfish'. If virtue is both a continuation into the future (the future that belongs to the overhuman) *and also* is 'your dearest self', then an act of virtue is like a perpetual return to itself. 'The thirst of the ring is in you', Zarathustra says, in the least ambiguous (but still cryptic) anticipation of the theme of eternal recurrence thus far.

As mentioned above, much of the section is taken up with an extensive, critical taxonomy of those who call themselves 'virtuous'. This seems to generate an interesting tension between two uses of the concept 'virtue'. First, there is an *ontological* account wherein virtue is, as we said above, the duty that a dominant will to power gives itself, irrespective of the content of that duty. Secondly, there is an *ethical* (for lack of a better word) account according to which virtue is only virtue if it seeks to create the overhuman; thus the stress in the section on what this or that type of human 'calls' virtue. This tension, though, is at least partly a misunderstanding, for Zarathustra is not contrasting what others merely *call* virtue with something like *true* or *real* virtue. On the contrary, naming things and above all picking them out as something valued or important is the basic function of life insofar as it forms a specific mode of life, such as a 'people' (see Part I, Section 11). The difference between the ontological and ethical accounts of virtue, then, is internal to the ontology. It is the difference between (1) a mode of being aligned to and consummate to its mode of being, and the virtues that express this alignment;[42] And (2) a mode of being that constitutively 'lies' about or flees from its own being and indeed whose virtue (the expression of its will to power, what is needed by the mode of life) consists of such lying or fleeing.

The section begins curiously with 'the voice of beauty talks softly'. Those who are virtuous, whose souls are already awakened, do not need the voice of 'thunder', and such a thunderous approach might be counter-productive. The danger of the thunderous approach was already alluded to at the end of Part II, Section 1. So, in accordance with that earlier passage, we can here ask whether Zarathustra has taught his 'wild Wisdom' to speak softly already? Well, to be sure, there are two or three of Zarathustra's most gorgeous images in this section, but the snout of a boar as plow is by no means one of them! So, the rhetoric of this section is not noticably distinct, then, except only that it is addressed to the curious situation of 'you virtuous ones'. The clue is 'shield'. Since his first book, *The Birth of Tragedy*, Nietzsche has thought of beauty as a kind of shield, something that preserves or even nurtures. Since virtue is thought of as the will insofar as it realises itself in a form of life – in contrast to the annihilating and creating acts that bring about such a form of life in the first place – it can be thought of in association with beauty. Beauty is newly achieved form, arrived at through overcoming and growth, and precisely because it is form it has stillness and the strength to preserve. If virtue is to be addressed, it should be addressed in the 'voice of beauty'. Thus also, 'beauty alone should preach penitence' in the previous section.

Section 6, 'On the Rabble', and a Note on Nietzsche and Social Taxonomy

This passage has an autobiographical ring to it, and is strikingly short on analysis or ideas. The rabble is the lowest form of human life, below all categories of human transformation. This is humanity not even at the camel stage; on the contrary, they are the 'filthy camel drivers' (Nietzsche no doubt imagined this a suitable ancient Persian epithet) dwelling by the well of life and poisoning it. There is a contract between the rabble and those in power who need them for power. Also, there are many types of rabble; the underclass is in itself divided: 'the power- and writing- and pleasure rabble'. This last is an important clarification. Nietzsche's social conservatism is not founded on conventional class or socio-economic boundaries. The rabble can be literate, they may even hold positions of power (rather than just being, *en masse*, a force that rulers must bargain with). Likewise, there is no necessary correlation of 'nobility' with social class or traditional feudal categories. Through Zarathustra Nietzsche aims to lash out against the contemporary social realities of the time, which does bring out the anti-democratic side of Nietzsche's rather underdeveloped political philosophy. The next section picks up the political theme a bit more successfully.

Zarathustra realises that even the rabble has its place in the grand scheme of life – even the rabble is '*needed* for life' – and that above all disgusts him. This means that the rabble is a function of life, through which something important for life's development is achieved. Zarathustra does not say what, unless it simply be the spur to discover the 'fount of pleasure' in the heights. Indeed generally in these kinds of passages such explanation is underdeveloped; the analysis of the ascetic ideal in *The Genealogy of Morality* is an exception. Being needed for life here also means that because of the relationality of will to power there is a comprehensive interlocking of all features of existence. This is a new idea in the book, only gestured at here. It will only be developed at the end of this part (section 20) and in the treatment of eternal recurrence in Part III. Here Zarathustra seems to be able to escape into the future; the later thoughts of willing back and eternal recurrence will close off this route, or at least complicate it considerably. The section is frankly rather dull, a rant without analysis, that serves as a mere negative foil for the dithyrambic epiphany of the overhuman that concludes this speech.

A Note on Nietzsche and Social Taxonomy

Nietzsche shares his outlook on social and political issues with a number of illustrious nineteenth-century social 'theorists'. We suggest that the anti-democratic impulse, his hierarchical taxonomies of social class and derogatory view of modern mass society is derived in part from German sources, but also from Anglo-American cultural criticism. The later German Idealist and Romantic generation tended to turn markedly reactionary, especially after the Vienna Congress of 1815. An example is the influential Adam Müller (1779–1829) who propagates a return to medieval feudalism. Fichte (1772–1814) combines the loftiness of his achievement as transcendental philosopher with an extraordinarily chauvinistic and at times racist vision of German politics (*The Closed Trading State*) and national identity (*Addresses to the German Nation*). Nietzsche's line on politics is more the Emersonian one: 'Every actual state is corrupt', writes Emerson in his essay on 'Politics'. Nietzsche follows Emerson in the assumption that 'nature is not democratic, nor limited-monarchical, but despotic, and will not be fooled or abated of any jot of her authority, by the pertest of her sons'.[43] For Thomas Carlyle, a friend of Emerson's (they share their enthusiasm for Goethe), this means that social organisation cannot be conceived of in terms of equality and democracy. Nietzsche broadly follows the line of Carlyle, who in his famous essay on *Chartism*[44] assumes that aristocracy is 'a corporation of the Best, of the Bravest', that it is within the 'nature of men . . . to honour and love their Best', and that wherever true aristocracy is still a corporation of the best, it is 'safe from all peril, and the land it rules is a safe and blessed land'. The crisis of the present, Carlyle reckons, can only be solved by re-instigating 'a *real* Aristocracy' (191–2), for 'Democracy . . . what is called "self-government" of the multitude by the multitude', was 'never yet . . . able to accomplish much work, beyond the same cancelling of itself' (190). Nietzsche shares the idea of a naturally hierarchical social organisation where difference is acknowledged and the integration of a people achieved through nobility who are predestined to lead. If it is the case that Nietzsche's notions of social and political constitution are significantly influenced by Anglo-American sources, then we must rethink the commonly held assumption that fascism could legitimately feed in this area of Nietzsche's thought. Nietzsche's doubts regarding mass society, the state, democracy and the emancipation of the 'lower classes' originate in a mainstream 'elitist' European context rather than a nationalistically deranged Germanic one.

* * * *

Section 7, 'On the Tarantulas'

This section proposes an elaborate (and frankly rather long-winded) analogy between the tarantula and those who propose 'equality' as the prime definition of justice. The latter are a far from specific group, encompassing Christianity (all equal before God), European and North American democracies, British utilitarian liberalism (each person's happiness or suffering is counted equally), socialism (to each according to his need), and equality before the law (thus the recap of the ideas from Part I, Section 7). As so often before, Zarathustra accuses such ideas of having a well-hidden and quite different motivation: in this case, revenge. The doctrine of equality is a revenge of the weak against the powerful (social and political power, and above all the power to set and enforce values). Accordingly, 'were it otherwise' – that is, were those now without power put into a position of power – their teaching would be otherwise too. And, indeed, Zarathustra suggests, many who now preach equality are the continuous remnant of a mode of life that once practised the opposite: 'world-slanderers and heretic-burners' (Nietzsche likely has in mind the sovereignty of medieval Christianity in Europe). Some such teachers even teach 'in favour of life', but must not be confused with Zarathustra. These passages should be compared to Part I, Section 19, the last time Zarathustra was bitten.

'Human beings are not equal' – this is the counter-assertion concerning justice. The state of human life is indeed one of differences in social, political or evaluative power, but this is not necessarily a situation requiring correction according to principles of justice. Inequality – in the sense of differences in political or social power, but more especially differences in approach to this or that problem, different values, talents and virtues – is a condition of growth. A situation is unjust insofar as it somehow blocks overcoming, the development of the human animal; justice consists of those social or political relations which promote the overhuman. Existing differences in power can, of course, be directed to the preservation of a mode of life; so one cannot simply equate inequality and justice. Likewise, the relation of friendship or love is, or should be, a relation of equals in rank, the one type of equality not recognised in the values Zarathustra criticises. The will to power is essentially relation, and this means that inequality is not a contingent feature of life, and equally necessary is that inequality means struggle, opposition and so forth. This way, these differences become productive. Even beauty – a form of life or cultural form achieved – contains 'struggle and inequality'. Thus the continuing circle of overcoming and achievement of what must be overcome. This notion is very nicely embodied in the image of steps (*Stufen*). Life 'needs steps' – that is, alternating moments of vertical upwards leaps of growth and plateaus, beautiful achievements of form, within which the momentum for further growth can build. Life also needs 'opposition among steps' – for there are 1,000 bridges and footpaths', and a struggle even among the highest; see also Part II, Section 4. Similarly, a few lines later, the images of arches and vaults that, by means of the one side straining against the other, achieve a height, beauty and a quiet strength, upon which yet another arch or vault can be constructed.

Section 8, 'On the Famous Wise Men'

In *The Gay Science* and especially in *Beyond Good and Evil* Nietzsche develops the notion of an 'order of rank', that is a classificatory concept for human types (and not just human types, but also drives, instincts or 'goods') as to their organic health, nobility and spirituality. This notion tries to find a way of understanding the *distribution* of fragmentary virtues and forms of degeneration (whether in peoples, soldiers, rabbles, priests or 'wise men') by way of what appears to be a 'linear' scale leading up to – and indeed *seen* from the perspective of – the free spirit. It is, ultimately, a scale of power, but seen on the analogy of a uni-directional quantity of *force*. Such a scale is not terribly successful precisely because it is uni-directional, since it is thereby unable to deal with the overlapping, multi-dimensional subtleties of Nietzsche's individual analyses. For example, the portraits of the 'superior humans' in Part IV would not be well served by putting them in some 'order of rank'. The modes of degeneration constitute a critique of modernity, we have argued. They also provide either a merely negative foil for the difficult task of characterising the 'free spirit', or (more interestingly) a portrait of a fragmentary mode of human life with 'gaps'. Thus, for example, the priests were termed 'heroic' and had 'capacious souls'. Likewise, in this section, it is imperative that we read without irony 'to your own honour I say this!', for partly through their wise men have peoples become great (Part I, Section 15; see note on Nietzsche and Social Taxonomy, with the commentary on Part I, Section 15).

An atmosphere prevails in this section of medieval feudalism, where the spirit of Aesopian fable is still alive. The famous wise men are of course philosophers. Zarathustra sees them at the beasts of burden stage of the spirit, that of the camel (Part I, Section 1), which takes on heavy burdens and which exhibits reverence always towards the outside (the people and their 'Thou shalt'). Or, in the image preferred here, they are at the stage of the ass, in the service of people and of powerful men (who are no less 'of the people'). Because of their importance to the preservation and power of a people, even their 'unbelief' is tolerated – an allusion to the many nineteenth-century varieties of atheism. (It is instructive to compare this 'lukewarm' unbelief with the addressees of the 'madman' in *The Gay Science*, section 125.) Zarathustra wants them to stop pretending, 'at long last to throw off the lion's skin altogether' (the lion stage is merely a disguise). The second half of the speech is taken up by Zarathustra telling it as it is to the wise men. Four times he asks them the rhetorical question: 'did you already know that?', covering four descriptions of the spirit's contribution to creative overcoming and advancement of the human. 'Spirit is the life that cuts into life' is the most evocative of these four. In other words, spirit in the human being is the manifestation of will to power to the level of conscious knowledge, cultural activity, principle or virtue; which thus has the reciprocal capacity to modify the underlying structure of the drives by way of practices of internalisation. Spirit can (if you will) perform vivisection upon itself. This is the quasi-Enlightenment praise of knowledge or understanding that Zarathustra has been giving since the last section of Part I. In *The Gay Science* such 'experimentalism' with oneself, one's mode of life and practices is developed as a methodology for a 'joyful' science (see *The Gay Science*, 7, 51, 319–24). This idea is found in *Zarathustra* in the various references to 'seekers', 'experimenters', 'tempters'. And in *Beyond Good and Evil* the notion of vivisection and cruelty even to oneself becomes a common theme (see, in particular, sections 55, 229–30).

There are several notions wrapped up here. First, that the advancement of the human requires painful sacrifices and, in particular, the sacrifice (the going under) of one's current wisdom, virtue and mode of life. Secondly, that humanity is the cruellest animal (see Part III, Section 13), meaning that cruelty and pleasure are closely associated – thus Zarathustra says, the spectacles of 'tragedies, bullfights and crucifixions'. Now, there are two explanations of this association. The first is that the cruelty is the expression of a reactive will to power, which just like in pity (also described in terms of a hidden and unhealthy pleasure) is able thereby to feel its own power. The other explanation is quite different. We need to go back to *The Birth of Tragedy* (which meditates almost continuously on the question of how could one feel pleasure at the spectacle of suffering) and the contrast between the Apollonian drive to surface, still form, pleasure and beauty and the Dionysian drive to express the primal suffering of nature. In tragedy, Nietzsche then wrote, the two drives are combined, each enhancing the other: the Dionysian insight is expressed in the carefully crafted 'middle' or 'dream' world of the Apollonian. Now, here ten years later, we have the contrast between a beautiful and still form, on the one hand – an accomplished mode of life, or its noble expression in some cultural form – and its turbulent and destructive overcoming, on the other. In both cases, the joy is the same, the joy of the creative act, but viewed, so to speak, from two sides of the moment of creation: the destruction of a form as the creation of a new form. Thus, in Part IV, Section 19.9 we read 'blessed be the vintner's knife' which harvests what is ripe for overcoming (see Part III, Section 14). The same contrast functions in the domain of knowledge. The 'errors' required as conditions of life – the simplification of things, treating them as the same and unchanging – are countered by the drive to cruelly peel away such appearance and try to think difference, the multiple, the continuously becoming. Insofar as this latter drive contributes to the further aligning of one's whole bodily existence to the nature of will to power – that is, to the furthering of the 'work' of the overhuman – then the cruelty that cuts into these 'errors' is motivated by one's yearning for the overhuman (see *Beyond Good and Evil*, section 230). The reference to Oedipus and the images that follow suggests that one 'gap' these clever, lukewarm men have is suffering of the spirit, unlike their cousins the priests, who have 'little minds'.

The final image is of a strong will or spirit making the sail of wild wisdom swell (become pregnant). The wise men are neither masculine nor feminine and certainly not sufficiently *both* to be productive and accompany Zarathustra. This in turn suggests retroactively that what was at stake in the main body of the section was a description of the movement of the will to power in its two objectifications of feminine and masculine. The reader should also compare the discussion of a different kind of 'wise men' (empirical scientists) in section 15, which opens with just this gender symbolism.

Section 9, 'The Night-Song'

The tone changes abruptly and without warning. Hereafter one of Nietzsche's favourite pieces of dithyrambic writing (see *Ecce Homo*, 'Thus Spoke Zarathustra', section 7), this section also marks a transformation, in three ways. First, it is the book's first 'song', but by no means the last. Although the book so far has hardly been in conventional prose, and employs a multitude of narrative and poetic devices, this 'song' signals a change in writing strategy and rhetorical mode that Zarathustra has been anticipating since the first section of this part. It is also, and quite explicitly, a move towards a mode of writing consummate to music (see note on Nietzsche, Music and Language, with the commentary on Part II, Section 17). The three sections 9 to 11 are special as a lyrical visionary insertion interrupting (at roughly the half-way point, thus dividing Part II into three movements) the standard critical discourse of the rest of Part II. This is no longer an anachronistic portrait of modernity as foil for a projection of the free spirit; instead, we have the discourse of epiphany. Secondly, Zarathustra addresses the section to himself. This is not new (we have had three such sections already in the Prologue), but nevertheless it is clear that we are moving away from the 'speeches of

Zarathustra' – pattern that dominated Part I and also Part II till now, towards a meditative and preoccupied Zarathustra.

Thirdly, the song is a lament. Zarathustra's leaving the philosophers behind in the previous section brings on a heartfelt loneliness and melancholy. The new determination and joy at bestowal that Zarathustra felt in Part II, Section 1 has already faded and now Zarathustra longs to be the night that receives light instead of the sun from which light always flees. The idea of the sun as essentially bestowing, as requiring a relation with what is dark, comes from the beginning of the Prologue, and is developed also in Part I, Section 22. Immediately after the *Ecce Homo* passage alluded to above, Nietzsche says that the poem depicts the 'solar solitary in the light' which is the suffering of a God (Dionysus). The answer to the 'riddle' of the poem is Ariadne, who symbolises the human potential for the birth of new forms and also the ability (unique among living things) to spiritualise this potential so as to accelerate it. Ariadne is the answer insofar as she too (or, through her the human) can become sun. Notice also the many astronomical metaphors Zarathustra employs here and elsewhere (for example, Part II, Section 5). His longing even extends so far as to tempt him towards spiteful revenge. The theme of this passage also suggests the young man in Part I, Section 8, whose loneliness leads to a similar enmity. Clearly, something is wrong; some new and even violent transformation of Zarathustra's own spirit is on the horizon.

Section 10, 'The Dance-Song'

There are two dance songs in *Zarathustra.* This points to the importance of the dance motif in the book. In this first dance song, there is a tremendously complex play with the number three on a thematic level. It is the second of the three songs in this part, which thus frame it; dance song itself is thus at the centre of the triadic dithyrambic set. Moreover, narratively it is constructed in three parts as a song within a narrative frame. Finally, it concerns a *ménage à trois* between Zarathustra, his Wisdom and Life. We suggest that in the complex layering of frames of the dance song the innermost core of ideas of *Zarathustra* is allegorically framed, curling around what Nietzsche in Part I, Section 22 called a 'ruling thought'. The central poem is not a soliloquy, like the others, but contains an imaginary conversation between three partners in a dance.[45] The first of the two outer parts of the frame seemingly lightens the tone; it has a 'retarding', loosening dramatic effect. Specifically, it continues the bawdy sexual innuendo of Part I, Section 18. The third section closes the frame with a return to the exhausted melancholy of the previous, and next, sections.

The introduction creates an atmosphere of Elysian idyll (we are harking back to the Isles of the Blest of Part II, Section 2) with overtones, so it seems, of scenes of Greek or Roman mythology as depicted in the paintings of Poussin and Claude Lorrain. Zarathustra walks right into this idyll of dancing girls in the forest, engages in some slippery talk, flaunts 'his little God' with the 'tear-filled eye', the 'lazybones' [*Tagedieb*, literally 'thief of the day'] awakened with a bit of 'chastening' to do his duty, and enters into sexual role-play, singing a song for 'Cupid' dancing with the maidens. (Of importance for later – Part III, Section 2 – is the description of the Devil as 'the spirit of heaviness'; see also Part I, Section 7.) Sexual fulfilment is presented here as an allegory of intimate communion with life. In Part I, Section 18 Zarathustra was on his way to women; in this section the deed is being done. Sex is an appropriate allegory of Dionysian epiphany and understanding of the nature of life and one's integration within it, for a number of reasons. First of all, because in sex the sensuality of the body most clearly dominates and consumes the 'little reason' of the 'I', and thus sexual fulfilment has long traditionally been associated with the ecstatic loss of self; secondly, because the creativity of the will has been imaged several times already as pregnancy, also the function of love and marriage; thirdly, because this creativity is conditional upon both masculine and feminine aspects of the self; fourthly, because the 'expenditure' of the self in sex (which is already a metaphor for the bestowing virtue) is a metaphor for the cycle of death and becoming (see the end of this section).

This prepares the way for the dance song proper, in the high style of elevated poetic discourse in the tradition of Hölderlin and the other German writers of poetic epiphany, like Bonaventura and Jean Paul, whom Nietzsche is echoing in *Zarathustra* (see note on Nietzsche and Epiphany, with the commentary on Part III, Section 4). The song proper is Zarathustra's adoration-of-life, delivered in the form of a dialogue, and which is being sung as the orgy is underway, a speech therefore that we need to think of as a Dionysiac encounter with the nature of nature, symbolised by sexual climax. Life is woman, often misunderstood by men; she now sets the record straight for Zarathustra. This involves what initially looks like more clichés: woman as changeable and jealous, for example. The first of these, however, is actually an exposition of the 'with women no thing is impossible' idea from Part I, Section 18. Underneath all our taxonomic classifications and biological descriptions in terms of regular cause and effect, life is protean, changing continually in order to preserve itself as life (thus again a reference to evolution; and see *The Gay Science*, section 26). Nietzsche often claims that human life has the particular distinction (or burden) of being 'unfinished' and thus constantly and rapidly changing (unless prevented from this by some illness or degeneration) whereas all other creatures in their development tend to reach relatively stable plateaus of development (this idea can be found in *The Gay Science*, section 143 and *Beyond Good and Evil*, section 62: the famous idea of the '*nicht festgestelltes tier*', the 'not fully-determined animal'). The second cliché (jealousy) is a complex metaphysical idea concerning the proximity of life and wisdom that expands upon the metaphor of golden sun and serpent on Zarathustra's staff. Thus the feminine principle that Zarathustra denigrated as woman in Part I, Section 18 in his erotic confusion is now more than rehabilitated. All life is a woman, including of course the life in one's own body. But so also is the wisdom with which Zarathustra answers her, the third party in this communion. Wisdom is *from* life, life (as encountered in one's body and – in Dionysian epiphanies – as encountered as such) is spiritualised as wisdom.

The 'you men always confer on us your own virtues' is a clearer statement of the idea (which we mentioned in the context of Part I, Section 18) that biological differences between the sexes necessarily manifest themselves at the level of psychology. Male philosophers have always known this, Zarathustra implies, but have nevertheless absurdly denigrated women precisely for not being men (see *The Gay Science*, section 68 and *Beyond Good and Evil*, section 232). However, it is also a swift critique of innumerable philosophies of life and nature that anthropomorphise, for example seeing purpose or reason in life as a whole. Nietzsche may have in mind here Stoicism, with its projection of the virtue of rationality on nature as such, which he discusses more clearly in *Beyond Good and Evil*, section 9; but there are innumerable other possibilities. The 'golden fishing rod' seems to mean that Life preserves Zarathustra from drowning (with a joke here on interrupted ejaculation) – perhaps because Zarathustra is an instrument by which Life can be 'changeable', or Wisdom made pregnant – analogous to the way that Zarathustra helps save his disciples from the human and from themselves. Of course, eventually they all have to go under (and coitus is resumed and completed at the end of the poem-section). The image of Zarathustra fishing is from

Prologue Section 7, and becomes increasingly common hereafter in the text, most significantly at Part IV, Section 1. (The fishing rod may also, of course, be another allusion to the whip, demanding that Zarathustra pay attention and . . . keep up.)

The interior dialogue is sequenced in accordance with the progression of the sexual dance act and the drama of bodily elevation. It ends with the, only slightly veiled, sexual climax, which coincides with the profoundest depth of insight, itself the moment of loss of consciousness or individual identity. The sexual act is thus advanced to the status of a model of physio-psychological health. It is one of Nietzsche's great achievements to have conceived, at this comparatively early stage and foreshadowing Freud, Jung and Reich, of a philosophical psychology that is built around a core of sexual health. To claim that the deepest communion with and understanding of nature can be achieved at (or at least conceived of as) the moment of orgasm amounts to a very radical proposition indeed and bears little trace of nineteenth-century stuffiness. The final third of the section sees Zarathustra in post-orgasmic state. The Elysian 'meadow is damp' (see also images of dew in Part II, Section 22 and Part IV, Section 14). Life has spent itself momentarily, it is now evening, which brings on unknown and nihilistic thoughts. As early as *The Birth of Tragedy*, section 7, Nietzsche discussed how the emergence from the Dionysian ecstasy is accompanied by despair. This is both a transition to the reflections on death and the past in section 11, 'the Grave Song', and also a cryptic glance forward to the harrowing thought of eternal recurrence.

Section 11, 'The Grave-Song'

This section contains a similar lament to 'The Night Song' and the third subsection of 'The Dance Song', although initially the mood is more bitter-sweet ('to this day I am the richest and most enviable man . . .'). Also, this section is one of the most clearly autobiographical, recounting Nietzsche's own life, including the recent failure of his would-be relationship with Lou Salomé, and his disappointment with the direction of Richard Wagner's later career ('you won over my dearest singer'). 'Glances and moments' is the necessarily inadequate translation of the German pun: *Augenblick* [literally, 'blink of the eye'] contains *Blick* ['glance']. The idea is of an ephemeral moment that, insofar as it can be seen as making one rich 'to this day' – that is, in so far as one's life *continues* it –, is redeemed from its mere ephemerality (from its 'grave'). This introduces, in a highly personal way, the theme of time that will become increasingly explicit towards the end of this part, and in Part III. The section ends with an account of how the 'murder' of these youthful pleasures and joys was 'overcome' through the will that demolishes graves. The will, though, is grimly determined, implacable. It is entirely lacking in the sense of lightness and play of Zarathustra's less personal accounts of the self-overcoming of life, and is thus not an entirely convincing act of overcoming. It is like a first draft of the transformation of Zarathustra that occurs in the second half of Part III. This tone is continued into the next section.

Section 12, 'On Self-Overcoming'

This section represents the first sustained and general treatment of the will to power (although our note on the section is part of Part I, Section 4). The addressees of this speech are 'the wisest', – by which Zarathustra means not his disciples, but those who are like 'wise men' or philosophers from section 8, but who are not merely servants to a people, but rather – perhaps even without being aware of it – creators of a set of values, and thus a way of human life or a people. Zarathustra reveals the 'riddle' of the hearts of the wisest. What philosophers may have called their 'will to truth' – the desire for knowledge that drives 'the wisest' – is in fact a will to the thinkability of all things. (Towards the end of the section, Zarathustra also dismisses as misunderstandings two other philosophical notions of will: first, Spinozism (the idea of 'will to exist') and second, quasi-evolutionary biology (the idea of 'will to life').) The notion of a will to truth is discussed also by Nietzsche in the first few sections of *Beyond Good and Evil* and see also section 187. There the question is: what is the value of such a will and to what or whom is it valuable? A conception of truth and a pursuit of truth are functions of a will to power, functions that make something possible: namely, the creation and maintenance of a mode of human life. 'Thinkability' means that all things shall 'bend themselves to you', bending both in the sense of being malleable to the will, and also bending in the sense of reverence (see especially Part III, Section 9). This thinkability means to interpret that which, in itself, is essentially not thinkable (the fervent becoming of nature) as a 'thing' or a 'world', and especially as things that can be shared in language, manipulated using practices, and bear sempiternal values. The notion returns us to the theme of Part II, Section 2; however, whereas the earlier section discussed 'thinkability' in order to advance the notion of immanence, this section does so in order to advance the nature of will to power.

This 'thinkability' is not a special case, something to be sought, reserved for philosophers; rather, it is what all will to power does, although of course only the strongest wills are able to refashion the whole world, and do so on behalf of a whole people. This is a creative achievement that, back in Part II, Section 2, is described as supplanting the notion of a creator-God. Here Zarathustra is calling these strongest the 'wisest'. The wisest not only create but also spiritualise their creation to the extent of it being a set of values or laws (as religious system or science, for example), they also have a 'healthy suspicion' of the real state of things. The end of this passage suggests that the wisest too might perhaps be able to ascertain the process itself, and the will to power as its basis. Weaker wills naturally tend to fall in line with their subordinate role; or else they steal power through sly means. There are a few references to rebellions by slaves in the text (fro example, Part I, Section 10; Part IV, Section 8); what Zarathustra has in mind with this stealing is something like the (infamous) notion of a 'slave revolution' in morality, as described in *Beyond Good and Evil*, section 46, where the underclass inverts values, so that, for example, meekness or poverty are valued, rather than strength and richness. See our discussion of Part III, Section 11.

However, the above account of the will to thinkability is not the end of the story. There are several additional ideas here. All life, in its essence, obeys. If its will to power is weak, it obeys something else; if strong, it obeys itself. The latter is more difficult, not only because of the burden of responsibility for those who command – in effect, life invests its future in the commanding – but also because this commanding life-will 'puts itself at risk'. In other words, eventually even the greatest must obey and yield to itself in the sense of becoming differentiated or alienated from itself, and thus going under. This happens in the interest of yet another leap forwards and upwards in the forms of life. Life herself says 'I am *that which must always overcome itself*'. So, every system of good and evil, every form of life however beautiful, is in danger not so much from 'the river of Becoming' (which here stands basically for the passing of time) but from the will to power itself, which continually abandons its old creations and wills anew. Thus, 'whatever I create and however much I love it – soon I must oppose both it and my love'. We should note that the 'self' in the title of the section does not refer to a particular human being struggling with his or her inherited set of drives and their misalignment to the nature of will to power. This section makes only limited contribution to Zarathustra's teaching as a set of practices of truth and growth (thus again it is unlike section 2). Rather, this section is much more straightforwardly 'ontological' in character. The 'self' being referred to is the mode of life of a people, or the existence of a system of good and evil. These must be overcome, from within 'themselves', and that means from out of the will to power that previously brought them into existence. Notice that while here life only is defined as essentially will to power, there are hints here, and it becomes explicit in *Beyond Good and Evil* (op. cit.), that all nature, even that generally described as lifeless or inorganic, is will to power.

Zarathustra asks that the wisest – who he claims are already doing as he describes, without realising it – to at least talk about the plausibility and implications of the will to power as the basic principle of life. This request for a shared discussion is heartfelt, insofar as it recalls the loneliness of section 9, which of course followed the wholesale dismissal of the famous wise men. The reader should compare the 'at least *talk*' here with the notion of 'hypothesis' in *Beyond Good and Evil*, section 36. However, this sets up a false contrast between the will to thinkability that is creative, and the will to knowledge that resists the superficial and strives for an understanding of the former (see our discussion of 'cruelty' in section 8). This contrast is false because it is not an accident that the 'wise men' have some understanding of the process ('healthy suspicion'), nor that Zarathustra should call it, precisely, 'healthy'. The manifestation of a healthy mode of life as creativity and its spiritualisation as a wisdom that has insight into that creativity are two sides of the same coin – they are both aspects of what it means to be aligned to the will to power. Zarathustra describes a permanent evolution in the sphere of human existence, initiated and speeded on by those who are in accord with the will to power in nature, because they can understand and adapt it. The overhuman is not a mode of life (a species), but the situation where life spiritualised in human activity participates in its own continual development. Nietzsche describes such a continual growth under the heading 'great health' in the fifth book of *The Gay Science*, (section 382, and he quotes himself at length later in *Ecce Homo*): 'a health that one doesn't only have, but also acquires continually and must acquire because one gives it up again and again, and must give it up'.[46] This then becomes one of the principles of *Zarathustra*'s narrative structure, explaining Zarathustra's repeated advancing (into the human) and retreating (back to solitude); the changes of strategy, writing style, and mood; repetitions of ideas that are never exactly repeated, but recast, expanded, applied, modernised; the self-satirising by Zarathustra, and occasional undercutting of his authority.

Section 13, 'On Those Who are Sublime'

This section continues the account of the warrior or hero of values which we have seen before, most notably in Part I, Section 10, including even the repetition of key notions there such as ugliness and sublimity. However, where in the previous part this sublime role corresponded most closely with the 'camel' stage of the spirit, here the sublime hero is clearly at the 'lion' stage: primarily an annihilator, one who becomes free and lonely, but not yet a creator. As exemplars of such 'sublime ones', Nietzsche may have in mind Kant, Goethe or Schopenhauer – all thinkers that he consistently praises for their role in offering epochal and devastating critiques of complacent, metaphysical systems of values (see, for example, *The Birth of Tragedy*, section 18). However, of course, Nietzsche *also* condemns these same figures for not being thorough enough, for falling back into the same traps they previously identified, and even for replacing one system with another, which would make them more akin to the 'famous wise men' (Part II, Section 8). This is not a contradiction. The Self is a complex of competing drives, all will to power, and these drives manifest as, for example, virtue, the heart's commitment (such as desire or revenge), or a metaphysics (an interpretation of the world as 'thinkable'). If one is fortunate, there will be one, dominant drive (and thus one virtue and an unblinking gaze towards the overhuman), but even many great souls are not fortunate – and in the Night Song (in a serious and melancholic mood) or in Part I, Section 18 (in a comic mood), we saw that even Zarathustra has other, opposing impulses. A single philosopher thus might in one regard (or at one point) be a spirit-lion, annihilating systems of value and freeing itself for creation, while in another be in thrall to the spirit of revenge.

The sublime one, like the spirit-lion, is battle-hardened, serious and sombre – however, he cannot create beyond the negative struggle. This negativity suggests Kant's destruction of metaphysics, mentioned above, but also the more recent tendency that Nietzsche observed in his nineteenth century towards *nihilism*. The images of this negativity are many: 'I saw no rose there', 'shadow' or 'shade' in opposition to 'his own sunlight', 'evil' (cf. the end of the previous section), and so forth. (The shadow imagery in the section is remarkable; please see our discussion of Part IV, Section 9.) He is a 'penitent of the spirit' – the hero recognises in himself the operative presence of unhealthy or unproductive drives and, as if they were a sin, he struggles to overcome them. He pays penance, but has not himself *redeemed* them, transforming them into 'heavenly children'. That is to say, he is *sterile*. The image of the bull ploughing the field is an image of fertility (agriculturally, literally; sexually, metaphorically; and mythologically through the image of Zeus's abduction of Europa to Crete). This image is confirmed by the last line of the section: the feminine soul, abandoned by the hero, is 'approached' by the over-hero. This alludes to the story of Ariadne, abandoned by Theseus (again, the bull and Crete connection) but taken as wife by Dionysus. The secret to this section is that the hero must become *both* masculine and feminine. He or she must achieve beauty through one or more of the following: realising him or herself in and as a healthy, aligned form of life; achieving virtue as allegorical herald of will to power as its ruling thought (see Part I, Section 22.1); creation of a noble cultural achievement that through beautiful form affirms life; devising new tablets of values that command a mode of life to align itself with will to power; or a moment of rest and epiphany in which the will is momentarily 'unharnessed' and in which the beauty of all immanent existence is reflected. (On the latter, see Part II, Section 2, Part IV, Section 10; and also the representation of sexual ecstasy in 'The Dance Song'.)

There are a nice few lines on 'taste' near the beginning. '*De gustibus non disputandum est*' is the famous phrase to which Nietzsche refers. The traditional idea is that in at least some domains of sense, my taste is my own, and no amount of persuasion on your part will get me to like, say, anchovies. But, how far do these domains extend? Many traditional aestheticians argue that in the case of art there is indeed a purpose and a productivity to disagreements (see Kant's *Critique of Judgement*, section 56). Something might be learned or noticed, opinions might be changed, made more subtle, more cultured. Zarathustra here is not interested in the niceties of philosophical aesthetics; his point is more elemental: taste is a form of evaluation, the interpretation of the world as not only thinkable but as favourable or unfavourable with respect to the will to power that animates life. Disputing about taste then – about the beauty or ugliness of forms of life, or cultural forms such as literary or musical works, even about the significance of philosophical insight, since Nietzsche speculates on the proximity of the Greek words for 'wisdom' and 'taste' in *Philosophy in the Tragic Age of the Greeks*, chapter 3 – is one more arena in which the defining struggle of life occurs. 'Verily, my brothers, the spirit is a stomach' (Part III, Section 12.16).

Section 14, 'On the Land of Culture', and a Note on *Bildung*

The previous section, with its possible references to critical philosophers, eased us part of the way back from poetic epiphanies towards Part Two's more obvious task: the diagnosis and criticism of modernity. In this section, Zarathustra comes crashing back down to the ground of reality. Zarathustra turns into the mouthpiece for Nietzsche's *Zeitkritik* again, hurling poetic abuse at his contemporaries. We are back in the land of Bonaventura's grave-diggers, with some added post-Romantic metaphoric paraphernalia, the scarecrow ('men of the present' as hollow) for example, perhaps borrowed from Schubert's *Winterreise*. The central idea is that the human race in its present modern condition is constitutionally homeless. The Enlightenment has cleared away all superstition and belief systems, but these have not been replaced by new paradigms suitable to the scientific age, and moreover humanity now believes that on principle no replacement should be needed ('without belief or superstition'). Thus, this mode of life has been plunged into an empty vacuum of faithlessness. It believes itself to be entirely 'actual' – that is, it does not depend upon transcendent, imaginary, or historical origins of value, or narratives of value that rely upon anything but what is, here and now. This nihilistic actuality is the shadow-image of Nietzsche's conception of immanence, the latter stripped of the central 'procreative life-will'.

To be sure, this modern mode of life pads out it scarecrow-thin existence with a necessarily arbitrary choice of practices, styles or virtues from the past. Nietzsche may have any number of targets in mind with this criticism, but the then highly fashionable medievalism, both in Germany and Britain, is likely to be one. These targets are as artificial as the rational virtues of Part I, Section 2, since they do not and cannot belong to the mode of life as expression of its own will to power. Modern mankind – as Zarathustra says, piling rhetorical phrases on top of each other – is *incapable* of belief, *not worthy* of belief and therefore *lacks* all belief. Its pledge of 'actuality' means that its will to power refuses itself any expression of values, even those that might actually belong to it – or, if you prefer, its very lack of belief and values *is* its belief and value. A few people 'wonder' at themselves – Zarathustra cleverly integrates the narrative from Genesis 2: 21 with a gesture towards the running gender symbolism of the book: the moderns lack the female principle of creative productivity.

Modern culture is the mere sampling of everything that has gone on before *without* the possibility of synthesis. We can see T. S. Eliot's *The Hollow Men* (1925) prefigured, and the modernist poetic principle foreshadowed which consists of a technique of piling up a heap of broken fragments that no longer fit together and are 'shored against my ruins' of the past.[47] Notice also the prescient anticipation of twentieth-century semiotics in the formulation of cultural camouflage as a palimpsest of signs representing past cultural layering. This reads like a composition manual for experimental, artistic modernism of the T. S. Eliot, Joyce and Beckett-type. We are surrounded, indeed inundated, with past signs that have lost their once valid signifiers, so that we in turn have lost all orientation. In the modernists, this state of affairs is lamentable, but irreversible. In contrast to what we could call modernist nihilism, Nietzsche suggests that modern culture is not entirely doomed (though the flight into the empty future is a warning of the consequences). Zarathustra teaches the 'prophetic dream' of the overhuman as the new paradigm of belief, featuring the human in the role of both god and worshipper of a secular religion. On a par with Marx's 'classless society', the overhuman might be seen as the last great utopian vision, before the onset of twentieth-century realities produces nothing but dystopias. The notion of the hollowing-out of cultural substance in his own time is one of the key themes of all of Nietzsche's writings, and was enormously influential. Already in his first book, *The Birth of Tragedy* of 1872, Nietzsche compares contemporary culture after 1850 to the Alexandrian state of cultural decline in classical antiquity, suggesting that radically modern man has turned into a librarian of his own past. His critique of nineteenth-century historicism in 'Use and Disadvantage of History for Life' (*Untimely Meditations'* [1876]) describes a positivistic attitude towards the past that exhausts itself in an empty retelling and collecting. It should be pointed out, however, that the description of the arbitrary appropriation of the past in this section is slightly at odds with the parallel sections in both *The Gay Science* (section 337) and *Beyond Good and Evil* (sections 223–4). There Nietzsche discusses what he calls a 'sense for history', a peculiarly modern phenomenon that results in the same ridiculous spectacle described here in *Zarathustra*; however, in those two books he also sees in this new phenomenon possible avenues for the elevation of the human ('"Spirit" . . . eventually finds that this is to its own advantage': *Beyond Good and Evil*, section 224). Out of crisis emerge possibilities of the ascent of life.

A Note on Bildung

The title of this section includes the word '*Bildung*'. In *The Birth of Tragedy*, Apollo's identification with symbolisation and image-making creates an etymological opportunity to play with the possibilities of the word '*Bild*' ('image'). In German this can be put to a wide variety of uses; for example,'*Bild*' features in 'symbolic' (*bildhaft*). Another important use is made of '*Bild*' in the notion of '*Bildung*', absolutely central in all of Nietzsche's work, which – it is difficult to translate precisely – roughly means something like 'character training', 'education of the full person' or 'formation of the soul through education'. (Thus, we have the *Bildungsroman*, the novel dramatising education or maturation, a tradition that *Zarathustra* in a curious way continues.) *Zarathustra* elevates 'the child' to one of its key symbolic images. The accomplishment of over-humanity is dependent on successful educational training, continuing the line of great educational European texts, such as Rousseau's *Émile*. Two things should be noted about the term '*Bildung*'. First, since its root is image or figure, it means to give proper form or shape to something. Secondly, it is the other side, so to speak, of culture understood simply as the various products of human life. *Bildung* concerns the way in which culture in that ordinary sense reciprocally forms human beings and is formed by them. The relationship is clearer in English: culture cultivates. The other aspect of *Bildung* is that it occupies a firm place in German national ideology. Schiller, for instance, in the fragmentary poem *Deutsche Grösse* ('German Greatness', 1797), maintains that the French have their politics, the British their empire, both their capital cities with national theatres and museums. All of this, so Schiller maintains, 'the German' can do without, because he has his inner values, intellect, morality and language. Thus '*Bildung*' is a central element of German national ideology which is meant to help compensate for Western European achievements by turning them into shortcomings: '*Bildung*' suggests that Germans have depth of soul where other nations merely live on the surface of life. Nietzsche is fundamentally critical in *Zarathustra* of the notion of the old-style German humanist ideal of *Bildung* which has been hollowed out by the rise of mass society. This kind of *Bildung* suffers from the same detachment of cultural forms from life that is the general disease of the modern age (Nietzsche's critique of historicism is similar). In other books Nietzsche often comments on German universities in this regard (for example, *Twilight of the Idols*, 'What the Germans Lack', section 5). What is needed is a form of

Bildung that is a practice of internalisation. (See also our discussions of Part I, Section 7; and Part III, Section 9.)

* * * *

The speech ends with Zarathustra introducing the trope of 'homelessness'. Zarathustra has more in common with these homeless moderns than he lets on: the nihilism on the one side and the necessary annihilating 'lion' stage on the other both result in the condition of 'homelessness'. This image is also autobiographical. Nietzsche relinquished his German citizenship in 1869 in moving to Switzerland. However, he never acquired Swiss nationality, and was thus officially stateless. The lifestyle he led in the 1880s of constant travel and erratic changes of scenery was very unusual for an inhabitant of the nineteenth century (Heine and Rimbaud come to mind as rare exceptions). This underpins the philosophical reflections on the theme of homelessness and its many metaphorical implications in *Zarathustra*. Since Zarathustra is at home nowhere at present, he must make his home and haven the future of his 'children'. However, this is somewhat misleading, for nomads are not without practices of living (see Part III, Section 6, for example).

Section 15, 'On Immaculate Perception'

The key last term in the title of this section '*Von der unbefleckten Erkenntnis*' ('On Immaculate Cognition') is a pun on '*Empfängnis*' and thus a joke involving the virginity of Mary, mother of Jesus. Most translators choose 'Immaculate Perception' because it rhymes (better in fact than Nietzsche's German pun), and because visual perception is the chief metaphor in the passage. The cost of this transaction is missing the emphasis on a type of thinking or knowing, and also the reference to an absolutely central term in German idealist philosophy. Thus, 'On Immaculate Cognition' might have been better, or why not stick with 'On Immaculate Conception', playing on the already double meaning of that word?

In any case, the key metaphor is indeed visual perception. The moon 'loves' the earth, but is ashamed of that love – it represents a mode of life that turns away from life. It thus hypocritically manufactures a false form of innocence, keeps its distance, is sterile (the gender images are very similar to the critique of the famous wise men), deals only in images (the symbol of the mirror, and see Part I, Section 22.1), and casts only a cool, reflected light. There are two targets here: first a conception of science and scientific method as involving a disengaged, de-contextualised and impersonal mode of investigation, 'with a will that has died' (Nietzsche will have had in mind British empiricists, and August Comte, who coined the term 'positivism'). Zarathustra confesses to having been 'fooled' by this approach in the past; in this way Nietzsche may be referring to what is often called his 'positivist' period in his publications of the mid-1870s. (The reader should compare *Beyond Good and Evil*, section 207.) Zarathustra is calling for a science that also recognises the role of will to power in all perception and thought ('the day came to me' – the ruling thought itself, rather than its cold and pale reflection on the moon). Moreover, he is calling for a science that accepts as its scientific ideal not the fake innocence of 'pure knowing' but the real innocence of seeking the alignment of human life with the earth through seeking the overhuman. The sea does not just lie beneath the gaze of the moon moving slowly as tide, but 'wants' to rise to this sun (evaporate into the blue abyss). All of nature will seek to conspire in this science because such a science is nature itself, spiritualised (see Part III, Section 9).

Second, returning to the brief discussion of 'taste' in Part II, Section 13, Zarathustra is criticising a way of thinking about specifically aesthetic appreciation: disinterested, intellectualised and again will-less (Kant and Schopenhauer would be the most obvious names here). In contrast to these two false forms of innocence, Zarathustra contrasts an honest innocence (the idea comes from Part I, Section 13), one that recognises and is not ashamed of the role that the will to power (and thus the whole body, one's virtue and the aims of one's spirit) plays in all perception and cognition, indeed in constituting the world that might then come to be known. Thus, 'all depths shall rise up – to my heights!' Accordingly, beauty is not the object of a dead will but rather the 'unharnessed will' discussed in section 13. Such a will, released by the feminine from its endless masculine critical duties, means the beautiful might come to be and be sustained, that 'an image might not remain mere image'.

Section 16, 'On the Scholars'

By 'scholars' [*Gelehrten*] Zarathustra means university academics in the humanities and social sciences, such as Nietzsche's one-time profession of philology. (See note on *Bildung*, with the commentary on section 14.) In this section, leitmotifs deliberately remind us of several previous discussions – for example, the professor of virtue (Part I, Section 2). There it was the artificiality of his approach to philosophy dictated by the regularity of life as a professional teacher that led to a distortion of priorities and the inability to recognise important questions. Here we are presented with a similar case of professionally determined lack of insight; there is something here about the way that social institutions reflect modes of life but also reinforce and preserve them (thus here the idea of 'training', or of constructing a building to muffle the sound of Zarathustra's footsteps). The scholars, or learned ones, should remind us also of the scientists ('On Immaculate Perception'), with the difference being that what is coolly and abstractly reflected upon are not things (the world, with the moon pale above it) but the thoughts of others in the past. Thoughts that were once alive ('yellow delights of summer fields') are dried and ground to dust; in trying to rediscover the past, it is killed by being removed from its native soil – that is, a past mode of life. They are 'sheep', recalling the frequent images of herds and herdsmen and, in the implied connection with the people, also recalling the famous wise men. For the scholars, 'understanding' is some 'kind of nut-cracking' – myopically focusing on small, abstracted problems to be solved according to strict method. The image of ruined walls and poppies suggests the priests; scholars with their nuts and priests with their churches are both closed off from the 'clear sky' – from the nature of the immanent world as will to power – and the significance of these nuts and churches is an invented one (like the transcendent and unthinkable idea of God). There is thus a hint of something like the fabled scholastic problem of angels dancing on the head of a pin.

The passage overflows with other leitmotifs too – the swamp, the clock, spiders, poisons, dice, shade, hunger, child. We cannot discuss them all. Interestingly, though, the high density of such images, meticulously brought together here, shows that *compositionally* Nietzsche is not above having 'clever fingers' and 'multiplicity'. This self-mockery undercuts Zarathustra's bravura pose. Nor, on Nietzsche's part, is it true that he was not 'trained' in scholarly ways; indeed, his mastery of them led to a professorial appointment at a remarkably young age. However, in 1872, the publication of *The Birth of Tragedy* 'slammed the door', and he would never again be taken seriously by the community of philological scholars. Thus, in *Beyond Good and Evil*, the chapter title is not 'On Scholars' but 'We Scholars'; and in the new 1886 introduction added to *The Birth of Tragedy*, Nietzsche confesses that much about tragedy in the ancient world is still awaiting philological investigation. What is needed is not a wholesale rejection of scholarship and its methods, but a *strategic* use of them that, at the same time, remains 'above' them. See our discussion of Part III, Section 7.

Section 17, 'On the Poets', and a Note on Nietzsche, Music and Language

This section continues that work of the last two sections; they have clearly been a critique of particular approaches to knowledge or insight; now it is the turn of *poetic insight*. Zarathustra makes the link in a number of ways: the reference to 'knowledge' in the first sentence, to empiricism with the 'vat of memory', to Plato's treatment of knowledge in its relation to memory (*Theatatus*), and finally with the line that poets 'know too little', Zarathustra references Plato's famous discussion of the ancient quarrel of poets and philosophers (*Republic*, Book 10). For a section on poetry, it is, not surprisingly, full of allusions: in addition to those above we find the famous 'more things in Heaven and earth' line from Shakespeare's *Hamlet*, and a sustained set of allusions to the final lines from Goethe's *Faust*. This is the 'Chorus Mysticus', a description of transcendence made as Faust is taken up to redemption. Zarathustra takes it as emblematic of both great poetry and the dubious metaphysics of all poetry; line by line he rebuts it.

CHORUS MYSTICUS:
All that is ephemeral,
Is only an allegory;
The insufficient,
Here, becomes event;
The indescribable,
Here, is done:
The eternal feminine
Draws us upward.

The list of the crimes of poets is lengthy. The poets are guilty of positing as actual, or lying about the actuality of, that which is only allegory (specifically spirit – meant in the same conventional sense as in Part I, Section 4 – and permanence); repeating things that the 'old females' tell in the evenings (conventional doctrines and superstitions – see the beginning of the next section, and do not forget the whip: Part I, Section 18); of siding with the people and their 'wisdom' in petty resistance to learning (see Part, Section 8); and of the fanciful assumption of proximity with nature, the product of some idle laying about on the grass (a dig at certain strands of romanticism). The last third of the section gives the underlying pathology: a vanity and a desire to 'appear deep', such that the poet needs spectators of any sort, even uncomprehending herd animals that are never far from the swamp. (The need for witnesses should remind us of play-actors and lovers of neighbours.)

Notice, though, that this explanation appears to be precisely the 'why' for which the rebuffed disciple was originally asking. Having just apparently dismissed any scholarship, thoughts about previous thoughts (his own), he does the same thing himself. But that refusal makes him a mere oracle in whom one just has to 'believe'. Belief should be directed to the possibilities of human life, not to Zarathustra (compare Part I, Section 22.3); thus he calms down, smiles and says 'Belief does not make me blessed'. He then proceeds to give a sort of 'why'. The 'why', however, is not a reasoned argument, nor an accumulation of empirical evidence, nor a specific incident that can be remembered and analysed – it is more like a 'taste' (see Part II, Section 13), thus the repetition of '. . . for me' throughout the passage. So, after all, Zarathustra's scholarship concerning his own past is not quite the historicism of section 16. Instead, at stake are not thoughts and reasons at all, but *a mode of life*. This vanity of the poets leads nicely into the next section, with its critique of shallow things that make a big noise. Zarathustra predicts, however, that the poets will weary of their vanity and become 'penitents of the spirit' – a phrase used previously of those who are sublime (section13); that is, they will take up arms against their easy beliefs in the transcendent, permanent or romantic nature, become annihilators of the values behind such beliefs, and seek thereby to 'make up for being the child of my fathers' (section 14).

Notice that Zarathustra's tone here is anxious and distant. For the first time he is short with a disciple. Clearly, he is still troubled by whatever new insight brought on the 'Night Song'. Part of Zarathustra's mood is the self-criticism involved in including himself among the poets, and the overhuman among the dubious creations of poets. Zarathustra's/Nietzsche's attitude is more complex than the list of crimes in this section would have us believe. The key image here is the 'realm of clouds': poetry draws us spiritually higher, but only to a medium height that we then illegitimately deify. This may be a reference to an idea Nietzsche raised in *The Birth of Tragedy*: poetry functions by evoking a 'middle world' of fictions, mere appearances but anchored in cultural symbols and metaphysical insight. The clouds are, then, merely atmospheric (middle) phenomena and not 'heavenly'; also the satirical clouds of Aristophanes's play (a satire on the subject of Socrates); and finally too a reference to the stage machinery in a theatre. (And see the image of 'clouds' in Part III, Section 4, which also repeats other images from this section.) In the early work, this middle world of myths and 'allegories' does have a function, and so it does here, although a different one. Certainly, the function of such cloud-poetry is not metaphysical truth as the poet claims. The function of poetry is – or rather can be – the creation of allegory, the beautiful forms of which can be part of the 'tools' of overcoming. It is just this allegorical function that permits the poet at the end of the section to be transformed into a 'penitent of the spirit' – he who can write allegory has the talent also to *read* it, and thus critically to cut through the layers of allegorical spiritualisation behind the names of virtues (Part I, Section 22.1, and see also the pedagogical account of reading and writing in Part I, Section 7). That is, as their penitence, poets become keen genealogical philosophers. Zarathustra admits that he himself has to make use of this allegorical function of poetry: 'I am of today and former times . . .' Does this now mean that Zarathustra and his teaching have reached a point where the usefulness of a particular way of writing, and in particular the image of the overhuman, is past? Certainly, it is notable that mentions of the overhuman are much less frequent in the remainder of the book, but we certainly have not seen the last poetic song. On these points, see Part III, Section 12.2.

A Note on Nietzsche, Music and Language

Nietzsche's account of language and its relation to the underlying movements of the will dates back to the formative years around the conception of his first book, *The Birth of Tragedy* (1872). There are a number of sources in the early work, but three are of particular significance: first, there are scattered discussions of this matter in *The Birth of Tragedy*; second, there is a preparatory sketch for that book, entitled 'The Dionysiac World-View'; and finally, there is a famous fragment from 1873 called 'On Truth and Lies in an Extra-Moral Sense'.[48] Only the first, however, is an authorised publication of Nietzsche's. The others are sketches or abandoned projects. So, we need to be careful about our ascribing anything to Nietzsche that might simply have been something he was merely trying out.

In section 8 of *The Birth of Tragedy* Nietzsche combines a discussion of metaphor with a broadside rebuke of modern poetry. His argument is that we complicated, abstract-minded and generally talentless moderns have lost the faculty of appropriately contemplating an 'original aesthetic phenomenon' when we see one. Two of *The Birth of Tragedy's* aims are to construct a theory of symbolisation, together with a theory of what it means to be able to 'see' aesthetically. Nietzsche writes: 'For the genuine poet metaphor is no rhetorical figure, but an image which takes the place of something else, something he can really see before him as a substitute for a concept.' The 'something' might be a figure from a tragic play (for example, a God) or an emotional state. Metaphor is not then essentially a phenomenon internal to language (not a rhetorical figure) nor of thought (it is a 'substitute for a concept'). Metaphor, which we will take here as a species of symbolisation, raises the act of language to the level of a symbol which 'makes present' ('he can really see before him'). Poetry overcomes, at least to this extent and in this way, the limits of language, which is to merely represent and perhaps only represent something that is already abstract – that is, already *dead*. To be sure, even poetry is not in itself music, but with the aid of musicality and under a certain 'strain' it can attain symbolisation.

The central thrust of Nietzsche's account of language and perception is in the realisation that the rationality of systematic philosophy and the reasoning of mathematics and formal logic lead us *away* from insight into the nature of things, and not towards it. The great rational systems of modern Western philosophy are and must be founded on errors (see our note on Will to Power, with the commentary on Part I, Section 4; and *Twilight of the Idols*, 'Reason in Philosophy', section 5). (In the later work, these errors are identified as primarily moral in nature.) Thus, there is a hardening of linguistic (and conceptual) expression, language becomes disconnected from the forces of life, and in surreptitious service to the preservation of the mode of life of a people, who *share* a language (see Part I, Section 5; and Part III, Section 13). Modern thought systems bear no resemblance to the insights of the pre-Socratics and to what originally inspired the 'dithyrambic dramatists' of the early Greek musical culture. In 'On Truth and Lies in an Extra-Moral Sense', Nietzsche supposes a hierarchy of forms of human expression in terms of their proximity to a direct sensory stimulation of the body (affects, movements of the will towards satisfaction or realisation). This hierarchy extends (in ascending order) from the pre-linguistic 'nervous stimulation', through immediate metaphors (images) that retain a vital connection to perception partly because we are aware of them as metaphors, and then to the solidified and abstract language of 'positive' science and 'systematic' philosophy. Each stage is a higher objectification of the will (in Schopenhauerian language), but also a loss of connection to the body, nature and to existence. Each stage is also a 'creative' or 'artistic' achievement of semblance. After music, poetry belongs to a relatively early stage in the process of the subjective appropriation of the movements of the will. 'Free' poetic expression finds a way back behind the stages of linguistic hardening. In poetry the metaphor or symbol reconnects with sensations, with the basic physiological stirrings of the sensitive body, reactivating the original metaphor that led away from them.

This account of the possibilities of language to present experience remains unchanged, in at least some important consequences, right up to *Ecce Homo*. See 'Why I Write Such Good Books', section 1, where Nietzsche talks of his books as being 'about events lying completely outside the possibility of common, or even uncommon, experience – where it is the *first* language of a new range of experiences'; or see 'Thus Spoke Zarathustra', section 6: 'this return of language to the nature of imagery' – that is, away from abstraction, language 'returns' to the affective body. These experiences are 'new' for at least two reasons: either because they are experiences of health, ascent, the increase of power, or creation which have not been permitted, or have been consistently misinterpreted, for 2,000 years: or, alternatively, they are experiences of the growth of the human beyond its current state which, therefore, must be new. Thus in Part II, Section 2, Zarathustra said 'of time and becoming shall the finest allegories tell'. The communication of such states, in such a way that a genuine reader might be able to make of his or her reading a practice of internalisation, is a key goal of Nietzsche's poetry, and indeed also of most of his prose too (see also the discussion of great styles a few pages later in *Ecce Homo*, section 4.) Such experiences are not represented (as Zarathustra often says, not 'named'); rather, the style is, as in allegory, a movement, stimulation or *act*, and not an image (see Part I, Section 22; Part III, Section 9; this distinction between act and image is implicit in the famous last section of *Beyond Good and Evil*).[49] That is also why there is no contradiction in saying that Nietzsche's book is highly personal and also a work of philosophy of significance to others. Nietzsche's life is an experiment, in becoming comprehensive, in employing practices of internalisation, in 'wandering', in the body becoming sensitised to the will to power. His life is thus also an experiment in the metaphysical significance of affective states: these are experiences of previously unknown possibilities of human health, insight or growth.

Early Nietzsche is much indebted to Wagner's revolutionary aesthetic and to Schopenhauer's overall metaphysics. Even though by the time of the conception of *Zarathustra* he has fundamentally distanced himself from both, these early influences remain visible in some key areas of Nietzsche's later thought. Following Schopenhauer, Nietzsche's key idea is that music directly expresses the underlying reality of the will (the *Ur-Eine*) and is not a representation, image or concept of it.[50] This claim permeates the argument of *The Birth of Tragedy*. Thus, Nietzsche's early text was an attempt to adopt the principles of Schopenhauer's theory of music and Wagner's new compositional techniques by turning them into the foundations for his own work. This happened in several ways, but for us here the most important is as compositional imperatives for his own new style of philosophical explication, both on the level of language and organisation. One of Wagner's musical devices that Nietzsche especially favours is the idea of *Leitmotiv* or 'leading motif' which Nietzsche translates into a device of linguistic composition. The leitmotif device serves Wagner in structuring the vastly dimensioned musical canvases. Another key musical element of *Tristan and Isolde* (the one opera of Wagner that Nietzsche remained attached to) is a single, harmonically hybrid chromatic chord. It has entered the literature under the name of the 'Tristan chord', and it is reverentially quoted in a number of compositions central as manifestos to the modernist movement, for example in Arnold Schoenberg's *Three Pieces for Piano*, Op. 11 (1909), and Alban Berg's *Lyrical Suite* (1926). Nietzsche therefore had his ear on the ground when he elevated Wagner's opera to the status of an aesthetic-philosophical paradigm of a new era.[51] The developmental arch of Tristan is built on this harmonically unresolved chord, which features of the beginning of the Prelude as a minimalist harmonic symbol of the opera as a whole. The Tristan chord is constructed in this way: it contains two dissonances. At each resolution, only one dissonance is resolved, leaving the other dissonance open. By delaying the full release of tension for the duration of the four-hour opera, Wagner manages to turn the audience experience into a prolonged building of desire for resolution. The chord treats dissonance differently from the way it had hitherto been applied in 'classical' (for example, the first Viennese school of Haydn, Mozart and Beethoven) and Romantic music, down to Brahms and Bruckner. Traditionally, dissonance featured as a device primarily for portraying exceptional, extreme moments, either musical or extra-musical (e.g. psychological); that is, as an extraneous device and mainly for contrast to sanction the inevitability of harmonic stability. Wagner's Tristan chord is radically different because it turns dissonance itself into the centre of musical activity.

In *Ecce Homo* Nietzsche says that 'perhaps the whole of *Zarathustra* can be considered music' ('Thus Spoke Zarathustra', section 1). As Nietzsche's own '*Gesamtkunstwerk*', *Zarathustra* is a work of philosophy written in allegorical language that is through-composed like a piece of music. However, compared to *The Birth of Tragedy* we can perhaps see here a maturing of Nietzsche's faculties as a musical composer of conceptual language. He has now a vast range of techniques and devices at his disposal that allow him to vary his writing greatly regarding atmosphere, pitch, tone and register of language – always with a careful attention to musical phrasing and breathing. In parallel with Wagner's operatic experiment, we could call Nietzsche's style 'chromatic'. One secret of Nietzsche's stylistic specificity lies in the tension caused by using repetition to induce variation (of motifs, ideas, terminologies, and so forth). Rather than along the line of stringent logical explication, the development of ideas occurs through slight shifts of nuance and angle, so that the argument forms one long and 'undulating line' (that is Nietzsche's description of Wagner's melodic lines in section 21 of *The Birth of Tragedy*). The text opens up a 'web of complex relations' (the phrase is Darwin's) between ingredient components, 'a tissue being woven on a rising and falling loom' (Nietzsche with reference to *Tristan*: *The Birth of Tragedy*, section 21). For example, there are numerous leitmotifs in *Zarathustra*. The sea journey is one of them, so are times of the day and year, elevations and directions, geographies (caves, mountains, cliffs, seas, valleys), animals, shepherds, metaphors for sexual organs, and biblical images. Motifs appear, and reappear (never exactly the same) in Nietzsche's text at different strategic moments of development of the argument, underpinning it metaphorically and structurally.

And also the idea is new in *Zarathustra* of beating Wagner at his own game, by topping the achievements of the *Ring*-Cycle of operas with a different type of musical noise: that of musicalised language that does not seduce and lull its listeners into passive acceptance, as Nietzsche now accuses Wagner of doing (remember, Wagner is portrayed as a conniving sorcerer in *Zarathustra*), but one that conditions the listener/reader into independence of judgement and holistic life-practice. Parodistic undermining and satirical critique of his former musical role model have therefore become integral parts of *Zarathustra's* new 'musical style', even though, of course, Wagner is not the only object of Nietzsche's satire. Compared with the earlier work, *Zarathustra* reads like a tapestry, patchwork or pastiche of styles: *Zarathustra's* style is forged from a parodistic critique of other styles, more Rossini-style *opera buffa* than *Götterdämmerung*, more ironic *bricolage* (including self-irony: see, for example, Part I, Section 18 or Part II, Section 18, 'On Great Events') than relentless, uninterrupted questing. In *Zarathustra* two layers of allegorical meaning are interwoven: the allegorical and poetic imaging of language together with the organisation of the text (on a micro- and macro–level) in analogy to principles of musical composition (polyphony, leitmotivic networking of allegorical metaphors, theme and variation, counterpoint, building of tension through dissonance and the deferring of its resolution, harmonic development, symphonic superstructures, and so forth). In this way the linguistic allegory and symbolism are metaphorically enhanced by making them appear *as if* they were musical (the text is singing and dancing!). As Zarathustra falls into the bottomless well of time in Part IV, Section 10, the reader falls through the surface layers of imagery and structural symbolisation into new experiences of health, yearning, anguish or joy. Likewise, as Wagner in *Tristan* musically forever defers harmonic resolution, Nietzsche also endlessly defers both logical and emotional resolution not only to the end of *Zarathustra*, but beyond it.

Indeed, it becomes impossible to decide, for example, whether the four-part structure of the book (besides some other functions not relevant here) is meant as a mocking parody of Wagner's four-part *Ring* (with Part IV wielding the stylistic knife particularly relentlessly), or whether it was not also equally possible to align it with the four-part sonata form of the new Brahmsian type of post-Romantic symphony.[52] It would not be completely far-fetched, if we allowed ourselves to think syn-aesthetically for a moment, to construct a loose analogy between the four parts of *Zarathustra* and the four movements of a Brahms symphony, for example the *First Symphony* (1877). It would be a fun exercise, in fact, to find appropriate symphonic movement denominations: we suggest '*Rondo burlesque*' for Part IV. Whatever the case may be, the differences among the parts are more those between four musical 'movements' than those between the distinct stages of a discursively developed argument.[53]

* * * *

Section 18, 'On Great Events'

'Much ado about nothing', the reader might think, because the morale drawn from this parable is that the events that make the biggest noise are not the most important ones, a lesson spelt out approximately halfway through this passage. (*The Gay Science* is preoccupied with various noises; see, in particular, section 218). However, in its fantastical narrative, setting and rhetorical register, this piece of experimental writing is itself one of the loudest sections in the whole book. Are we therefore indirectly urged not to take it too seriously? The tone is that of wonderment but also satirical self-caricature. Zarathustra's shadow is seen flying through space, rocket-like; likewise, we have Wagnerian tuba-noise atmospheric effects. This section conveys its message by pointing to its own superfluity.

Again we have three subsections, with the outer two (appearance of, and discussion of, Zarathustra's shadow) framing the one in the middle. The first section is satirically couched in the style of a travelogue, a miracle encountered during a sea-journey (this brings Coleridge's *Ancient Mariner* to mind). The Mediterranean setting of 'The Isles of the Blest' (Part II, Section 2) is re-evoked. The autobiographical backdrop is Nietzsche's sea journey around the Aeolian Islands off Sicily with their regular volcanic activity, particularly Stromboli. The second part is the conversation between Zarathustra and the fire-hound. The devil-like fire-hound is an oxymoron: the shallow spirit of depth. In spite of all the thunderous histrionics, he flees back into his cave in the end with the tiny bark of a poodle. The satirical portrait of figures like Wagner (with his love of big effects and public platforms and adulation) or populist politicians and political philosophers (with their bellowing of 'freedom') is obvious. Those who create values, peoples and worlds do not necessarily make any noise, the world revolves around them 'inaudibly'. The third part is the report to Zarathustra. His disciples are eager to tell him about the miraculous flying man – so eager, in fact, that significantly they do not listen to his teaching. As it is reported to him, he realises that they have seen his own shadow, saying 'It is time! It is high time!'. High time for what, Zarathustra wonders at the end; in this way he (and therefore the reader) is being explicitly informed for the first time of the mission that is urgently awaiting him. This is to convey the doctrine of eternal recurrence, the major theme of Part III.

Who is this shadow? Zarathustra asks himself that question and thereby throws the reader into a little confusion: the image of the shadow is a complex and multiply valenced one. First of all, it is the *Doppelgänger*, an image frequently employed in Gothic writing and Romantic painting, here in a variant reminiscent of Schubert's *Winterreise* and Caspar David Friedrich's paintings of 'The Wanderer and his Shadow'. 'The Wanderer and his Shadow' was also the title of a section of *Human, All Too Human*; and the shadow returns as a character in Part IV. We also had a shadow in the stone, at the end of section 2. This last is a promising clue: it is the shadow as that which is cast *ahead*, into the future, urging Zarathustra on, the image after which he yearns (or should yearn). However, the *Doppelgänger* notion suggests that the shadow might be a cameo appearance by the author in his own text, a mover and shaker behind the surface noise. Nietzsche tells his own narrative mouthpiece to get on with things, a supreme piece of ironic narrative self-deprecation. What is the use of Zarathustra going on a sea journey to teach the theatrically posturing and hypocritical fire-hound when there is real work to be done? On a more serious note, we will soon find out that Zarathustra is frightened of his mission. Zarathustra's (Nietzsche's) waste of time with the fire-hound is therefore an act of procrastination, a kind of displacement activity to put off dealing with the most difficult aspect of Zarathustra's mission. It is therefore an important part of the text's interest in the workings of psychological phenomena, particular the psychology of the free spirit striving for self-overcoming. However, insofar as the flying shadow is a piece of theatre that distracts the disciples, Nietzsche is also indicating that his indirect, circumlocutory way of getting to the thought of eternal recurrence is the right one. If he just came out with it (without 'stammering'), no one would hear it correctly (which is precisely what happens three times in Parts III and IV). The section is therefore also a complex commentary on Nietzsche's compositional method, his strategy of 'teaching'.

Section 19, 'The Soothsayer'

This is a complex and nicely constructed section, continuing the narrative path from the previous section. It begins with the 'soothsayer' or 'prophet' giving a prediction, which may already be true, of a nihilistic age. The portrait is, in part, of Schopenhauer. Nietzsche was an enthusiastic Schopenhauerian for the first few years of his career. Since for Schopenhauer the underlying will is constantly striving and never achieving, the primary state of existence is suffering. This pessimism, from which Nietzsche has removed the viability of Schopenhauer's own solutions (the quieting of the will), and then combined with Nietzsche's analysis of the contemporary world, yields the soothsayer and his more radical nihilism. This prophecy affects Zarathustra, not, however, infecting him with the 'poison' of nihilism but rather causing him anxiety over how 'my light' – his teaching, his children – will be sustained through the coming age. He becomes ill, eventually sleeps and has a dream the meaning of which is not (yet) clear to him. In the dream, he is a night-watchman in the castle of death.[54] A storm pushes open the gate and blows in a black coffin; from the coffin 'spews out' thousand-fold laughter from the 'thousand grotesque masks of children, angels, owls, fools, and child-sized butterflies'. One disciple, Zarathustra's favourite, tries to interpret the dream. At this, Zarathustra looks as though he does not even recognise his disciples (another sign of increasing distance between them, like their not listening in the previous section). The end of the section makes it clear that Zarathustra considers this interpretation somehow wrong and, above all, *disappointing*.

This leaves us with at least two puzzles: what is the meaning of the dream? And what is the meaning of Zarathustra's rejection of the disciple's interpretation?

The second puzzle is the easier. The disciple casts Zarathustra in the Christ-like role of a redeemer who, on behalf of us all, triumphs over death. 'Your crutch, however, I am not', Zarathustra said back in Part I, Section 6. Their belief, yearning and efforts should be directed to the overhuman, not to Zarathustra (see also section 17). The key to the first puzzle, the dream itself, is probably the word 'overcome': 'From within glass coffins life that had been overcome looked out at me'. In Zarathustra's teachings thus far, death does not and could not 'overcome' life: rather, it is life as will to power that overcomes (some particular mode or aspect of) itself, even using death as an instrument of overcoming. Thus here is the image of carrying one's ashes up the mountain, that they might be transformed as Zarathustra was in his ten years of solitude (see Prologue, Section 2). The night watchman may have renounced life, but life as such has not and could not renounce *itself*. The castle of death is actually, or also, the castle of nihilism, maintaining itself in the belief that 'All is empty, all is the same, all has been'. As with death, so too nihilism must be seen as a means by which life can overcome itself (see *Twilight of the Idols*, 'Skirmishes of an Untimely Man', sections 43–4). That is why the recovered Zarathustra will invite the soothsayer and show him an ocean in which he may drown (in which nihilism may go under and be overcome). This overcoming of the sense of helplessness before the past and present is also the theme of the next section, with its notion of willing backwards. '[Y]et how shall this happen?' Zarathustra asks there. So, our interpretation of life overcoming is not the whole story: the arrival of the storm of life is accompanied by laughter, to be sure, but also horror. The overcoming of nihilism can be achieved through the book's next major idea – eternal recurrence – but this comes at a cost, one that Zarathustra is only just beginning to realise and is unwilling yet to name.

Section 20, 'On Redemption'

We are nearing the closure of Part II, and are (along with a terrified Zarathustra) left pondering the enormity of the task of what it takes to explain and implement the concept of eternal recurrence. This section contains the first sketch of Nietzsche's mature philosophy of history and of time. Zarathustra is prevented from going across the 'great bridge' – his own transformation is brought to a halt – by a group of cripples and beggars, and he is addressed by a hunchback. The hunchback asks him 'to take a little away' from the burden he carries (a reference to Jesus's miracles of healing), in return for their belief. Zarathustra cynically answers the man that his identity is complete with the hump, and is destroyed if the hump is taken away or ignored. The people say this, so why shouldn't Zarathustra? This already should make us a little suspicious. The hunchback with his extra burden carried from the past into the present and future is also, metaphorically, the spokesperson for all humans. This becomes clear when Zarathustra addresses his disciples: 'fragments and severed limbs and dreadful accidents – but no human beings' (see Parkes's endnote on this passage).

This brutal answer is a deflection of the fact that Zarathustra cannot perform this miracle, not literally (he is not Jesus), nor figuratively (again let us recall 'your crutch, however, I am not': Part I, Section 6), but above all not metaphysically. The will is prisoner to time, realising with great pain that what has happened cannot be undone. The evolutionary shape of human development (both biological and historical) including degenerative mishaps cannot be put right by an act of the human will. There are three types of freakish evolutionary aberrations: malformations, missing limbs or organs, and overspecialisation.[55] These are, again, meant both literally and figuratively. The naturally created variety of human types, including the accidents along the way, means that the individuals of the species are like fragments of a whole that does not (yet) exist.

This means that the thorny problem needs to be solved of how to make the past with everything untoward that has already happened in it (the hunchback's burden, the fragmentation of identities, the 'dreadful accidents'), a meaningful foundation of a future that is envisaged as a holistic unity of man and nature. The will is furious that time is not running backwards, but it is at least possible for it to reconcile itself with time by redeeming the past so that it be no longer a burden to time that runs forward (see the anticipation of this idea in Prologue, Section 4 and Part 2, Section 11). Zarathustra uses the image of the stone barrier covering the past in an allusion to the stone sealing Jesus's dead body in his sepulchre. The story is in all four Gospels, although Matthew (28: 2) has the additional detail of the angel of the Lord rolling away the stone, and sitting upon it (compare the dwarf in Part III, Section 2.2). A redemption of the human past which healed the hunchback of his hunch would be a miracle – an intervention into the course of natural events by something outside of nature. The Christian conception of time is a time in which such miracles can happen, but only through the grace of a transcendent God. The suggestion also follows that Christian morality and indeed the Christian conception of time is all of a piece with the spirit of revenge, which is the will exacting punishment for its incapacity to will backwards.

Redemption in connection with the overhuman is the faculty to redeem the past itself such that it is a domain of affirmative will. This is not a miraculous change to the past, or an equally miraculous disentanglement of the past and the present or future. Rather, it is a change in the will's relation to the past, that is, in the image of the past that causes it so much pain. This is a problem Zarathustra had failed to fully address so far. It now dawns upon him that it is not sufficient to proclaim creative willing as it is flowing from the overabundance of energies in the human type newly aligned with nature. For, as long as this kind of creative willing takes place in a temporal vacuum (akin to his description of the artificiality and arbitrariness of the past in the 'land of culture'), it will always be haunted by the spirit of revenge, as long as it does not include the past as its basis. So, we can distinguish between a merely 'formal' conception of creativity, and a richer, materialist or historical conception. We will develop this idea further in Part III, Section 2. The will needs to be reconciled with time through some kind of extension of its power into the past. Zarathustra has changed from a historicist position at the beginning of the section (he is just recording the types of the fragmented mess around him), to diagnosing the 'folly' and 'madness' of the will, and finally offering a prophecy of the healing of time. Zarathustra anticipates a redemption of the past such that the 'it was' is transformed into a 'thus I willed it'; and not, however, merely as resignation and acceptance, but rather as an absolute affirmation of the whole entanglement of the past as it surges towards the future. Thus, near the end of the section, just before Zarathustra falls silent (as if he had let something dangerous slip out), the refrain 'will backwards' becomes 'want (or desire) backwards [*Zurückwollen*]'. The will wants and has, as its object, the whole of the past back, again. What, though, makes this possible? It is eternal recurrence; Zarathustra is still unable to bring it to the surface, and certainly unable to tell his disciples. The section demonstrates again that one of the leading ideas of *Zarathustra* is derived from the (mostly German) tradition of the '*Bildungsroman*' ['educational novel'] (cf. note on *Bildung*, with the commentary on section 14). It shows its hero in transition. In fact, he is momentarily paralysed by the monstrosity of the task. His disciples have stopped following where he has taken them. He is found out by the hunchback who is suspicious that behind Zarathustra's silver-tongued double-speak lurks both an unspoken thought and a weakness.

One related problem lies in the incompatibility of past and present fragmentation with the future Dionysian holism of overhuman's *unio mystica*. Because of the specialisation of learning in the modern period, because of nihilism that refuses all values including even those that might authentically belong to it, because of Christianity that has turned one aspect of the body (spirit) against the rest, because of philosophy that has substituted artificial rationality for the 'great reason' of the living body – for all these reasons among still others, the modern human is at best a piece of a full human. We are reminded of our gloss on passages earlier in this part, such as 'On the Priests', where admirable virtues were found isolated, and there were 'gaps' in the spirit. Zarathustra walks 'among human beings as amongst fragments of the future'. He includes himself – 'Zarathustra is all this' – but also thereby excludes himself, for he is *all* this. As a prophet of the overhuman all his 'composing and striving' is therefore devoted to bringing all these fragments 'into one'. This bears marked similarities with what Walter Benjamin later calls the 'tiger leap' into history, the desire to go back in history because the present is deficient, and from salvaging the broken fragments of the past, to fuse history back together again as a continuum. Until the will can will backwards, 'all "it was" is a fragment, a riddle, a cruel coincidence'. What does this mean?

It cannot mean that the affirmation of the past in 'wanting back' shows that, judged against the whole of the past development of human life or nature more generally, the apparent fragments of humanity are not in fact fragments. This would be a version of a Leibnizian solution to the problem of evil, that it is a problem of our limited perspective. Nor can it simply mean that in the future overcoming of the human, and the realignment of the drives constituting the self with the nature of will to power, any fragmentation too is overcome. A dependence on the future does not remove the pain of willing backwards (if it could, the promise of eternal life would not be an instance of the 'spirit of revenge'). Zarathustra briefly outlines (as a possible but rejected solution) the reasoning within a cosmic version of the spirit of revenge. It preaches that all life deserves punishment, eternally, but this is rejected as 'madness'. Likewise with the Schopenhauerian solution ('willing should become not-willing'). We are left with a statement, not a solution. Now, part of Zarathustra's solution will lie in the redemption of the notion of contingency (see our discussion in Part III, Section 1) – thus here the repeated stress on 'accident' or 'coincidence'. However, we will have to wait until Zarathustra has managed to give us the full version of the thought of eternal recurrence (which begins in Part III, Section 2) to explore these ideas further. (See in particular Part III, Section 12.)

Section 21, 'On Human Cleverness'

This section is an interlude within Zarathustra's personal struggle with the new idea of eternal recurrence. Zarathustra has a 'double will': to overcome himself towards the overhuman but also to remain supported by the human because he is being 'swept' up and away. This is a metaphor for the double necessity of dealing with the human. For, first of all, it is by remaining human and being fully within social relations, by writing and reading and otherwise engaging with one's time, that one might be able to aid the human in its overcoming, and not be swept away in vain. A hermit could not have the bestowing virtue, properly speaking. However, secondly, precisely the will towards this overcoming makes such engaging difficult and even repugnant and one would like only to flee from the flies in the market-place. How is it that one is supposed to fulfil this double necessity? Through 'human cleverness', of which Zarathustra names four varieties.

The first variety is to lack 'foresight', to not look out for oneself, but 'roll with the punches' (to use a phrase Nietzsche would no doubt dislike). To have foresight would be disengaging from the 'anchor' in the human. The second is to allow the vain their vanity, both because this vanity hides a profound modesty (being unaware of who one is, and thus needing onlookers: see Part II, Section 17) and because the spectacle of vanity makes life 'good to watch' and lifts the heavy heart. The third is to not be put off by conventional attitudes but to seek out evil, which is a 'bliss' and 'worthy of wonder'. For otherwise, the wise, the best and the wickedest are frankly disappointing and not likely to anchor and engage one in the human. Finally, Zarathustra's human cleverness allows others their disguises of 'the good and the righteous', and also disguises oneself even from oneself. (To the mask is contrasted the ideal of a 'realm where Gods are ashamed of all clothes', that is where the health and beauty of the spirit is such that a mask would be a lowering of oneself.) The mask, role or persona means a shield whereby what is dispiriting is kept at bay (cf. the allusion to beauty as a shield in Part II, Section 5), but also means both an instrument for engagement with others (the struggles that need to be fought happen in all sorts of social and intellectual domains; cf. 'all the names of values: weapons they shall be' in Part II, Section 7) and a place where one's self-identity is invested or found (not only the vain need to be seen as this or that in order to *believe themselves to be* this or that).[56] At this level, the section is a manual for the free spirit to solve the problem of living among humans, not as he or she must, but as he or she cannot. However, this close to the end of Part II, and surrounded by sections depicting an anxious Zarathustra avoiding the 'abyss deep thought', the anchor in the human takes on another meaning. This section is thus also yet another diversion or delaying tactic.

Section 22, 'The Stillest Hour'

This is Zarathustra's leave-taking. He must leave his disciples again and return to solitude because he is not yet strong enough, or humble enough, or child enough to carry on into the next phase of his teaching and self-transformation. The message is delivered through a voice (another female persona, the stillest hour) in a dream. His 'terrible mistress' is not identified with any conventional part of the psyche, such as soul, heart or spirit. Moreover, though 'hour' is a feminine noun, what speaks to him without voice in the dream is 'it' – the neuter pronoun – and 'it' speaks to him 'at the stillest hour'. This makes it difficult to align it with the gender symbolism we have been tracking throughout. The 'voice' is most similar to the flying shadow of section 18, but the status of that shadow was hardly unambiguous; and here in this section we get a repetition from section 2 of the shadow as the image of what is to come. In other words, this dream conversation is delicately constructed by Nietzsche so as to be unassimilable to any conventional narrative tags, such as *conversing with his heart, listening to the voice of reason* or *voice of heaven*. This gives a mystical atmosphere (like the 'Chorus Mysticus' at the end of Goethe's *Faust*) and thus removes any suspicion that Zarathustra's ails are simply psychological or individual in nature and not also metaphysical.

In any case, the result is that Zarathustra takes stock of the situation. For example, he believes he has made no impact on human beings or modernity (the voice reassures him: 'the dew falls upon the grass . . .'; see the use of this image in Part IV, Section 14). Most importantly, he admits the discrepancy between what he already knows (a knowledge that has gradually grown inside him and changed from a feeling to premonition [section 20] to actuality) and what he feels he is capable of carrying out. The repetition of the child image makes it clear that it is Zarathustra himself who has to perform the three transformations outlined in Part I, Section 1. The realisation of the full extent of what is now needed comes to him as a shock and he is overcome by it at the end of this section (the violent eruption of laughter should remind us of the dream in the soothsayer section), nearing a breakdown before his second retreat back into his cave.

Part III

Section 1, 'The Wanderer', and a Note on Contingency

While the first two parts commenced with Zarathustra in the mountains and about to go down to his teaching, the third part commences with him just having left his disciples and beginning the long journey back to his 'home' – the cave in the mountains. The perpetual wandering image – recalling Odysseus's long journey home – is meaningful in at least four ways. First, it is autobiographical, as Nietzsche was effectively of 'no fixed address', living in a series of rented rooms mostly in Switzerland or Italy. Secondly, it is also descriptive of the narrative of this book, which cycles through various themes and strolls off on detours and diversions. Thirdly, the wandering refers to the dominant image patterns in the book which are all about motion: going down, over, climbing up, flying, dancing, and so forth. It is of the essence of the will to power to be wandering, achieving stillness and beauty only briefly in cultural forms and modes of life: 'Whatever I create . . . soon I must oppose it' (Part II, Section 12). The fourth meaning concerns methodology, the avoidance of single scholarly specialisation and thus a kind of wandering through problems, languages and strategies. This was introduced in Part II, Section 7 and Zarathustra will return to the idea again at the beginning of Part III, Section 7, where we will discuss it in more detail.

A Note on Contingency

Part III contains most obviously a meditation on the 'abyss deep thought' of eternal recurrence and its significance. The first hint of this here is 'in the end one only experiences oneself'; this is elaborated upon by way of a discussion of the nature of accident or chance. Zarathustra says, 'The time has flowed past when accidents could still befall me'. This idea is a natural extension of the problem of willing backwards (Part II, Section 20), and also appeared in the line 'Come on, old heart! A misfortune misled you: enjoy this as your – good fortune!' (Part II, Section 21). If one could be 'redeemed' to the point of willing that which one did not, in fact and at the time, will (that is, as a matter of the objective history of the artificially decontextualised self; in the ordinary sense of will) – if one could accept and indeed affirm the whole – then the notion of a merely contingent or accidental event, as something that arrives from outside the sphere of the will, evaporates.

Likewise, as Zarathustra will say in Part III, Section 4, if one's world has been redeemed from purpose – from an overriding sense of what life is supposed to be like, or an overall narrative of progress, salvation, enlightenment or what-have-you – then also redeemed will be the concept of contingency. 'The total character of the world . . . is for all eternity chaos', Nietzsche writes in *The Gay Science*, section 109. It is not alive, not an orderly machine, not organised, not unified or planned, neither elegant nor beautiful in its movement or action, and should it all eternally recur (as Nietzsche suggests even in that passage in *The Gay Science* passage) then it returns as a noise rather than a 'melody'. What is follows its necessary course without that course having a sense. The distinction between contingency (the unexpected and thus also the creative) and necessity can only be made from a position that has transcended (or rather imagined itself having transcended) the immanence of nature through illegitimately interpreting order and purpose into things. (See *Twilight of the Idols*, 'The Four Great Errors', section 8; and 'Skirmishes of an Untimely Man', section 49.) This idea also leads directly into an analysis of possibility upon which, in the next section, eternal recurrence seems to rely. Will to power and with it the aligned mode of life is aligned to or consummate with *that which is* and not struggling (in vain and with more than a hint of the spirit of revenge) against it. In *The Gay Science* (section 276), Nietzsche famously calls this '*amor fati*', the love of one's fate (the idea is in play even at the very end of Nietzsche's career, in *Ecce Homo*, 'Why I am so Clever', section 10). Importantly, though, this 'not struggling' and not having any accidents 'befall me' does not mean a kind of Stoic indifference and placidity, as if one has simply been melted into the world as a whole (see *The Gay Science*, section 306). (Where 'whole' means that which is, without exception; it does not mean thinking that which is under a concept and thus treating it as a unity. If the latter, one could again meaningfully distinguish between necessary and contingent elements.) The Dionysiac moment, to be sure, involves a kind of ecstatic destruction of individuation, an insight into the whole by *being* the whole – but such a state cannot be maintained. Rather, there are '1,000 bridges' to the overhuman, and there must be difference and struggle for life to advance (see Part II, Section 7). However, one can affirm these 1,000 bridges even as one's best enemy.

* * * *

Section 2, 'On the Vision and Riddle', and a Note on Eternal Recurrence

This section contains, in the guise of a Gothic fantasy, the explication of the doctrine of eternal recurrence. In Part II, Section 20 the problem of time was posed, but left unresolved, partly because it was deliberately couched in the inadequate language of Christian miracle (resurrection and salvation). The intention of Part II, Section 20 was to show the link between the conception of time and cultural systems of value, especially Christian morality. Here now, the language is more geared towards analysis of the 'physical' or rather ontological aspects of time. This was (in Part II, Section 20, and is now still) the question: how can the will be redeemed from its vindictive, impotent relation to past time, and with it how can past time be resurrected from its status as dead time and elevated into the living foundation of the future? Zarathustra's slip of the tongue – he says 'want back' – seems to imply a double action: wanting to go back in time into the past, and wanting time back. This current section gives a detailed explanation of what this might mean.

As so often before, the ship-narrative is a frame supporting another. The inner narrative here though is very complex, spanning two subsections and including three individual settings. So, we have two initial situations (scenes 1.i: on board the ship and ii: a walk upward into the Alps), which spawn three events (2.i: at the gateway of the moment; and 2.ii: the memory of childhood; and 2.iii: the riddle of the shepherd) and finally returning to the first frame (scene 2.iv: the address to the sailors on the ship). The narrative devices provide playful variations on the duality of opposites and their reconciliation. For example, note the juxtaposition of the two title elements: although Zarathustra recounts the vision as something he '*saw*' (the word and thus tense is emphasised), a vision is of its nature *futural.* He is remembering the future. Similarly, the riddle is largely backward looking in its narrative material, but in the transformed shepherd also contains the shadow of the future. Inscribed into the present world of the sea journey is thus the past world of Zarathustra's struggle and the future of his epiphany. Indeed, to an extent the figure of the shepherd refers us *back* to the world of Greek or Latin mythology, even though we are astonished to realise that the action is firmly placed in the Gothic North amongst stark, ragged rocks in the mountains. (The dog[57] also links the narrative with past events, this time on an autobiographical level: as the note informs us, the howling of the dog occurred when Nietzsche's father died.) Somehow, however, the shepherd is historically and geographically displaced here. As high up as he is found, no grazing would be available for sheep. An element of classical Southern European mythology has been teleported into the harsh Northern climate of Gothic fantasy. Nietzsche is deliberately confusing the sense of historical space and time here by concocting this hybrid mixture of North/South, an almost modernist 'rendering-strange'-device (Brecht and Kafka come to mind) that would fit in with the main brief of this section to show as obsolete *the notion of linearity of time.*

We should note three things immediately. First, Zarathustra is on a lonely sea journey, though he is not travelling alone. There are *two* passengers on board, the second having come from the Isles of the Blest (by now we can regard the reference to this Elysian place as one of the many Leitmotifs of the text). In the light of Part II, Section 18 we suggest reading this as Zarathustra being accompanied by his shadow

('The Wanderer and his Shadow').The shadow had a mystery voice in Part II, Section 18 (an ironic authorial intrusion urging him on), and perhaps again in Part II, Section 22 (the ambiguous voice demanding he give expression to eternal recurrence). The shadow has always been cast ahead of Zarathustra, his next step; the text suggests that he is the origin of the rumours, which precipitate Zarathustra's address. Secondly, the second 'initial situation' serves as another frame, but is never returned to or resolved. It remains open like the Tristan chord; or perhaps we are to think of Zarathustra as perpetually *ascending*. Finally, as we are following Zarathustra going higher upwards into the mountains, we are at the same time getting further inside Zarathustra's inner dream world. An inverse proportional relationship is created between physical outer verticality (striving upwards from sea-level to mountain heights) and psychological inner depth – this has been one of the leitmotifs of the books since the beginning. Both of these are ways of leaving behind the 'surface'. This relation forms a spatial equivalent to the notion of time meeting up with itself in the present moment of the now. In this way the anti-linear space-orientation of the narrative metaphorically supports the propagation of the new philosophy of time.

Zarathustra recounts his vision to the sailors. The more he strives upward, the more Devil inside him comes out and tries to weigh him down – the Devil as a parasite (recall Part I, Section 8). 'The spirit of heaviness' takes on the shape of a persuasive dwarf carried along on Zarathustra's shoulder and constantly interfering sarcastically, even nihilistically, with his thoughts. Much is made here of the metaphor '*mit klingendem Spiel*' ('ringing play': a reference to German military marching music – not, that is, very light and playful) as a symbol of courageous and defiant battling with this enemy. The dwarf bears similarities with Wagner's dwarf Mime who, in Wagner's opera *Das Rheingold*, wants to steal the ring. He also features in the third opera of the cycle, *Siegfried*, still plotting the stealing of the ring for himself, where he engages Wotan in a protracted riddle competition. Also, in the way the dwarf spurts his nihilism, he strangely resembles Goethe's Mephistopheles in both parts of *Faust*, a spirit who 'forever denies, and quite rightly so because everything that is being created is worth in turn to be destroyed'. Zarathustra presents the dwarf with the alternative: 'Dwarf! You! Or I!'. In *Faust* it is the Devil who facilitates the transgression for Faust. Here Zarathustra himself grasps the final complications and earth shattering mysteries, while the dwarf sits uncomprehending. At the start of the vision (2.i),

Zarathustra uses the dwarf as a sounding board for the explication of the principle, increasingly wrong-footing him until he in the end calls him lazy and degenerate: 'lamefoot'. This is a reference to Oedipus, and the dwarf is thus also a tragic view of the world. The self-quotation that Nietzsche chose as epigraph to Part III now makes a great deal of sense.

A Note on Eternal Recurrence

The vision of eternal recurrence commences with the 'moment' as if it were the nuclear cell of all time in which the past and future fuse together and switch around. The concept is that of 'the present moment in time', as the sensually perceivable concretisation of abstract time, comprising and compressing time. The 'rock in front of me' (complete with a parody of an angel of the Lord sitting on it) brings to mind the tomb-barrier covering the dead past in Part II, Section 20. The will there was enraged by its inability to roll this barrier away. Here, it has been rolled away to the side, or perhaps never stood in the way at all, and the gateway of the moment stands open. The gateway is the interface of the two time dimensions of past and future, the latter its outward-facing direction, the former its reverse-facing one. The whole scenario is constructed like a physics demonstration. From the moment, past and future extend in linear lanes in opposite directions for an 'eternity' and 'another eternity'. To this moment the past leads up, and the moment 'draws after it *all* things that are to come'. The moment is thus the model of becoming: it comprises the difference between past and future, and from out of this nuclear difference all time is spun. In that sense it contains past and future in their entirety. Insofar as the moment is not understood in isolation from past and future, as, for example, a now-point, then the double eternity of time is concretised in the moment. (Notice that all-important notion of the continuity and indivisibility of time; that is the tie-in with Nietzsche's critique of the 'actualness' of the land of culture, and the 'last humans' of Prologue, Section 5.)

The moment as so conceived contains the possibility of creativity – it is the moment of birth, eruption, bursting, explosion, sudden insight or exclamation (as in the 'it cried out of me' a page later). This conception of the moment thus links up with the watershed image (see Part II, Section 1 and Part III, Section 16.1). Nietzsche evokes such a 'midnight moment' in *The Gay Science*, section 87 and again at *Beyond Good and Evil*, section 240, curiously in a passage praising the artistic gifts of Wagner.

The moment is both time as continuous becoming, itself fully tangible and rescued from abstraction – *and* also 'timeless time', eternity folded and wrapped.[58] That is why in the initial description of the moment, the opposite directions of time from the moment are *also* described as where the two ways of time 'confront one another head on'. The sensual tangibility of time in the moment, understood as the Dionysiac insight into nature and time by way of dissolution of the self, is an important theme throughout the book; as we have seen, it is often imaged as the sexual act (Part II, Section 10; Part IV, Section 10).

The second element of the vision is the notion of the return or circularity of time.[59] The dwarf pronounces with blasé nonchalance what has been struggling for recognition in Zarathustra for so long, namely the notion 'that time itself is a circle'. Zarathustra chides him, not necessarily or primarily because what he says is wrong, but because the dwarf does not take it seriously. (This is far from the last time this will happen.) The moment that contains the difference of past and future as the nucleus of time is equally determined by what is in the past and will happen in the future; for each moment both dimensions have the same validity, the same property of being spun from out of it, because all things are 'knotted together'. Thus again, the moment as absolute difference of past and future is also the moment of 'timeless time'. Each moment then is a repetition of itself in this limited sense: it returns as becoming. That is to say, it 'returns' again as the nuclear difference of past and future, again the tangible fullness of time and also timeless time.

But Zarathustra speaks of the return of *things*. Here is where a new notion enters the scene. 'Must not whatever among all things *can* walk have walked this lane already?' Here, to say 'can walk' the lane of time means to be a possible existence or event. In the immanent sphere of nature, and across the eternity of time, there is no unactualised possibility. In order to describe something as possible that never occurred in the past and never will in the future, one would have to 'stand' at a transcendent point outside the world and employ laws of nature that are not immanent to it.[60] (The dwarf, sitting on the rock, is thus not on the path, but viewing it from the side – thus his lack of comprehension, thus the ease with which he can say 'circle'.) Such possibilities are empty. They serve as a negative warning of how little we understand the knotting of things, and are the product of the human ability to create abstract descriptions of nature and then use them as 'laws'. (The point should remind us of the discussion of the compatibility of contingency and necessity in the previous section: a contingent event would be understood as one among many possible events.) Thus all things that 'can walk' on the lane of time – that is, everything that is possible – must have already been actual. That everything would of course include this moment itself, and include also all those things that are possible in the future. The 'eternity' of the past and the 'other eternity' of the future turn out to coincide. Zarathustra's voice has lowered to a whisper: 'must we not eternally come back again?' The result we obtained from meditating on the moment – the equal validity of past and future – turns out to have been an anticipation of this idea of the *return* of past and future.

That was the 'cosmological' or 'metaphysical' account of eternal recurrence (one version of it, anyway). Nietzsche explores it further in his notebooks.[61] What follows is a quite different version, eternal recurrence as existential test. The first posits as a metaphysical truth the eternally recurring nature of all things. The second asks 'what must the human being be like who could affirm, from the ground up, his or her existence within an eternally recurring world?'. This second version would seem the meaning of the riddle passage that follows here, and also the treatment of eternal recurrence in Nietzsche's next book, *Beyond Good and Evil* (section 56; see also section 39). There is a third version also which is quite Kantian in content, resembling closely several formulations of the categorical imperative (particularly the formulation in terms of a maxim as law of nature: Kant (1968) IV 421). This third achieves its classical expression in *The Gay Science*: '[T]he question in each and every thing, "Do you want this again and innumerable times again?" would lie on your actions as the heaviest weight!' This idea is intended to make momentous, indeed sacred, every decision one makes by showing it to be integrated into the fabric of eternity and thus showing every decision to be an affirmation (or denial) of existence itself.[62] The health of life under such conditions would have to be the life in which regret or guilt is inconceivable. There is no reason, of course, why these three versions (and others) could not *all* be what Nietzsche 'had in mind'. And, indeed, in trepidation of what is coming, Zarathustra's voice lowers to a whisper, and the riddle begins. The first version is nothing but a thought, and incomplete on its own; what matters is what that thought *does*, which is the question posed by the second and third versions.

Zarathustra poses this second version in the form of a riddle (scene 2.ii, iii). Thus we have an abrupt scene change, precipitated by the sound of a desperately howling dog. This first sets off a memory (autobiographical for Nietzsche) of a howling dog at midnight, of which the current howling is a repetition; and then we get a physical change to a different mountain environment with the asphyxiating shepherd. In the light of the above reading of the metaphysical eternal recurrence, the riddle can be solved as follows. The biting snake is the overwhelming nausea that comes with the idea of eternal recurrence. For not just all joys recur, but also all sorrows, pains, shame, all the pettiness, smallness and cruelty of human beings, the accidents and fragmentation and the waste. This becomes clearer if we return to Part II, Section 20. The will which cannot will backwards is released from that torment (the torment that causes the spirit of revenge) by the thought of eternal recurrence – because if past and future coincide, and in every moment 'confront one another head on', then willing forwards *is* willing backwards. This is the destruction of the discontinuous model of time (nihilism), the merely linear model of time (the spirit of revenge) and also the Christian model (linear plus transcendent miracle). However, this redemption seems far-fetched and simplistic. At the very least, it carries a still more terrible cost: one has to will the return of the whole of the past, and the future as its repetition. Moreover, insofar as one is in the moment, as past flips over to future, the self is implicated at the 'centre' of cosmic history. I am the active and willing agent of that repetition: in brief, I 'cause' all pain. '[T]he strength of a spirit would be proportionate to how much of the "truth" he could withstand,' Nietzsche writes in *Beyond Good and Evil*, section 39. (The reader should also compare *Beyond Good and Evil*, section 270.)

Such insight might drive one back into the arms of religion (*Beyond Good and Evil*, section 59: 'wounded children'; and see Part III, Section 8) if it does not destroy one altogether. The highest response would not be to 'withstand' it at all, but rather to not feel it as a 'weight'. The being that could do this – could bite off the head of the snake – would no longer be human; it would laugh joyfully because life is ascending and recurs ascending. This is the shadow of the overhuman. Notice that the 'Bite off!' is not cried out by Zarathustra, but by 'it' – perhaps the same voice, then interior, as in Part II, Section 22. The point of making this identification is that this is the voice of Zarathustra's total being, all his drives, virtues, knowledge and affections crying out with a 'single cry'. Zarathustra is no longer paralysed by the thought of eternal recurrence, he is no longer silent, but he is also no longer just an 'I' (a conscious, speaking, spiritual being – the 'ego'). This *integration* of the self is precisely what seemed to be lacking in Part II, Section 20. Eternal recurrence solves the problem of the fragmentation of the human insofar as it is an instrument for the alignment of the ensemble of drives with the nature of things as will to power. That is, it provides us with an image of what it would mean to be whole, and not a fragment of a human. This alignment is possible, and (in accordance with eternal recurrence) *always was*. That is the *ontological* meaning of being whole; however, there must also be *materialist* or *historical* meaning. The 'work' of heralding the overhuman involves the task of creating that new form of humanity from out of the fragmentary materials at hand. Only a comprehensive soul might achieve that, a being that understands what the ontological model of wholeness means in terms of historically determinate human modes of life (see our discussions of Part II, Section 20 and Part III, Section 7).

The amount of foreboding and the rhetorical noise in the run-up to explication, Zarathustra's breakdowns and histrionics, authorial interventions and so forth – all this cannot deflect from the fact that the actual substance of the theorem of eternal recurrence is a sober hard-core of a new theory of time based on 'scientific' thinking. Like Darwin who was concerned with the impact that the theory of natural selection might have on human cultural identity, Nietzsche concerns himself with the possible consequences of his new insight.

* * * *

Section 3, 'On Blissfulness Against One's Will'

The first part of this section is a meditation on Zarathustra's children, by which he means not only or not specifically his disciples, but any achievements of growth in the life of the human. Notice that Zarathustra must 'perfect' himself for the sake of his coming 'children' – that is, for the sake of the validity and efficacy of his teaching. Accordingly, the section alludes to several episodes in Part II where this need for him to perfect himself was announced, though Zarathustra did not immediately listen: most clearly, the flying shadow, the dream after the soothsayer (the reference to doors flying open), and the Grave Song. Now, for his children, he 'evades' and pushes away his happiness in order to get on with things, but it refuses and 'pursues' him (thus the title of the section). Zarathustra's work, and the happiness of that work (imaged as a woman in accord with the earlier image of pregnancy and children), travels with him, for wherever his work is to be done 'there *are* isles of the blest'. Notice also that Zarathustra discusses two stages in the life of his 'children', imagining them as trees: their 'first spring', followed 'one day' by their separate planting, as a test. (This passage repeats an image from *The Gay Science*, section 106.) We have already commented that Zarathustra's disciples thus far have been anonymous, mere foils for his teachings. They were grouped together like these newly planted trees. In Part IV this changes: the 'superior humans' are individuated at least to the extent of being allegorical types (and some, like the sorcerer, are clearly individual satirical portraits).

Nevertheless, even now the abyss-deep thought of eternal recurrence is kept in the depths, not allowed to surface. The dread of that thought has not yet been overcome in him. Section 2 was the most sustained account of it we will get, but let us not forget that it was couched within a vision and a riddle that still awaits and asks for interpretation – and, at the end of it, Zarathustra was still 'yearning' for that transformed laughter. Here, he asks himself: 'When shall I find the strength to hear you burrowing and no longer tremble?'. Zarathustra then prophesies: 'Once I have overcome myself in that, then will I overcome myself in something even greater'. This is both a general claim – about continual overcoming – and a specific claim, namely that once Zarathustra has the strength to 'summon up' the thought of eternal recurrence, another overcoming will have to present itself. This is either the task aligning the spirit and heart to the mode of life that welcomes eternal recurrence (that is, he is alluding forward to Zarathustra's convalescence in Part III, Section 13 which continues to the end of the part), or an allusion to the task of coming to terms with the superior humans in Part IV (named, at the end of the book, the trial of pity).

Section 4, 'Before the Sunrise', and a Note on Epiphany

A Note on Epiphany

This section is a Dionysian dithyramb. In *Ecce Homo* Nietzsche claims to be the 'inventor of the dithyramb'. This is both true and not true. Associated with communal celebrations of the god Dionysus in an early, post-Iron-Age stage of Greek culture, the dithyramb is a form of sung and danced poetry and one of the first ever literary utterances at the beginning of European culture. However, no specimen from this early period has survived, only poems written when the form's origins were already old. The problem is therefore that nobody knows what the dithyramb originally was like. Nietzsche thinks he does. In *The Birth of Tragedy* he talks about the decline of the Dionysian dithyramb in the New Attic dithyramb, particularly as employed in Euripides' *Bacchae*, a mannerist re-creation that cannot, Nietzsche assumes, be compared with the subconscious intensity of the rapturous devotional language of the original poetry. Plato links the dithyramb with the birth of Dionysus, Aristotle (and Nietzsche, following him here) with the origin of tragedy. All that remains of it are therefore fragments, later works, mentions in philosophy and aesthetic theory, and recent literary re-evocations, including Hölderlin's late numinous poetry in free verse and Schiller's 1796 *Dithyrambae*. Nietzsche is the first poet to have recreated, from an intimate philological knowledge of early Western cultural history, the dithyramb as he thinks it must have been originally meant and sounded. Whether the recreation is accurate or not is beside the point, though, for the style is one of Nietzsche's most original contributions to the literary history of the late modern period.

Nietzsche's notion of dithyrambic covers a number of different forms of exalted, elevated writing in this book: the range is from euphoric, to phantasmagorical and dream-like (or nightmare-like), to visionary and epiphantic, and finally to free verse ode. They all have in common that the articulating subject seems grabbed by an outside force that speaks, or sings, through it. In *Ecce Homo*, Nietzsche describes the elemental, almost annihilating power of his 'inspiration' that led to *Zarathustra*. It hit him like an irresistible force and made him yield. 'I never had a choice', he writes, it was 'a rapture whose colossal tension occasionally finds release in a stream of tears, in which involuntarily the pace is at times forward storming, at times slowing down; a total being-outside-of-oneself . . .' This is not the first time Nietzsche talks about his out-of-body, out-of-mind experience. He also, for example, describes this act of being ravished by a numinous, anonymous force in 'An Attempt at Self-Criticism' (a much later added introduction to *The Birth of Tragedy*), where he claims that 'a *strange* voice was speaking here'.[63] *Zarathustra* is the purpose-build theatre of foreign, holy voices that have taken over Nietzsche, as well as his protagonist Zarathustra.

This is what seems to be happening in these passages: meaning all of a sudden shoots together and finds free-flowing expression in a literary form that is meant to seem unhindered by conscious interference from an artistically planning mind, a form of what André Breton later called *écriture automatique*.[64] In this way Nietzsche is anticipating what many twentieth-century modernists – Breton is a good example – only managed to accomplish with a great deal of conscious effort (or alcohol and various other toxins): namely to make the subconscious speak with its own, inimitable voice. It is not 'stream of consciousness', strictly, because this type of writing could really best be characterised as 'stream of the subconscious'. A similar phenomenon is found in those many passages where Zarathustra finds 'himself' conversing with some aspect of himself – his heart, soul, Life, Wisdom, Stillest Hour, or something else, unnamed. This, as we suggested, indicates that Nietzsche's conception of the self is not originally unified, but is rather a system of struggling drives, and thus 'voices'. Although, of course, in religious traditions, the 'voice' that seizes control and talks through one is thought of as coming from *outside*, that is, from a God or demon who is not part of or identical with the Self – here Nietzsche suggests something quite different. The voice that speaks to or through Zarathustra should perhaps be thought of as the voice of Dionysian life *within* him, the spiritualisation of his alignment to will to power, and which often chastises him for his all-too-human struggle. One of the reasons for Nietzsche's choice of Zarathustra as cicerone is his association with early history, where (he imagines) these voices still spoke without inhibition and could be heard clearly. In Nietzsche's work the modernist idea is anticipated that forms of artistic expression at the end of history come to resemble those at the beginning, as we can see in Joyce's *Ulysses*, for example, or Ezra Pound's *Cantos* and Eliot's *The Waste Land*.

Nietzsche's writing of epiphany, even though highly original, can be located in a tradition of ecstatic writing. Nietzsche himself places his poetic ventriloquism in the tradition of pre-Socratic poetry, that of the dithyramb. Other forms of early poetry show similar features. For example, Sappho's of Lesbos or Pindar's odes belong here. There is also a rich seam of numinous writing in the modern period, particularly after 1770. Some *Sturm und Drang* writing breaks down the barriers of regulated poetic or narrative discourse, for instance some of Goethe's (1749–1832) early 'Promethean' poetry, and also Herder's (1744–1803) 'stream-of-consciousness' eulogy on Shakespeare. There is also a large body of epiphany-writing in the Romantic period, not just in German literature. To hear nature speaking directly is one of the foremost aspirations associated with the writing of that period. Thus, Coleridge was often overwhelmed by fantasies stronger than what he could consciously control. *The Rhyme of the Ancient Mariner* is one of many examples. We should also look at Nietzsche's compatriot Hölderlin (1770–1843), whom Nietzsche revered. Hölderlin was a highly original poet and tragedian who, like Nietzsche, suffered a mental breakdown in later life. In fact, Hölderlin and Nietzsche are the two most illustrious cases of the 'mad' modern poet/philosopher. Hölderlin's epistolary novel *Hyperion* contains much writing in the style of Nietzsche's Dionysian interludes. Part II, Section 10, for example, makes deliberate reference to it. Hölderlin's late free verse poetry, modelled on Pindaric and Horacian odes, is the foundation of Nietzsche's own dithyrambic poetry.

There is one writer who needs mentioning here, we think, because his phantasmagorical prose fantasies bear remarkable similarities to Nietzsche's dream sequences in *Zarathustra*. This is the aforementioned Jean Paul (1763–1825), a late Romantic and fiercely individual writer. Jean Paul's literary style is like Nietzsche's (and Thomas Carlyle's, incidentally) torn between biting satirical *Zeitkritik* and surreal exaltation of dream imagery. Interspersed in all of Jean Paul's often voluminous novels and prose works are passages of seemingly uncontrollable flux of the imagination. Thus in his novel *Siebenkäs* ('*Seven Cheese*') we can find a 'Dream within a Dream' sequence. Here also is one of the most striking examples of a ravishing cosmic voice speaking in the atheistic night fantasy entitled 'Speech of the Dead Christ Addressed Downwards from the Edifice of the World, that there be no God', one of the darkest pieces of writing in German literature and totally unique in content and form. There, Jean Paul writes:

> And as I fell down and into the illuminated edifice of the world: I saw the elevated rings of the giant serpent, the serpent of eternity, which had coiled itself around the All of the Worlds ['*Welten-All*'], – and the rings sank down, and it doubly encircled the All –, and then it wound itself around nature a thousand fold – and squeezed the worlds together – and ravishingly compressed the temple of infinity together into the Church of a Burial Ground, – and everything grew narrow, dark and fearful – and an immeasurably extended bell-hammer was to toll the last hour of Time and shiver the edifice of the world asunder . . . as I awoke.[65]

* * * *

Back here in *Zarathustra*, the time is just before sunrise, before even the 'blushing' colour of sunrise – but also after the dark of night ('you conceal your stars'). The sky is a pure 'light abyss' – it is the symbol of the immanent wholeness of all things. Translating '*Himmel*' as 'heaven' here is possible, but risky, unless the specifically Christian connotation is intended, which is doubtful here; in German there is only one word for both 'sky' and 'heaven'.'Heaven above me' possibly refers to Kant's famous adage (cf. *Critique of Practical Reason* II, 205) 'the starry sky above me, and the moral law inside of me'. In contrast to Kant, the experience of the 'light abyss' stimulates the 'godlike desire' to transcend, grow and fly beyond itself 'into your height' – 'that is my depth'. The height-depth connection as discussed in the Prologue and Part III, Section 2 is reaffirmed here. The first third of the section praises the sky as the 'sister-soul' with whom Zarathustra has learned self-overcoming and affirmation (see Part III, Section 14). The second third gestures towards the sustained cultural critique of Parts I and II with the image of clouds. The clouds stain this beautiful sky, drift beneath, without proper elevation or the appreciation of elevation (thus the images of halfway, partial, impure and so forth – and see Part II, Section 17).

The final third of the section (up to the last few lines with the image of 'blushing' sunrise) elaborates upon the theme of affirmation and the redemption of contingency, discussed most recently in section 1. To do this, Zarathustra employs religious imagery: yea-saying, blessing, baptism and so forth. This is a kind of natural religion. Zarathustra, like a priest, blesses each thing as 'its own sky, as its round roof, its azure bell and eternal security'. The world, and all things, are redeemed from the idea of an eternal and transcendent will and purpose. Without purpose, each thing is the thing that it is, without foundation in transcendent law, essence or idea. Each thing is the result of a game of chance played on the sky as a 'God's table'. Zarathustra, understanding this, restores the innocence of things. For each thing, its will to power is relationally extended into *its* abyss and *its* depth, and it is free for its own serenity or exuberance (the image of dancing). In an inversion of Plato's account of cosmic law and chance in the *Timaeus*, there is just 'a little reason' and because of this 'a little wisdom is no doubt possible'. There is just enough reason to create the possibility of 'folly'. This means at least four things: it means the 'great folly' of the will which leads to the spirit of revenge (Part II, Section 20); it means the folly of the human spirit that produces descriptions of things and believes them to be eternal laws (see our discussion of Part III, Section 2); it means Zarathustra's 'little wisdom' which often makes him act like and appear a fool, madman or jester; but it also means the folly involved in irony and laughter, the ability to see the whole progress of things as a spectacle (again, see Nietzsche's choice of epigraph to this part). The dithyramb ends with a part preview of the poem 'Midnight' in 'The Other Dance Song', Part III, Section 15.3: 'The world is deep – and deeper than ever the day has thought'. When it appears, the poem repeats in condensed symbolic form the theory of time outlined in the vision of Part III, Section 2.2.

The day is the time of human consciousness, philosophical enquiry, planning and doing and making. With dawn, then, epiphantic wisdom must now be silent. Accordingly, the next section will return (albeit briefly) to the business of cultural critique.

Section 5, 'On the Virtue that Makes Smaller'

For the most part, this section repeats material we have seen before, in Prologue, Section 5, for example, or Part II, Section 14. It is a portrait of the modern European: the key metaphor is obviously smallness, beginning with the delightful and thoroughly modern depiction of rows of houses like children's toys. Smallness here means: modest in ambition and definition of happiness (mere contentment; notice the repeated image of sitting around the fire at night – compare section 6), accordingly modest in what is considered virtue (and this virtue is born ultimately of fear, it is 'cowardice'; thus, 'even what you abstain from weaves at the web of all human future'), small in the difference between the roles of male and female, small in the difference between leaders and followers ('even those who command dissemble the virtues of those who serve'), modest in strength ('Some of them can will, but most are merely willed', or again 'half-willing'). Particularly interesting is a smallness in scope, which contrasts with Zarathustra's 'many ways and questions'. This indicates a methodology that does not rely upon a narrow specialisation, but *spans* them – we will return to this idea in section 7. Smallness is not merely a state, but a *process*: 'You are crumbling away'. It is a process of the ever-diminishing of the possibilities of the human. The idea of moderation (that virtue is always a mean between two vices) alludes, rather crudely, to Aristototle's account of virtue in the *Nichmachean Ethics*; other sections (the previous section, for example) pick up this idea with the phrase 'half-and-halfers'. But this is not moderation or modesty, claims Zarathustra, but *mediocrity*.

Let us point out a couple of passages of particular interest. First, notice the repetition of the idea that 'small people are *needed*' (see Part

II, Section 6). Formerly, we were only able to interpret this notion in terms of the strategies that life as such must follow in its self-overcoming. Now, we can add to this: the notion should be seen as an integral part of the idea of eternal recurrence and especially the redemption of contingency. Second, notice that here, as with many of the passages in Part III, Zarathustra realises that his teachings are in vain (see, for example, sections 8 and 9, and contrast Part II, Section 22). These people 'know neither how to take or to retain' – there is a certain minimum level of nobility required even to recognise a teaching that is not simply more of the same. Zarathustra should not be that surprised, though, since this was the lesson he learnt in the Prologue, and why he sought disciples thereafter. Imagine, then, his disappointment with his disciples in section 8.

Finally, towards the end of the section, we come across a famous, oft-quoted and probably oft-misunderstood passage: 'Do whatever you will – but first be such as are *able to will*'. At first glance, this passage plays into the hands of those who read Nietzsche as a relativist and indeed also a nihilist. However, being able to will, or, in the next sentence, loving oneself, are not default states, but achievements of individual or collective development. This development can only happen insofar as the spirit aligns itself, or becomes commensurate to, the world as immanent will to power and the challenge of eternal recurrence. From this does not, to be sure, follow any specific *content* of one's virtue – there are '1,000 bridges' to the overhuman and the noble struggle among these is part of the conditions of human growth – but there do seem to follow certain structural limitations or, if you will, 'meta-virtues'. These are spiritual descriptions of the ontological structure of being 'able to will' – that is, of any such health and alignment. They are necessary for such health precisely to the extent that the structure of will to power or the thought of eternal recurrence are necessary for it. These 'meta-virtues' include those alluded to here: honesty concerning grounds (so that love of your neighbour not be a mask for 'bad love of yourselves'; Part I, Section 16); the 'welcoming' of contingency and *amor fati* (here, love of oneself); creativity rather than reactivity or passivity (having the capacity and 'right' to will); as well as those we have seen elsewhere, and above all the feeling of overrichness, and thus the virtue of bestowing. There is nothing in Nietzsche to suggest that even these 'meta-virtues' (and the metaphysical ideas to which they are attached) might not be historically contingent, and there might be modes of human life whose aligned health must be differently characterised – be that as it may, these meta-virtues comprise the frame with which Nietzsche worked. That is, the critical engagement with the history of morality, the contemporary European scene, and the prophetic vision of a humanity to come, all are characterised within this frame.

Section 6, 'Upon the Mount of Olives'

There are many autobiographical references in *Zarathustra*. The metaphors of place very often closely resemble the geographical locations of Nietzsche's varying residences (such as the Alpine scenery of the Upper Engadine) including Nietzsche's winter places, when he took up quarters either in Italian Adriatic or Southern French seaside resorts. This spawns another metaphor of homelessness, with the triple meaning of an allusion to Nietzsche's personal lifestyle, his lack of a home nation, and a reflection on what it takes to philosophise under modern conditions. Like the man, his philosophy is not rooted in any particular spot of soil, as the German word '*Heimat*' implies (see Part II, Section 14, which not only ends with this idea but also contrasts it with the superficially similar idea of nihilistic 'actuality'). Both Nietzsche and his philosophy are therefore forced to take the entire world, indeed the universe, as an anchorage – their 'azure bell', as Zarathustra expresses the idea in section 4. There is a corresponding 'toughness' virtue in Nietzsche's philosophy, which can ill afford the luxury of metaphysical comforting or Christian solace.

The winter cold of the physical environs renders itself well as a climactic or seasonal metaphor: the cold winter of the soul, of European civilisation, and so forth. Again we find here a contrast between North and South – the North (particularly Germany) cold, hostile, nationalistic, intellectually abstract, innately committed to human equality, and so forth; the south fertile, creative, adventurous and welcoming but not to just anyone. Nietzsche works on the anthropological, cultural, climatic, historical and symbolic possibilities of this contrast throughout his career (see especially *The Gay Science*, section 291; the poem 'In the South'; and *Beyond Good and Evil*, Part IX, and we will have a poem on the theme in Part IV, Section 16). In terms of narrative style, Nietzsche gets close in his winter vignettes to late Romantic idioms, particularly Schubert's *Winterreise* comes to mind.[66] The writing builds on the contrast of Jesus praying in the warm climate of the Mount of Olives for a future place in a heavenly beyond, and Zarathustra who develops the sun-seeking side inside himself and is empowered to do so by an environment hostile to human life. The first third or so of this section is in praise of a very modest lifestyle indeed, without the comfort of 'pot-bellied fire-idols', of opulent beds, bright lighting or hot baths. The writing is frankly rather sanctimonious, although good-humoured enough. The key idea here is of a philosophical life-practice that cultivates 'love' (for the lover, the friend, and for the overhuman) and 'mockery' of both enemies and 'all pity'. These are the kinds of things we had in mind when introducing the notion of practices of internalisation in Part II section 8. We will discuss these issues further in the next section.

Zarathustra constructs a symbolic apparatus from the luminous winter sky, just as section 4 did from the pre-dawn sky. The idea is of an austere silence so deep that its grounds do not betray themselves to any inspection. The flat, round luminosity of such a sky (or of such a soul) is a kind of shield, protecting one from those who would pry, steal or pity. But this shield does not function through veils or masks, but through a complete transparency. Let them see me cold, Zarathustra (or, rather, Nietzsche) says, how little they know of my Mount of Olives – that is, of my spiritual and not just spiritual journey exploring and making my home in what is South to all Europe. This description of a certain kind of defence brings to mind Part II, Section 21. Notice that 'the origin of all good things is thousandfold'. The idea here is that those things (here, the virtue of the 'long and luminous silence' like the winter sky) which are conducive to ontological health of body and spirit crystallise *in multiple* from out of the nature of things. The world is thus full of things that have turned out well and are allegories and inducements to health (see section 12.17, complete with unintentionally comic example). Those things opposed to such health tend to be products of misunderstandings, narrow circumstances, petty revenges, or conceptual over-simplifications. The line 'suffer coincidence to come unto me' is a beautiful joke on Luke 18: 16. Coincidence, in its innocence, is the new version of a Kingdom of God (the passage should be compared also with section 1).

Section 7, 'On Passing By', and a Note on the Comprehensive Soul

Apparently, this is a portrait of the 'great city' – the specifically modern phenomenon of the large, dense urban centre. The city is imagined less as a geographical phenomenon than as a particular mode of life. However, there is a curious feature about this 'portrait': it is introduced through the figure of 'Zarathustra's ape', someone who has borrowed some of

Zarathustra's ideas and ways of speaking – and even by the standards of this book is decidedly manic, 'frothing' – but is clearly no 'great soul'. What this means is that we have a double portrait: the city and also a certain kind of social observer and critic. Zarathustra's ape criticises life in the city while being a part of it, and thus from out of self-loathing and insecurity, and revenge for the fact that 'no one has *flattered* you enough'. It is not that the critique is wrong so much as that its grounds are suspect, and ultimately (for the ends that Zarathustra is pursuing) the motive is more important than the content (the point is similar to the one we made about the dwarf's words in Part III, Section 2). 'Where one can no longer love' – that is, where one's desire for the overcoming of the human sees no fertile ground and 'nothing is to be made better' – then one should 'pass by'.

An important feature of this section is the emphasis on Zarathustra's wandering and detours. Despite his desire to return to the mountains, he does not go directly there: the meaning of this metaphor is that his 'ascent' has to be a 'wandering', and as wide and thorough a wandering as possible. The wandering motif is another aspect of the homelessness and the philosophical life-practices of internalisation discussed in the previous section. Nietzsche is interested in how a daily routine (the mundane aspect of a mode of life), and especially one that is not fixed, might contribute to the overcoming or realignment of desires, drives and habits – or indeed the opposite: whether such a routine is a product of, and serves to reinforce, laziness or cowardice. He thus discusses a critical 'history of every day' (*The Gay Science*, section 308). Indeed, in *Ecce Homo* Nietzsche writes at length about the significance of nutrition, climate and so forth – he recognises that these things are not normally considered important for thinking, but that is a result of the dominant idealisation of spirit and mind with respect to body. Again, Nietzsche's mode of life makes up the practices that make him 'so clever'. Likewise, he discusses the value of 'brief habits' – immersing oneself in a way of acting, speaking and thinking but in such a way as to not become its captive – which we are inclined to relate to the idea of a comprehensive soul (see *The Gay Science*, sections 295–6). What Nietzsche is after is a new conception and practice of *Bildung* – one that cultivates down to the level of body (see *Twilight of the Idols*, 'Skirmishes of an Untimely Man', section 47). Activities should be practices of internalisation – this basic principle applies to small, daily habits right up to 'higher' activities: for example, at *Twilight of the Idols*, 'What the Germans Lack', section 7, Nietzsche discusses thinking as a practice, as akin to dancing.

A Note on the Comprehensive Soul

This wandering is thus a description of a method of enquiry and critique, one that is deliberately comprehensive, multi-disciplinary, eclectic and welcoming to accidents. This contrasts nicely with the narrow, nut-cracking, specialised methodology of the scholars (Part II, Section 16), or more recently the smallness of scope in section 5 (and see Part III, Section 12.19). Only in this way can the philosopher of the future perform the task of synthesising all the 'fragments' of human beings (represented here primarily by isolated virtues, separated by 'gaps') which Zarathustra evokes in Part II, Section 20. In Part III, Section 2 we distinguished between the ontological problem of human wholeness (which is a problem concerned with the nature of time and will to power, and thus with the structure of ascending life) and what we there called the historical problem. The latter is the issue of imagining the aligned being not just as an ontological form but as a concrete historical form of human life. One needs to be able to see to the ground of such fragments in order to ascertain what service they might offer, in this or that context, to the yearning of life for new human forms. Evolution has to be historically managed, so to speak. (And yes, there are places where Nietzsche seems to approach the idea of eugenics, for example, in *Beyond Good and Evil*, sections 203 or 251; however, more often ideas of breeding are used metaphorically to think about cultural or spiritual hybrids.)

To achieve that synthesis, it is not enough to be cognisant of the notion of eternal recurrence. One must inhabit that thought materially and historically, and still affirm it. So, in this context, that means a philosopher must be, or pass through, such fragments. Thus for example Nietzsche's praise of 'brief habits' in *The Gay Science*, section 295. In *Beyond Good and Evil*, section 211, Nietzsche writes that the philosopher must take on many roles and masks 'in order to run through the range of human values and value feeling and *be able* to gaze with many eyes and consciences'. (See *Republic* V 475 c and also *Beyond Good and Evil*, sections 61 and 212: 'unity in multiplicity'.) Similarly, Nietzsche claims to be a 'master' of 'switching *perspectives*', for being able to see one of many human healths from the point of view of sickness, and the many varieties of sickness from the point of view of health (*Ecce Homo*, 'Why I am so Wise', section 1). Nietzsche's methodology deliberately avoids disciplinary boundaries (the reference to boundary stones in this text is not unique to *Zarathustra*; see *The Gay Science*, section 4) for these are institutionalised metaphysics. These passages both indicate that the comprehensive soul is part of a method of enquiry that is able to understand perspective, and thus the underlying will to power, by being methodologically mobile and familiar with alternatives. But beyond being a method, this is also a characterisation of the aligned and healthy being: a being that is in some sense 'at one with' the whole of its exterior without being either desensitised (the Stoic ideal) or dissolved into that exterior (destroyed by Dionysian insight).[67] For example, in *Twilight of the Idols*, 'Morality as Anti-Nature', section 6, Nietzsche writes, 'we are increasingly opening our eyes . . . to that economy in the law of life that can take advantage of even the disgusting species of idiot, the priests, the virtuous – *what* advantage? – But we ourselves, we immoralists, are the answer to this . . .' In Part III, Section 13, in the middle of his convalescence, Zarathustra says, 'How could there be an outside-me!'. Or again, 'In just this expansiveness, this willingness to accept oppositions, Zarathustra feels himself to be the *highest type of everything that exists*' (*Ecce Homo*, 'Thus Spoke Zarathustra', section 6). The idea of the comprehensive soul ties in also with the nature of language in this text as a form of action or invocation (see our discussion of Part I, Section 7; Part III, Section 9; see also Part IV, Section 7 where Zarathustra says 'only the one who does, learns'). Language use in this book is the communication of inner states – not ones we know and already have names for, but new states which thus can be internalised, leading to transformation.

These ideas of wandering and of the comprehensive soul should also be seen as another meaning of 'going down' to the human or 'becoming' human: solitude is only ever a temporary phase of philosophical movement. Only the comprehensive soul – the soul that has through practices of internalisation made itself comprehensive – is able to ascertain both the needs of human life as a whole and also the resources to achieve it. That is, first, its yearning for higher and more powerful (that is, more ontologically aligned) forms of humanity as the overcoming of precisely *this* historical mode of life; and secondly, *also* the physiological and spiritual resources, embodied in human beings, cultures and histories, available to achieve those needs. (See also our discussion of Part III, Section 12.11.) Finally, we should notice that this comprehensiveness is not an individual project, or even a communal one, but the work of ages. Nietzsche writes, 'All good things are inherited: anything that is not inherited is imperfect, a beginning' (*Twilight of the Idols*, 'Skirmishes of an Untimely Man', section 47; and see our discussion of section 12).[68] This relates to the idea that one must be physiological and spiritually ready for transformation even to *hear* Zarathustra.

****

Section 8, 'On Apostates'

Throughout this text, the question arises of how it is possible for Zarathustra's message to be understood correctly. Nietzsche is aware that in spite of the carefully constructed poetic qualities of this text and the fail-safe guidance provided by its allegorical signposting, there is scope here also for misunderstandings by the reader (and how!). This section shows one possible consequence of a misunderstanding of Zarathustra's message, expressed on the level of difficulty of relationship with his disciples, a problem area first introduced in Part I, Section 22.3. In Part I his disciples were too close to him for mutual comfort. Here they have grown too distant for the doctrine to be maintained and applied successfully. In this way, the effect of the text on a reader is being discussed. Unlike Jesus, Zarathustra insists on physical and spiritual separation from his disciples. Since there is no church to supervise and reinforce the doctrines, its adherence is entirely dependent on personal perseverance. This section is a warning to the reader of how easy it can be to lose the willpower and strength to follow the new philosophy.

At the end, we discover that Zarathustra has been in The Motley Cow, the town of his first disciples and a place in which he invested much hope. He is retracing his ground, travelling back from the Isles of the Blest through earlier episodes. Here, he is near home. His first disciples have turned into apostates by falling away from Zarathustrianism which preaches the end of God: they become apostates by *returning* to God. Again, the projection mechanism is at work whereby inner confusion, weakness or burden ('cowardly Devil within') becomes the invention of an external power to redeem the inner chaos. Praying is back, piety, a degenerate form of community spirit (unlike the social institutions of friendship or marriage that Zarathustra advocates), and trifling moralising. We get a long list of specifically modern forms of religiosity (including fashionable spiritualism). Towards the end of the section is an overheard conversation of a pair of 'dried-up night-watchmen'. They are compared to 'light-scarecrows'.[69] These two are leading a theological conversation as if it were gossip about the failings of a local dignitary. Zarathustra laughs convulsively: it is past time for such doubts now. This passage is indicative of the failure of this section's analysis: for the falling back to religion is not distinguished from the original religion, nor is it explained (for example, in terms of the psychology of revenge or heaviness). Thus, the section does not actually serve to warn readers and disciples. Nevertheless, the section is important narratively, since this is both Zarathustra's last stop before returning home and also the scene of his biggest disappointment as teacher and prophet. The crescendo of failure contributes to the burden with which Zarathustra wrestles in section 13.

There follows one of the most famous passages emanating from Nietzsche's atheistic critique of the spirit of religion: the ancient Gods of Greek and Germanic mythology did not die (as Wagner's *Ring*-Cycle would have us believe) a protracted, 'twilight' death through abdication. The polytheistic Gods died in an explosion of laughter about the pathetic claim for supremacy over them issued from the monotheistic God of Judeo-Christianity – a God, so Zarathustra claims, who did not understand that through his hegemonial aspiration he laid the foundations for his own demise. Such monotheism forced a mode of human life that could only exist as a disease or perversion of life generally and which had, eventually (and after centuries of widespread suffering and human stagnation) to go under. Godliness in a healthy, sustainable and fitting form – one aligned to the nature of life – is that 'there are Gods, but no God'. By this Zarathustra does not simply mean a polytheism as a variety of theistic belief – throughout Zarathustra has been saying variations on 'what are Gods to me'. Rather, he means a 'polytheism' that comprises a knowing symbolic projection of differentiated human ideals (see *The Gay Science*, section 143), insofar as these ideals are themselves consummate with the nature of life and existence. The sacred is widely distributed, as a result of the liberation of things from purpose (see section 4). The worship of Dionysus (see *Twilight of the Idols*, 'Skirmishes of an Untimely Man', section 49) would comprise practices and festivals that celebrate the earth as the sacred site of both aligned beauty and of the ascent of life.

Section 9, 'The Return Home'

At last Zarathustra returns to his 'home', the cave in the mountains. But it is not the cave itself or even the animals that welcome him first and most, but 'solitude'. For Zarathustra/Nietzsche, wanderer of no fixed address, 'solitude' *is* home – although, to be sure, this most frequently took the form for Nietzsche of a first-floor room in the house of a grocer in Sils Maria. He imagines solitude personified as a stern but ultimately welcoming mother, who insists on the difference between solitude and loneliness. Loneliness is being among humans and being so 'wild and strange' to them that one is forced to disguise oneself for one's own health (this idea comes from Part II, Section 21). 'Solitude' recounts three moments when Zarathustra encountered such true loneliness (Prologue, Section 10; Part II, Section 9; and Part II, Section 22), and also says that the advantage of solitude is that 'here you can talk freely about everything' and moreover, all things 'want to ride on your back' (like small children playing). Both of these points are expanded upon in Zarathustra's own voice. The former idea is discussed in terms of 'pity's little lies' and this is called 'my greatest danger'. The latter point is spoken of as 'all Being wants to become word here'. Zarathustra feels the freedom of being home and back in solitude as a being able to speak, and be spoken through, by being and becoming. This whole section is about the philosophy of language: solitude is the mother who taught Zarathustra to speak (in the ten years prior to the Prologue).

The most obvious point is that whatever happens in solitude, in the mountains, it does not happen among humans: everything there is 'mere talk', and this is repeated in references to 'jingling', 'cackling', 'noise', and so forth. Language there is systemic lie. The ordinary humans of the herd or people are unable to be honest, but rather, their deepest wisdom is still a turning-away from the nature of Being and from themselves too; therefore, their language too circulates among fabricated, deceitful or illusory entities, motives, values and aspirations. Languages are devised to serve the interests, and perpetuate the constitutive errors, of a mode of life. In the world projected by such a language, there is literally no place for will to power, eternal recurrence or becoming. Because of the necessity of playing a game of disguises – including even a disguise from oneself – philosophical language suffers even among the otherwise honest ('I learned to mix up words'). What Zarathustra has been calling 'honesty' – where this has to do with the recognition of one's own nature as will to power and of the ground of one's own virtues – is the condition of philosophical truth. It is not that the possible ontological truth of language relies upon some kind of direct or ostensive language, for 'on every allegory you ride here to every truth'. So, there is no praise here for plain speech, or an attempt to define artificial, formal languages with precise definitions. Only an allegory (*Gleichnis*) can, it seems, avoid 'oblique (*versteckte*) . . . feelings' and 'talk frankly (*redet gerade*)'.

For some further help in this, we should notice a feature of the language throughout this passage: it is about events, movements, the becoming of things. Zarathustra can 'shake out all grounds', things 'come caressingly', Being wants to 'become' word, and Becoming wants to 'learn to talk'. Ontological language is *not descriptive*, it appears; rather, it is an action or more specifically an event of the will. We already observed that the words of Zarathustra's ape in Part II, Section 7, though in some sense they might have been employed correctly and even be descriptively insightful, still *do harm*. Conversely, throughout the book, Zarathustra's gift or bestowal is not a theory of things, but a teaching and a work. Language is a key manner in which will to power can employ spirit to further itself and feel an increase in power; spirit can thereby become a teaching – or, for that matter, a preaching, a warning, a law, a social convention and so on. ('Only the one who does, learns': Part IV, Section 7.) This spiritual action either contributes to human overcoming from out of an alignment to the nature of things, or else it does harm – and it is in the contribution or harm that its *ontological truth* consists. Ordinary human language is also act, but it universalises its own validity and the validity of the values it embodies by calling itself description and truth. Ontological language is, first of all, aware of this feature. Being is will to power that wants continually to overcome itself; through the language of spirit it can contribute to this overcoming. That is to say, Being realises itself in ontological language, Being wants or desires such language. Thus, here, we have the images of proximity and even affection between Zarathustra and 'all things' – through him, they seek language. The treatment of what we have called ontological language should be compared to Part III, Section 13, and our note on Nietzsche, Music and Language, with the commentary on Part II, Section 17. (Please see also the images of sun and sea at the end of Part II, Section 15; and see the nature of Life's love for Zarathustra in Part III, Section 15).

Section 10, 'On the Three Evils', and a Note on Perspectivism

This section has two numbered subsections. In the first, we have another of Zarathustra's surreal dream sequences and some of Nietzsche's finest descriptive writing; in the second, an waking repetition of the dream in which Zarathustra appraises three 'vices' traditionally most 'cursed'. The dream of weighing the world is beautiful, but impossible – to stand 'beyond the world', even though it be a finite world, is precisely the presumption of the transcendent that Zarathustra has so often derided. The dream itself tells us this, for Zarathustra is both 'beyond the world' and yet in the 'foothills' – that is, metaphorically in the *middle* of the world, halfway between the valleys and mountains. Likewise, Wisdom comforts dream and dreamer, but 'secretly', because during the day she says, 'Where there is force (the 'weight' of the world, and counterweight on the scale; 'force' also here stands in for all study of physical nature), there *number* will become mistress'. As invention and abstraction, number is 'constant falsification of the world' (*Beyond Good and Evil*, section 4). That is, number – precisely what would be needed to determine the world's weight – is an unavoidable error for those who would measure forces.

In the dream the world – which is so slandered by those eager to be otherworldly, but is here said to be 'humanly good' – comes to be weighed in three richly symbolic ways: apple, tree, and shrine. Together they form an organic metaphor of an integrated correspondence between man and nature: the apple, as fruit from the tree (of knowledge; also Newton's apple of gravity, recalling the mathematised 'force' from just above), and the world as shrine, sacred place for worship *of itself*. These objects are also metaphors for the three central character traits to be analysed in the subsection that follows. Zarathustra identifies them as the 'three evils' of the section's title. They are 'sensuality' (*Wollust*, meaning enjoyment of the senses, but with a healthy dose of specifically sexual pleasure), 'the lust to rule', and 'selfishness'. All three are sins in Christian moral thought, but here recast or re-evaluated as three *virtues*. The apple is sensuality. The tree that has bent down is 'lust to rule' (the image is repeated in the desert poem in Part IV, Section 16, stanza 6). The shrine is selfishness. Just before the end of the first subsection, Zarathustra then anticipates the analysis to follow by a series of three questions to which the newly designated virtues are answers. So, what is 'best' from the dream comes to be weighed during the day – during the period of philosophical contemplation and coming to know. It is not a weighing of the world from outside it, but a weighing of attributes of the spiritualisation of a higher will to power from *within* the world, and indeed from a perspective *aligned to* the world.

The first of these questions poses a more complex interpretative problem; we will return to it in a moment. The second and third 'evils' are deliberately provocative. The 'lust to rule' is described in two ways: first, as a tyrannical torture even for the tyrant, which eventually extracts from a populace the 'great despising' – a first step in the advancing of humanity which is the will to go under ('away with *me*!'). We can easily imagine a dictator of a Medici type as so vividly characterised in Machiavelli's *Prince* or Jacob Burckhard's *Civilisation of the Renaissance in Italy* (Nietzsche's distaste for this kind of dictatorial abuse of power, seen as particularising and fetishistic, is documented in Part III, Section 12.12) However, secondly, lust for power is also the 'bestowing virtue', the attempt to raise up that which is not yet elevated. It is thus an answer to the question of what compels the high down to the low. Selfishness is the name for the 'self-enjoyment' of a health and fully aligned body and soul; such selfishness wishes and knows itself capable of creating a world ('around which each and every thing becomes a mirror': see also the end of Part II, Section 13); such selfishness should be pronounced sacred and blest – it is a shrine, and also an answer to the question of what 'bids even the highest – grow up farther?' Keats's sealed 'casket of the soul' in his *Ode To Sleep* comes to mind. There follows a rather familiar rant about those who are timid or wish to be 'selfless'. They will be first against the wall when the transformation comes.

Now, let us have a look at that apple. Certainly, the sensual qualities are emphasised in the touching of the apple, obviously enough. The praise of sensuality is meant to recall the critique of the despisers of the body (way back in Part I, Section 4). However, thus far in the book the noun *Wollust* has been used in a negative manner (a typical example would be 'a little lust and a little boredom – that has so far been their best reflection', said of the poets in Part II, Section 17). So, Zarathustra is re-evaluating even his *own* account of this vice/virtue. However, the question Zarathustra poses at the end of the first subsection is not (directly) about the nature of the body, it is about *time*. 'On what bridge does the now go to the someday?' Undoubtedly, then, we are meant to recall the symbolic significance of the various moments of ecstatic sexual pleasure (especially Part II, Section 10). These are moments of Dionysian submergence of the self, which precisely because the contact with body is at its most voluptuously or ecstatically intense, and the screening mechanisms of culture and spirit dissolved, yields insight into and alignment with the constitution of the world as such. The sensuously full Dionysian moment thus also leads (in the combination of feminine and masculine) to the pregnancy of Wisdom; that is, to the creation of a future (the overhuman). Similarly, we saw in section 2 an account of the moment as the sensually perceivable nuclear difference of past and future, the very becoming of becoming, but also a compression of all time which, from within the moment, will be spun out. Sensuality here is thus the thanks of the future to the now – the created or envisaged future giving thanks to the moment of transformation or alignment in which it was begot; physiologically, sensuality is the spur to develop, create and indeed procreate. Also, it is allegory of future happiness – the shadow image of and insight into the future it inaugurates. Finally, it is 'reverently preserved wine of wines' – sensuality in the now is the culmination or distillation of past that coalesced in this moment and which points forward to the future; see our discussion of Part III, Section 12.

A Note on Perspectivism

This whole passage is a nice example of what is often called Nietzsche's 'perspectivism'. 'Perspective' means three things for Nietzsche, all of them based upon familiar optical phenomena. First, as in the classical tradition of European painting, it is the creation of an illusory depth on a flat surface. This is a metaphor, for example, for philosophies of morality that seem to see profundity and even a transcendent God, though they are looking at mere surfaces. Secondly, there is perspective as the fact that that which is nearest and in the 'foreground' seems largest and most important. This serves as a metaphor for all those values or principles that seem self-evident, but only because they are in the foreground and what lies in their depth is not seen. So, this metaphor of perspective invites what Nietzsche calls genealogical analysis, the uncovering of the hidden grounds of 'obvious' evaluations; likewise, it invites a critical analysis of the values implicit in positivism (which takes information from the senses at face value). Thirdly, perspective is the idea that each individual viewer will have a different and unique optical view point. For Nietzsche, this is a metaphor not, as it is so often used, for relativism so much as for the relationality of will to power. All three of these ideas feed into Nietzsche's 'perspectivism'.

Something is 'valued' when it enhances the will to power's feeling of power. I value those things, then, that serve to preserve, extend, grow, defend or what have you. Value or morality is the spiritualisation, or interpretation, of an affect of power; will to power is always relational, and thus 'there are no experiences other than moral ones, not even in the realm of sense perception' (*The Gay Science*, section 114). However, because morality is an interpretation of an affect, likewise 'there are no moral facts' (*Twilight of the Idols*, 'Improving Humanity', section 1). 'Whatever has value . . . has it not in itself . . . but has rather been given, granted value,' writes

Nietzsche at *The Gay Science*, section 301 – this is another way of saying that there could be no thing (and no value) 'in itself'. It also follows that there are no genuine moral universals. Where you and I value the same things, because these things both have the same function for us, we have a morality in common. A historical people (for example, the Romans) tends to be defined as having a certain set of values. Values become entrenched in history, in societies and institutions (churches, universities, police forces), and ultimately in bodies – my values are an expression of my physiology, at bottom, while my physiology is the result of a long process of selection by and for a people. Nietzsche's notion of 'genealogy' is the strategy he employs for peeling back the layers of such entrenchment, so as to reveal the historical or psychological development of values (which are often quite different from their appearance). (Here, see, for example, Part I, Section 5, 'On Enjoying and Suffering the Passions'.)

Now, on one level, Nietzsche's perspectivism requires that we see the diversity of human values as a basic biological given. The consciousness which might make an 'objective' judgement concerning something is, Nietzsche claims, itself a spiritualisation of a system of drives that makes up a mode of life. Thus the 'falsifications' of nature that arrive at concepts of substance or essence (the names of things) are motivated by a desire for the preservation of a mode of life – for an example of such an analysis, see the treatment of science in Part IV, Section 15. A 'good' cannot be objectively judged 'good'. Deciding between them can only be made from within a perspective, and thus the decision is already made in advance. (See *Twilight of the Idols*, 'The Problem of Socraces', section 2 and 'Morality as Anti-Nature', section 5: 'life itself values through us *when* we posit values'.) However, that is not the end of the story. For Nietzsche does seem to posit a set of meta-virtues (see section 5). Above all, there is a perspective that belongs to the ascent or decline of life in one of its forms; a being realigned to the will to power and eternal recurrence is able to form more 'comprehensive' and 'honest' evaluations. In 1888, the last year of his sanity, Nietzsche uses the expression 'revaluation of all values' (for example, *Ecce Homo*, 'Why I am a Destiny'). By this he means to assess the historically held values of his own and other cultures on the only possible 'scale': the health of human life as a whole. In what way does a value contribute to, or detract from, the possibilities of the human? So, here in this section we have two contrasting valuations of traditional 'vices'. The first valuation is made according to the will to power of those (declining, diseased) modes of life that have dominated

Europe under the hegemony of Christianity. The second is the value from the perspective of a (ascending, healthy) mode of life yet to come, or still only a fragile rarity, but which is fully aligned to the nature of human life in general and its constitutive desire for enhancement. *Universal* philosophical justifications of values *per se* are an absurdity; indeed, philosophy seems to have the job of ensuring that the above perspective character is not discovered (and thereby indirectly protecting a mode of life; see Part I, Section 2, 'On the Professorial Chairs of Virtue'; and see also our discussion of descriptive language in section 9).

* * * *

Note that the three virtues appear to parallel the triadic structure of the psyche as outlined in Part I, Section 4.[70] At the same time these three qualities are also the three symbolic directions of the will to power of the free spirit, directions from which the allegories of time, space and location throughout the text's narrative are derived: (1) sensuality is the Dionysian moment as depth; (2) lust for power in its incarnation as bending to the low and bestowing virtue becomes the travels of Zarathustra, the search for disciples and the wandering among peoples and places; (3) selfishness, which wants to extend the image of the self across the world (not as political or social power, but as creativity) in an act of becoming yet higher, gives us the dimension of height. Finally, note that, in accordance with the extension of the concept of will to power from the organic to the inorganic in later writing (see our discussion of Part I, Section 4), so the concept of 'perspective' or 'interpretation' moves from the merely human domain to a characterisation of the nature of existence itself (see *The Gay Science*, section 374, which is in Book 5, added in 1887).

Section 11, 'On the Spirit of Heaviness', and a Note on Reactive Will to Power

A Note on Reactive Will to Power

The Spirit of Heaviness is an allegorical figure we have seen before (as early as Part I, Section 7, then in Part II, Section 10 and Part III, Section 2). It is generally linked with the Devil or 'my devil' – not in a theological sense, but as the 'arch enemy' of lightness, flying laughter and any 'God who knew how to dance' (Part I, Section 7). The spirit of gravity is not a character in the narrative (although it was personified in the dwarf of Part III, Section 2), or even a human type – rather, it is a symbolic characterisation of the *reactive* will to power. What does this mean? (1) It is life that wishes only to preserve itself and not to advance or go under (thus the 'weighty words and values' that are universalised across a people or the human as such: 'good for all, evil for all'); (2) it is spirit that acts by holding back or holding down other spirits, or itself, and this revenge originates in a 'bad love' of itself (see our discussion of 'bad love' in Part I, Section 16, 'On the Love of One's Neighbour'); (3) it is exemplified in one of several metaphysical positions, such as pessimism (the Schopenhauerian idea that the world is, and will remain, essentially suffering: 'every upthrown stone – must fall': Part III, Section 2), nihilism (all values and all beliefs are false), and also in the banal saying that everything is simply good (the immediate reference is to Leibniz and the 'best of all possible worlds' theodicy; the less direct reference is to those who have no taste of events in their relation to the health of life; relativism; the 'yea-haw' of the ass returns in sustained parodic form in Part IV); (4) as spirit it acts against the 'honesty' we discussed in Part III, Section 9; it misunderstands the ontological basis of its evaluations and even more the nature of the life that it is (and thus here we have 'often the spirit lies about the soul'); thus morality is a spiritualisation of life that completely ignores the interests of life (*Twilight of the Idols*, 'Morality as Anti-Nature', section 6); (5) its values are formed not just as a response to but as an *inversion* of others (that is, not creatively, and not in joy but in revenge), in an attempt to annul or sidestep the powerful (including even the desire for self-overcoming that characterises all life as such): see, for example, *Beyond Good and Evil*, sections 62, 195; (6) it is a mode of life whose necessity and value for the health of life lies in its being an enemy to be overcome, in the titanic strength that must be found to overcome it ('I learned how to stand and walk and run. . .': and see section 12, subsection 2), and in the build-up of energies that might one day explosively emerge (see *Beyond Good and Evil*, Preface; and *Twilight of the Idols*, 'Skirmishes of an Untimely Man', sections 43–4). All human beings bear this burden 'almost from the cradle'; some, though, take on all such burdens gladly that they might prove and improve their strength and some day be transformed – thus the repetition of the camel image from Part I, Section 1.

* * * *

The passage begins, as so often in this book, rather curiously as if in an attempt to wrong-foot us through honesty. We have an appraisal of Zarathustra's capabilities (or perhaps the appraisal is of Nietzsche). His speech is 'of the people', (though presumably, unlike the people's, without shame?); certainly his speech sounds strange to those who make words their profession (for example, professional academics, journalists); his hand is a 'fool's hand', scribbling on anything, and so forth. His stomach, though, belongs to a bird of prey, especially in its opposition to and struggle against the Spirit of Gravity. Finally, Zarathustra/Nietzsche possesses the capability to 'sing a song' (compose poetry but more generally to use the kind of language praised in Part III section 9), though he be 'alone in an empty house' (that is, not needing witnesses, like a play-actor does).

The image of taste returns at the end of the passage, and it is there that we discover the meaning of this self-appraisal: 'This – is just *my* way'. Zarathustra/Nietzsche has achieved insight and overcoming using the dispositions of the spirit that were at hand. Thus, there is no '*the* way'. Again, this is not really a claim about the relativity or subjectivity of all values, or about heroic individuality (these are the ways in which the passage is almost universally interpreted, and not only by Frank Sinatra). Rather, it is about the manner in which one – being the particular living being one is, at such and such a point in history – discovers and pursues one's virtue and contributes to overcoming following one's taste (see our discussion of taste in the commentary on Part II, Section 13). The spirit of heaviness starts out as 'my enemy'. However, in the second part of the section it is clearly *others'* enemy too, though only insofar as that other is a free spirit and 'wants to become light and like a bird' (that is, the spirit of heaviness is not 'evil for all', but also not for just one). Zarathustra is disingenuously confusing two questions here. We have here first of all the question of 'the way', which cannot be answered in general. Also, though, given the ontological ideal that the free spirit sets for him or herself, what must any 'way' be like? Clearly, it must be characterised by 'dancing' and thus opposition to the spirit of gravity, but what, if anything, follows from this? This is the problem, we discussed in the commentary on Part III, Section 5 under the heading of 'meta-virtues'. One of those meta-virtues is the notion of the comprehensive soul (see our note on this topic). Which ladders you should climb cannot be answered; but there must be many. It should not be surprising then, in the very next section and despite all the talk here about 'my way', that we have Zarathustra sitting among half-written tablets – symbols of the fact that his teaching entails *some* meta-content concerning 'the way'.

Section 12, 'On Old and New Tablets'

Subsection 1 shows us Zarathustra in front of his cave, taking stock of what he has achieved so far: he is in limbo, awaiting the call to return to human beings. This call will happen in the last section of Part IV. The laughing lion is an adaptation of the transformation of the spirit imagery in Part I, Section 1 – there the lion spirit lacks the innocence of the child. Here, that innocence is figured as laughter. Zarathustra has 'old shattered tablets about him and new ones too – half inscribed'. The new code could never be fully inscribed, of course, for a number of reasons. First, because there is no '*the* way' (section 11; in other words, each situation of overcoming must be different because differently fated, although what overcoming means can be described, thus the meta-virtues). Secondly, because the moment that it was inscribed (the moment a new mode of human life was achieved) it would already be on the way to being shattered. What emerges in the sections that follows is a terse, aphoristic recapitulation of previous themes, with many explicit gestures and self-quotations towards key narrative moments. It is a recapitulation, though, with differences: these themes are stated as they appear now, having been recontextualised and modified by the ideas that followed. We can see this very clearly already in subsection 2 (which also happens to be one of the best passages). The themes of Part I, and especially the idea of the creator of values, are there seen in the light of the notion of eternal recurrence. We will only offer comment where these recontextualisations yield particularly interesting fruit.

Notice in subsection 2 the reference to 'hotter souths'. The whole of this book is a highly fictionalised recreation of the dawn of European morality, which was not, strictly speaking, in Europe at all. This South is a seething cauldron of creativity, but also of innocence. Also notice here that Zarathustra's means of communication must be to 'speak in parables and like poets hobble and stammer: and verily, I am ashamed that I must still be a poet!'[71] This is one of those interesting moments where the text explicitly reflects upon its own allegorical and poetic style. The characterisation of poetic language as hobbling and stammering is noteworthy because it clarifies Nietzsche's literary aesthetic. 'Stammer' only occurs two other times in (Prologue, Section 5 and Part I, Section 5). The second of these is significant: the unique configuration of drives that is a virtue would be destroyed if it entered language as a *name*. Poetry is the detour language must take in order to avoid that problem, to act in and on the reader rather than being names or images. However, the complaint that Zarathustra must still be a poet is not (or not just) a reference to the inadequacy of poetry, or to Nietzsche's own poetic gifts, but indicates his shame that the world should still be in need of poetry and thus that the revolutionary moment is still outstanding (see Part IV, Section 10: 'At Midday' poetry is no longer needed!). Zarathustra will give up being a poet when the Gods are ashamed of all clothes (all mediations, in other words). The pertinent theory of ontological language, and thus the poetry of will to power and eternal recurrence, was dealt with in section 9 (see also section 13 and our note on Nietzsche, Music and Language, with the commentary on Part II, Section 17).

Finally, we have a lovely passage on the 'blissful mockery of moments' and 'thorn of freedom'. It is 'mockery' because while in the moment time is compressed, that is so only on the condition that it is the nuclear difference of past and future, the becoming of becoming (as we expressed it earlier) – a moment never *is*; also because the moment as an achievement of a beautiful form or state is something that must immediately be overcome. Necessity is freedom – the being that is aligned with the nature of being is necessary (that is, he or she is indeed the course of fate), but also free. This freedom means at least two things. First, the aligned being is free by *being* the course of fate, rather than subject to it, struggling against it, misunderstanding it. Secondly, that being is free by being powerful enough to occupy that course, accept that responsibility, and feel its power as freedom (see *Beyond Good and Evil*, section 19; and *Twilight of the Idols*, 'Skirmishes of an Untimely Man', section 38). The former point at any rate is far more Spinozistic, and indeed Stoic, than Nietzsche generally lets on. The difference from these earlier thinkers lies partly in Nietzsche's praise of sensuality and the affects generally (see section 10, 'On the Three Evils' especially) – thus the word 'blissful' here.

The 'alignment' of the self to the nature of being is not an alignment of reason or understanding, for these are mere echoes of the system of drives which themselves are an objectification of will to power. Rather, the alignment is the reorganisaton of the system of drives, in their becoming (that is, not as a fixed system), so that their spiritualisation no longer denies and evades will to power, nor the desire for enhancement of the feeling of power (blissfulness, joy, voluptuousness). But this also means playing with the 'thorn of freedom' – the requirement to will all, eternally – and thus a parallel intensification of melancholy, pain and woe. The account of freedom is continued in subsection 4. It continues the Kantian theme we first noticed in our discussion of Prologue, Section 4. For Kant, the only coherent theory of freedom is that the will gives itself its own law – that is, it commands itself rather than being commanded. But here, the commanding and obeying motif should call to mind the language of 'On the Thousand Goals and One'. There we identified this distinction as mapping onto the symbolic language of masculine and feminine. So, the masculine capacity to command (or rule) is incomplete, impotent or goes astray, without the feminine capacity. Creativity in the domain of values can be achieved only through the productive relation of masculine and feminine aspects of the human organism. The notion of alignment will have to include this; in that way the idea of freedom is related to the masculine/feminine distinction.

Subsections 11 and 12 should be read together. The former begins with a meditation on Zarathustra's pity for the past that has been forgotten or erased, but ends with an outline of the need for a new form of nobility (see note on Social Taxonomy, with the commentary on Part II, Section 6). Every 'generation' interprets the past as the unique route to itself, and justification of itself. Nietzsche's generation saw just this happen in Bismarck's race to legitimise the new German state. Thus, the 'great despot' or 'some prince' is both a reference to Bismarck and to Machiavelli's manual *The Prince*, advising those in power in the art of how not to lose it. Here it is argued that attitudes towards the past are interconnected with hierarchy, so that the lower humans have an understanding of history concomitant with their restricted horizons. (See note on Social Taxonomy.) The nobleman is a 'free spirit', an emblem of a finer sort of human that has risen above both the 'rabble' and the 'despotic' by virtue of his or her inheritance of nobility together with self-overcoming and alignment with the will to power. Nobility will redeem the past by receiving its justification only from the future (this is made clear in the next subsection). It can only do this, however, by assembling the possibilities of the human from the past, as fragments of virtues. Thus nobility too interprets the past and present, though in a manner more comprehensive and less exclusive, and also not as a bridge to *itself*, but towards its overhuman ideal, 'your *children's land*'. (See note on The Comprehensive Soul, with the commentary on section 7.) The reader should compare the parallel passage in *The Gay Science*: such a noble being would 'feel the history of humanity altogether as his own history . . . the dutiful heir to all the nobility of past spirit' and finally 'the first of a new nobility' (*The Gay Science*, section 337).[72] (Notice there also the link that is made between this idea and that of bestowal. Finally, the golden oars image that shows up there can be found again in subsection 3.) Zarathustra rejects authoritarian rule: dictatorship means an illegitimate channelling of power for particular, unhealthy reasons. This needs to be borne in mind when we want to understand the use made of Nietzsche's theories, particularly the will to power, by the Fascist movements, both Italian and German. Only through falsifying Nietzsche's positions or through misreading them has it been possible to make political use of them in that manner.

Subsection 25 is a meditation on the idea of a people, and of a new people of 'experimenters' (or 'searchers'). All human society is an 'experiment' – this means that expressed in terms of life and evolutionary growth, the purpose of a people is to create the conditions for its own overcoming. To be sure, the society may itself be great, beautiful, and yield astonishing achievements. That is its moment; but it thereby has tremendous resources for further enhancement. And within a society there is a struggle, of a broadly biological nature, for the commanders who can best lead it to its overcoming. Thus, society is not a 'contract' (a reference to Locke and Rousseau, among others) – that is, a rationally arrived at state of organisation. Rather, human society (with its values, institutions, laws) is objectification of a mode of life and ultimately a will to power.

In an astonishing twist of argument, Nietzsche makes it clear in subsection 26 that he can combine a vicious attack on Christianity and Christian morality with enthroning the figure of Jesus as a role model for the overhuman. Not those who have been called evil (by 'the good') do most harm in hindering the progress towards overhumanity; it is those whom Zarathustra calls 'good', the self-satisfied, complacent bourgeois, the '*Biedermann*' of Bismarck's militaristic and economic boom-land of Germany. This is what Jesus saw for his own time when he branded the 'good' as 'Pharisees'. In this he was as little understood by his contemporaries as is Zarathustra/Nietzsche. Jesus was, had to be, crucified for creating new values. However, even Jesus did not ask the critical question, posed by 'the second one' (presumably Zarathustra): 'whom do they hate the most?'. Only this question reveals that what is at stake in the creation of values is the survival of an existing people and the possibility of an elevated future, an ultimately biological/evolutionary struggle between modes of life.

Section 13, 'The Convalescent'

At last Zarathustra has the strength to summon up his 'abyss deep' thought (compare Part III, Section 3), but only in a kind of sleep-walking state (he is not said to be awake *himself*), imagining it as a part of his soul still on the pallet. When it comes up, though, Zarathustra is filled with disgust and collapses. His convalescence then occupies the rest of Part III. The rest of this section is a dialogue between Zarathustra and his animals, which is notable in itself since the animals have never hitherto spoken – the reference is likely to be Wagner's hero Siegfried – but this symbolises a new stage of insight into, and proximity to, all of nature (see also Part III, Section 9). However, the phenomenon initially leads Zarathustra to a largely negative reflection upon the nature of language and communication. It is 'refreshing', 'lovely' and beautiful to hear the animals 'chatter',[73] but words and 'tones' are deceptive, making us believe that the 'eternally separated' can be bridged in this way. This briefly expressed idea probably refers to no less than three claims about language: that moments in the constant development of a thing are 'bridged' by a proper name, and the development thus effaced; that similar individuals are bridged by abstract or collective nouns and thus their specificity lost; and finally that two human souls might be bridged by speaking and understanding, giving the illusion – which can of course be very useful and also emotionally important – of a coming together. Within those illusions lies another: that there *is* an outside at all. This is both a reference to the comprehensive soul, and also to the notion that, within immanent Being, a field of will to power, there could not be 'eternal separation' any more than there could be an eternal 'everything is firm' (Part III, Section 12.8). The treatment of language here should be contrasted with that in Part III, Section 9, with its account of the possibility of ontological truth. Only for the philosopher who has already critically taken apart the deception of language, as part of his or her ontological honesty and realignment of spirit, will 'all Being' want to 'become word' (Part III, Section 9). There is a sly dig at Wagner here: yes, in a magic moment Zarathustra hears the animals talking, but what do they say? They chatter and sing fairground songs.

The references to beauty and illusion recall the concept of the Apolline from *The Birth of Tragedy*. (See the discussion in Part II, Section

8.) Thus, Zarathustra is preparing the way for his smiling rejection of his animals' précis of the notion of eternal recurrence. It is not that their account is factually incorrect – indeed, Zarathustra repeats 'how well you know'. As 'chatter (*schwätzt*)', it necessarily fails to capture the Dionysiac and ontological truth of the thought. It is too easy, too descriptive, the same thing Zarathustra said to the dwarf in Part III, Section 2. He calls them 'pranksters and barrel-organs (*Schalks-Narren und Drehorgeln*)' and singers of 'hurdy-gurdy (*Leier-Lied*)'. In the first of these terms we can hear an echo of the jester, who wants merely to jump over (see previous section, subsection 4). In the second, the *Dreh* means to turn or crank, and thus a reference to eternal recurrence as a contained, examinable *mechanism*. In the last term *Leier* also means 'lyre', and is thus a reference to Apollo. What we have here is an Apollonian beautiful appearance of eternal recurrence, a consolation to their convalescing master. The animal's version emphasises the joy of eternal recurrence ('those who think as we do are already dancing'); Zarathustra's version emphasises the profound disgust at the return of the small. The latter cannot simply be leapt over, it cannot be disposed of with 'hurdy-gurdy' words, but of course the latter is also not where Zarathustra's convalescence is taking him. The animals *do* know that he must 'sing', and (if we include the next section) Part III ends with three songs. Zarathustra must discover the specific joy that arises when Apollonian beauty is inhabited by Dionysian insight – this is also the merging of feminine and masculine. In three different ways, the three songs that end this part do just that.

During the seven days (the period of time that *creation* takes) when Zarathustra was first wrestling with this 'disgust', the animals, cruelly it would seem, first 'slipped away' and then 'simply watched'. But in this they were following Zarathustra's own suggestion – 'better yet, leave him lying – in Part III, Section 12.18. Their 'cruelty' then was a mark of respect and appropriate shame, just as is their silence at the end of the current section. The animals chose well their moment to introduce the soothing balm of their chatter. Nevertheless, this leads Zarathustra to a meditation on human cruelty. '[I]ts most evil is necessary for its best', and both must become greater. His torment is that the extent of both evil and best are 'so very small'. With this we return to the metaphor of Part III, Section 5, and reach the crux of the matter: the eternal recurrence of the small. This was the narrative significance of Zarathustra's disappointment in Motley Cow just before his return home. Its consequence might be a 'loathing for all existence', an existence in which such smallness is integral, necessary, eternally recurs and is eternally destructive to all that is higher.

Section 14, 'On the Great Yearning'

Zarathustra is 'conversing with his soul', giving expression to yearning for overcoming. The style is high, hymn-like, foreshadowing 'future songs' – here, the next two sections, and those of Part IV. Like Life and Wisdom before, the Soul is gendered as feminine. Originally entitled 'Ariadne', this section offers a male speaking voice, the 'I' which appears to be the past and present of Zarathustra, his total life-struggle as critic, destroyer, teacher and prophet – all are imagined as gifts to the soul. (See the similar evocation of the 'sister-soul' in section 4, the divine sky as sacred companion.) Such virtues or activities have generally been symbolised by the masculine. In this moment, the hands of this 'I' have 'become empty'. There is nothing more the masculine drives can achieve. The task is passed to the feminine who must now give birth. This description of two discrete stages of transformation is only an allegory. Only as a complete being – and that means both masculine and feminine – can Zarathustra 'go over'. The 'I' addresses the female object of his eulogy, entreating her to transformation, to song. The soul is a 'vine with swelling udders' (that is, pregnant with song, the 'future songs'), it will give birth when the vintner's knife cuts it (an image of broad symbolic meaning: birth, death, completion, beginning, the moment of transformation). The song will then calm the seas[74] so that the golden bark of Dionysus (the vintner and 'the nameless') can come, and Ariadne will become a demi-god.

Note that for the first time (even though we had seen many earlier references to Greek mythology) the historical horizon of this section is consistently that of classical antiquity. Numerous references to different aspects of the myth of Dionysus are woven into this passage: wine; seafarer with an escort of dolphins; eternal recurrence associated with the seasons (Dionysus dies cyclically and is put back together again by Zeus, his father). The homing in onto Greece must be regarded as a most significant development given Nietzsche's own very close, long-standing attachment as a former philologist to Greek culture. His first book was devoted to chronicling the development of Greek art using the tool of two interconnected cultural forces, nature's 'artistic drives' which he named after two central deities in Greek mythology: Dionysus and Apollo. Here, as there, Dionysus symbolises the depths of reality, the surging destructive and creative will to power that underlies all appearances and all affects. What is new is that Dionysus here in *Zarathustra* has also a more specific symbolic function, as the deified projection of the ideal of the overhuman; or, rather, the God that tempts humans (or experiments with humans) to ever higher and more fully aligned forms of life. It almost serves as a summary of Nietzsche's philosophy here to say that he sees these two symbolic functions as the same. The figure of Apollo is only ambiguously present in *Zarathustra*. To be sure, the theme of appearance (and specifically, still, beautiful and consoling appearance) has not disappeared – indeed, it was evoked in the previous section. However, Apollo has here become a *function of* Dionysus: the will to appearance and form is an aspect of Dionysiac nature. At the end of *Beyond Good and Evil*, Nietzsche calls himself the 'last disciple and initiate of the god Dionysus'. This God is fond of humans precisely in that they are 'pleasant, brave, inventive animals . . . they find their way around any labyrinth' – and thus he gestures to Ariadne, the symbolic form of Dionysus's love for human possibilities. Dionysus, the deified ideal of growth, ascent, health and also destruction, loves human beings only as the self-overcoming species. He would like to make humans 'stronger, more evil, more profound' and also 'more beautiful'. Back towards the beginning of that section, Dionysus is said to have 'understanding of how to appear [*scheinen*] – not like what he is but like one *more* compulsion for his followers to keep pressing closer to him'. With this treatment of 'appear', Nietzsche signals that the productive dynamic of Dionysus and Apollo as separate drives is replaced by a dynamic of overcoming with its rapid alternations of destructive overcoming and beauty.

We might go so far as to suggest that the 'I' here is meant to be Theseus, who in some accounts of the myth did not simply abandon Ariadne on Naxos, but did so precisely to yield to Dionysus – that would mean that this section repeats at greater length the image at the end of Part II, Section 13. Alternatively, the 'I' is Dionysus, love-struck and trying to woo her, as several versions of the myth suggest – trying, in the terms of this book, to tempt her to the attainment of her own divinity – and her imminent song would be her acquiescence. In any case, Dionysus in his multiple symbolic functions must be both masculine and feminine. Zeus carried the child in a makeshift womb on his thigh; in several versions of the myth, Dionysus was also disguised as a girl to hide him from an understandably jealous Hera; and one of his symbolic roles was as God of seasons and thus of rebirth. So, the arrival of Dionysus is thus an image of the *whole* human. Ariadne represents human possibilities in general and more specifically here the necessity of the feminine aspect of Self in human creative transformation, after the exhaustion of the masculine impulses. Note also that Ariadne gives symbolic expression of the overflowing fullness of wisdom and the realigned Self – to sing is to bestow, as muse (see the first lines of both Homeric epics). What is coming, Zarathustra prophetically suggests, is a form of life where masculine and feminine are not separated and unreconciled.

In the travel imagery of the soul, awaiting union or reunion, the soul that sings is also the expressive aspect of the Self, the part that faces outward into the world. The soul here is the worldly objectification, and especially the futural objectification, of the Self. One model for this idea of the soul going out of the self into the world, in a kind of out-of-body experience of the Self, can be found in Eichendorff's (1788–1857) post-Romantic poem *Mondnacht* ('Moonlit Night', around 1835). As one of the best-known German poems of the period, it will have been familiar to Nietzsche; indeed, Nietzsche set a poem by Eichendorff to music, namely *Das Zerbrochene Ringlein* ('The Little Broken Ring', 1863). Nietzsche would surely have known Robert Schumannn's (1810–56) version.[75] The poem starts with the lines '*Es war, als hätt' der Himmel/ die Erde still geküsst*' ('It was as if heaven/ had softly kissed the earth') and ends with the following four-line stanza: '*Und meine Seele spannte/ Weit ihre Flügel aus,/ Flog durch die stillen Lande,/Als flöge sie nach Haus*' ('And my soul expanded/ its wings wide/flew through the quiet lands/ as though she was flying home').

Assuming we can count this section as song-like, Part III ends with three 'songs'. They form a loose narrative sequence, since section 15 would appear to be the song announced at the end here, and section 16 with its image of the wedding would seem to complete the romantic comedy of Zarathustra and Life. However, all may not be quite so simple, as we will see at the end of section 16.

Section 15, 'The Other Dance-Song'

We are still within the frame of the end of section 13, with Zarathustra conversing with his soul. The sequencing suggests that this is the song that Zarathustra bids his soul sing. It is also 'the other' dance song, continuing on from Part II, Section 10, with the same personification of Life. The song divides into three: first, there is an Arcadian narrative of the double-valenced pursuit of Life, who teases and flees, reminiscent of many a mythic chase of (or by) a nymph, which ends in frustration and a threat of violence; secondly, there is a dialogue between Life and Zarathustra; thirdly, there is a brief poem whose lines are between the twelve strokes of midnight. We call the first part 'double-valenced' because Zarathustra professes both love and desire but also fear and hatred, for Life; she is both innocent and child-eyed, and also a witch and a dangerous snare. (This doubleness might be related to the story of Apollo and Daphne.) The second part begins with Life pleading, and she says 'must one then dislike the other just because one does not love from the ground up?' He whispers something in her ear and they sit down together, now on soft meadows in the cool evening.[76]

This little episode is just as teasing for the reader. Zarathustra, in fact, does love Life from the ground up (that was explicit in the first dance song), and all the more when Life must be hated. Thus the ambivalence: his love of Life is desire for Life's creative overcoming of itself, and thus must be partly rooted in despising (see the end of Part I, Section 17). In the first dance song we learned that Wild Wisdom resembles Life very closely – and is all the more alluring for that; Wisdom is founded on, and seeks to align itself ever more closely with, Life. Here, we have a kind of inversion. Life is 'jealous' of Wisdom; Life responds to Zarathustra only because of wisdom. Zarathustra is that mode of Life that is able to advance Life, he is the channel, so to speak, through which Life achieves its longed for future – only thus is he one of life's 'favourites'. This we have seen, for example, at the end of Part II, Section 15, or Part III, Section 9. Please also see our discussion of ontological language at that latter reference. In this little drama, though, Life suspects he wants to leave, thus suspects he does not love her. Zarathustra has had to overcome the desire to escape from Life, through weariness, nihilism, heaviness or because life has become the object of disgust; for example, at the end of the first dance song, and again in the 'The Convalescent'. In each case this is an urge to be overcome, at least in favour of the 'free death' (Part I, Section 21), the death aligned to Life rather than opposed to it, death from out of total devotion to Life. Perhaps, though, this overcoming happens not once but *each* midnight (this is suggested by Life's words here, and also by the parallel passage in Part IV, Section 19). The cycle of the day, like the cycle of the seasons, signifies a continual process of overcoming and growth. Moreover, if Life only loves Zarathustra out of jealousy of his Wild Wisdom, and that Wisdom is not complete (he has not yet overcome the weight of the thought of eternal recurrence), then her jealousy and thus love will not be 'from the ground up'.

What, then, does he whisper to Life that brings them so close? The obvious answer is the thought of eternal recurrence, the dominant idea of this Part III, which has not yet been alluded to in this section, but is referred to in the poem with which the section ends. This thought, after Zarathustra's convalescence, is no longer a wish to leave Life. '[A]ll joy wants eternity', declares the deep midnight. Thus, having been whispered to, Life now knows Zarathustra's love for her. Moreover, with the completion of Zarathustra's Wisdom, her jealousy and thus love must have reached a climax; Wisdom and Life here become merged, bound together like the image of serpent and eagle at the end of the Prologue. Life too now loves 'from the ground up'. The eternal recurrence is the whispered Wisdom – but it is merely hurdy-gurdy song unless it is also the proper spiritualisation of a 'Self' that has bitten off the head of the snake. The whispering of eternal recurrence, then, mutually seals their love like a wedding vow – and indeed the nuptial ring is precisely the dominant image of the next section.

The poem is employed again in the penultimate section of Part IV, and we will discuss it further there.

Section 16, 'The Seven Seals'

Recall that *Zarathustra* was originally published in just three parts. Part III ends with a ceremonial confirmation of what has been achieved in the book as a whole, and specifically through Zarathustra's convalescence. This is high poetic style again, in the form of an ode to eternity. 'Life' is revealed as 'Eternity', Zarathustra's bride. There is a poetic pattern with the last three lines of each of the seven sections repeated (with only a change in punctuation), like a chant. The title reference is to the *New Testament*, The Revelation of St John, Chapter 5, which narrates the Book with Seven Seals. The opening of these seals initiates the apocalypse. In contrast to the apocalyptic destruction envisaged in the Bible, the seven seals here initiate the *affirmation* of a newly found world of the future. In Nietzsche's extraordinary imagination, the apocalypse becomes a wedding march! The seals are here not lifted, as in the Bible: they are put on, sanctioning and sanctifying. Nietzsche is never entirely straight-faced, though. The nuptial ring of rings is (among other things, as always) a re-interpretation of Wagner's mythical *Ring of the Nibelungs*. The whole project of the doctrine of eternal recurrence thus moves into the context of Nietzsche's emancipating himself from Wagner by providing a more far-reaching, more radical philosophical reading of the ring-trope.

Seal 1 positions the gloomy pessimism of the soothsayer (reminiscent of Ahasverus, the Wandering Jew) against Zarathustra's yea-saying gaiety. Seal 2 affirms the destructive work of critique. With Seal 3 Zarathustra seats himself with the 'Gods', at their gaming table, the earth. Seal 4 concerns the genealogical work that shows the common and inversely valenced psychological origin of both good and evil ('well mixed'); more, though, it concerns the necessity of that mixture and the aligned being as channel ('salt'). Seal 5 says Amen to Zarathustra's questing for the future, risking a sea without shore. He has been on a journey where 'far and away space and time sparkle'. Seal 6 celebrates a philosophy that has declared the physical elevation of the dancing and laughing body to be its 'Alpha and Omega'. Seal 7 is the affirmation of 'song' as the natural language of man seeking physical liberation and completion. Words are heavy; poetry can make light of the heaviness of language by musicalising it. Music is the most adequate symbolic form of expression for a humanity about to be transformed (see section 12.2 and note on Nietzsche, Music and Language, with the Commentary on Part II, Section 17.).

The three sections that end this part would appear to be three songs in a narrative sequence, as we described at the end of our discussion of section 14. All three take place outside the main narrative space (Zarathustra in the cave), and all take place in the internal narrative space of the convalescent Zarathustra conversing with his soul. The first and third of these (sections 14 and 16) are in part recapitulations akin to the 'Old and New Tablets'. The second resumes an allegorical narrative from Part II, the last brings it to a close with a wedding song. They all include the masculine-feminine trope as their main thematic axis, and, moreover, that trope is evoked at symbolically crucial stages (in section 14, pregnancy and the moment of birth; in section 15 the moment of absolute proximity and love; in section 16 the 'nuptial ring of rings').

However, this reading of the three last songs as a seamless narrative sequence leading to consummation is troubled by some elements of section 16. First of all, there is the curious hypothetical form to the seven seals 'If I am a soothsayer . . . Oh how should I not lust . . .' The grammar suggests necessity, to be sure: to be such a soothsayer would *require* that one lust after eternity; to not do so would be to be incomplete, dishonest, a play-actor or unhealthy. Thus all of Zarathustra's teachings and all his masks lead to eternity; it is as if all the thematic threads of the book are knotted together at just this point. Nevertheless, the grammar also suggests incompleteness: everything is caught in the possible space of this hypothetical, awaiting only a minor premise for a whole cascade of conclusions. Also, in the last of the 'seals', we find again (just like at the end of section 14) an invitation to 'sing'. It is not over until that lady sings. Once again, as always, we appear to be just *before* the moment of transformation itself, teetering on the edge of the future. The event of the song would be the event of transformation of the human, but the transformation of the human would render all songs redundant (see section 12.2; and also Part IV, Section 10). So, in addition to being a narrative sequence, these three songs are also three different or alternative statements of the same awesome, imminent event. Nietzsche/Zarathustra has pushed it as far as possible, but this future could never arrive *within the book*. After all, the book's primary function is not to describe the life of Zarathustra, it is to act so as to effect a revolution and ultimately to invoke, in and for us, the readers, the god Dionysus.

Part IV

Part IV was published separately and as a privately financed print run. Much speculation has gone into the significance of this final part and its link with the rest of the text. In the *Nachlass*, Nietzsche puts forward numerous ideas as to its role and significance, including at one point the plan to add another, a fifth part. *Zarathustra* is thus two books: one with three parts, one with four. Each can be legitimately defended as a proper object of our philosophical and literary attention. In discussing the end of Part III, we did so with little reference to Part IV. Now, it is time to explore the alternative. There are a number of arguments that help us make sense of the four-part structure. One of them is the assumption that, as a form of parody of Wagner's *Ring*, the four parts of the text of Zarathustra ironically imitate the four-part structure of the operatic cycle.[77] Likewise, the book can be investigated as symphonic in structure, since the classical symphony form had four movements. Another, very exciting, argument is that Nietzsche is adhering to the tetralogy-model of Greek tragedy,[78] whereby three connected but distinct tragedies are followed by a fourth drama: not another tragedy, but a satyr play, a satirical contrast to the previous three and a commentary on them. Indeed, Zarathustra is not so much the highly strung prophet here, but more like an old philosophical faun who roams the woods meeting contemporaries and getting it wrong, rather like the Wotan in Wagner's *Twilight*. Satire, and not so much the serious, poeticised philosophy (section 19 is one notable exception), nor the euphoric poetic epiphany (again, with the key exception of section 10), is the dominant stylistic pitch of much of the writing here, culminating in the ribaldry of the sections that follow number 12, 'The Last Supper'. This key symbolic event at the foundation of modern Western European culture is here satirically demolished by turning it into the forum for the simultaneous praise and critique of those strangely deranged creatures, the 'superior humans'. Who are these superior human contemporaries? They are ass's heads in a fool's gallery.

Part IV has a tighter and more continuous narrative than any of the previous three. With its focus on individual allegorical portraits, it resembles Part I; however, these portraits are not just subject matter for Zarathustra, they are part of a broader symbolic story. In this part, Zarathustra takes on a new role. In hosting the supper he turns into a hybrid between an earth-bound Socrates and an atheistic Jesus. Part IV brings together, through the device of a communal dinner, the divergent antagonistic positions in the various areas of the book's critique: religion, science, social morality, politics, aesthetics. They are all under one roof, as it were: that of the cave, Zarathustra's earthy, sybaritic church. These gathering individuals are the 'superior humans'. They are 'superior' or 'higher' in that they stand out from the all-too-many through having internalised, made part of their mode of life, some aspect of Zarathustra's teaching. They are all allegorical portraits and some are clearly satirical re-imaginings of real individuals (for example, Schopenhauer or Wagner). What seems initially difficult to understand is the futility of the gathering of guests and their entertainment. As the night progresses, they become more and more whole, but it is clear that they do not in the end transform, they are unable to further Zarathustra's work, and cannot bear fully the thought of eternal recurrence. Zarathustra is failing here, and he admits it at the end. Is this *Zarathustra* turned novel of disillusionment *à la* Flaubert's (1821–80) last novel *Éducation sentimentale* (1869)? On the final pages, Frédéric, the novel's anti-hero, is overcome with the realisation of the futility of all he has achieved and done.[79] Or is this the *Twilight of Zarathustra*, Nietzsche's cryptic reference to the failure of the gods in Wagner's last *Ring*-opera? Only the final scene with its mystical sign of hope, and a hope closer than ever, keeps Part IV distinct from these two models.

The Dionysian satyr play or 'goat's song', the deflating fourth part of Greek tragic tetralogies, is the appropriate form. Dionysian ribaldry satirises modern forms of degeneracy as they emerge from within the crisis of the Platonic and Christian traditions. Socrates and Jesus are the two representatives of spiritual escapism and ethical life-denial. In the Last Supper, the explicit reference is to Jesus's last episode with the whole group of disciples before his crucifixion, including the gesture by which arguably the most important church institution is initiated: the Eucharist. However, in Nietzsche's inventive hands, it also contains an implied reference to Plato's *Symposium*, one of the richest and most elaborate of the dialogues where Athenian literati, including Socrates, discuss the origins and history of love and of knowledge. Nietzsche is here rewriting these important incidents, in the same way as the book as a whole is creatively rewriting the birth of European morality in the historical figure of Zoroaster. The German words for both events superimposed upon each other here are '*Abendmahl*' for Last Supper and '*Gastmahl*', the translation of *Symposium*.

The general lowering of tension in the mainly satirical style of Part IV puts the first three parts in sharper profile: there Nietzsche had attempted, by means of gradually increasing poetic concentration, to drive the present time of the narrative as closely as was conceivable right up to a point of revolutionary turn-around. But this was also the point where Nietzsche had to let go, because it is in the nature of the utopian vision that its realisation is out of reach of the visionary; the prophet never reaches the promised land. The highest intensity of poetic conjuring cannot achieve the realisation of the future in the present, other than perhaps in poetically evoked vision. Only for the poet (who also calls on the resources of music) is it possible to write this kind of philosophy.

Zarathustra's hair has turned white; he is now a wise old man, our contemporary – all-too-human again perhaps – who can deal more calmly, indeed, sometimes even nonchalantly, with challenges. For he knows that the seeds of his message have been sown out into the world and are beginning to bear fruit. It seems likely that the portrayal of Zarathustra in Part IV picks up to an extent on Goethe's (and, inspired by Goethe, Karl Immerman's) notion of 'renunciation'. Goethe's sequel to his first *Bildungsroman*, *Wilhelm Meister's Apprenticeship* ('Wilhelm Meisters Lehrjahre', 1795–96) was called *Wilhelm Meister's Journeyman Years, Or the Renunciants* ('Wilhelm Meisters Wanderjahre, oder die Entsagenden', 1821–9).[80] Immerman's seminal *Zeit*-novel, *The Epigones* of 1836, is built around this notion of renunciation: the titanic extremes of youth and forcefully original artistic creation ('Storm and Stress' [*Sturm und Drang*]) are being replaced by an equilibrium of the Self, more in tune with what is humanly possible and culturally conceivable. To the end, though, Zarathustra does not let go of his belief that it will be possible to overcome this kind of epigonal pessimism. Nevertheless, Zarathustra has largely lost the frantic, yearning side his character shown in the earlier parts. There is another feature that can now come to the fore in Zarathustra's character: he can make fun of himself and lampoon some of the positions he had been tackling in more serious ways before, a self-ironical streak that in turn separates Zarathustra from Wilhelm Meister who hardly ever laughs, let alone about himself.

One function of Part IV is for Nietzsche therefore to clarify his critique of contemporary culture. Here now these positions are turned into portraits of (near) contemporaries, Schopenhauer, the French and German Kaisers perhaps, Wagner, maybe Feuerbach, socialist egalitarianism, contemporary positivistic science, specialisation, and so forth. The poetic intensity of Parts I to III may be broken now, the suspense of the story line suspended in favour of a much smaller-scale narrative, but if we read *Zarathustra* as a kaleidoscopic compendium of cultural critique, then this final part adds a sharp edge to the first three parts. This fits in with the Goethean programme of critique as part of character reform through renunciation. Grown-up Goethean man goes out into the world and tackles it head-on. Goethe's (and Immermann's) novel features extensive discussions of issues topical and relevant at the time, education, for instance. It is *Zeitkritik.*

Section 1, 'The Honey Sacrifice'

The 'honey sacrifice' is a ruse, first so that Zarathustra can speak still more freely than even he can as a solitary (compare Part III, Section 9; presumably the animals are incapable of such 'wicked' ruses), and secondly as bait (the honey of his happiness) to catch 'human-fish' with (Matthew 4: 19). Both these signal yet another new phase in the teaching of Zarathustra: he needs again to pass beyond the phase of the solitary, but rather than going down once more, he will raise human beings up to his mountains. This fishing is 'wicked' both because his teaching will be called 'evil' by those down below, but also because of the deceit of the baited hook. It is a deceit because happiness is not an end in itself for Zarathustra – it is merely the affect that belongs to the state of being aligned to or consummate with the needs of life's overcoming. The words 'Become the one you are!' refer back to *The Gay Science*, section 270, and from there to Pindar (we have seen several similar expressions). Here it is an emblem of the fact that spiritualisations are not inversions that turn away from life; one must align oneself with the fact that one is a living body with a specific historical fate. This involves an intellectual recognition, of course, but more importantly a change at the level of the system of drives such that their spiritualisation is just such a recognition. This is a process that Zarathustra has undertaken and to which he will lure others. Notice the reference to the '*hazar*', the 1,000-year division within Persian historical thought; this idea continues the notion of the people of the overhuman (Part I, Section 22).

Section 2, 'The Cry of Need'

Zarathustra sees 'beside his own shadow another shadow'. Through Zarathustra, his allegorical medium, the author is having another debate with himself about his influences. This section is a portrayal of the links and differences that connect Nietzsche with Schopenhauer's philosophy (we have identified the latter as the soothsayer earlier). Reminiscent of the Devil tempting Christ in the desert (for example, Matthew 4: 1–11), the soothsayer 'of the great weariness' is tempting Zarathustra to commit what both think of as his ultimate sin: compassion, the Christian 'virtue' of pity. This is a mirror image of the biblical story. Here the nihilistic tempter wants Zarathustra to deviate from the path of re-evaluated values, fall back into the old Christian ways of valuation, and commit what was formerly a deadly 'virtue'. The soothsayer thinks he has driven Zarathustra into a corner by indicating the cry of need from his own creation, 'the superior human'. He launches into a speech where he denies Zarathustra his happiness in a world where 'all is the same, nothing is worthwhile, no seeking avails, nor are there Isles of the Blest any more!'. In the biblical story Jesus find the strengths to reject the Devil in recognising his work for what it is, conjuring tempting realities that are nothing more than chimeras. Here, Zarathustra emerges from out of his attack of existential anxiety by recognising as unreality the soothsayer's claims that the real world is no longer recognisable as paradisiacal. He can now reject the tempting spirit of pessimistic nihilism ('No! No! Three times no!') in the firm conviction that the real world is still beautiful.

We have already discussed the concept of pity – how in appearing to be a benign impulse to help, it is more often a 'lustful' play for power through demeaning. Those most worthy of pity would be precisely those most damaged by it (the ugliest human, one of the guests to come, is the clearest example). However, Zarathustra's rushing to defend the 'superior human' whose cry of need he can hear, his repeated claim that no one shall come to harm in his 'realm', his wish to 'set everyone who is mournful on firm land and firm legs again' (section 6), and the whole evening's events all express a virtue already dangerously close to pity.

Zarathustra's pity would be for the superior humans. By these are meant human beings who are the first fruit of Zarathustra's teachings; they have in part learned the 'great disgust' for the current state of the human, and have the strength of will and creativity of the spirit to do *something* about it. However, whatever furtherance they give the project of the overhuman, they must also be allowed to 'go under'. The superior humans, however, also represent modes of humanity that Zarathustra has overcome in himself (they are *also* self-portraits). They are thus enemies, too. Zarathustra turns the Christian moral requirement of love of one's neighbour into the worldly demand of the love of those farthest away (Part I, Section 16) – that is, love for friends and enemies insofar as this is love of the overhuman. He extends the laws of hospitality towards the soothsayer once more by inviting him as a guest into his cave. This Über-Schopenhauer is prophesying the end of the world, Nietzsche its beginning in the overhuman.

Section 3, 'Conversation with the Kings'

Unless we count the soothsayer, the first of the 'superior humans' that Zarathustra encounters is in fact a double act: two kings, with a 'laden ass'. Again, this is a biblical reference: Jesus's entry into Jerusalem (by way of the Mount of Olives) is on the back of an ass (a symbolically low creature), which he had sent two disciples to obtain for him (the incident is recorded similarly in all four Gospels). Here, the disciples have the ass, but not yet the master. (There might be another, and more subtle, biblical reference to the magi – or 'kings' as medieval tradition would have it – who search for the new-born Messiah. After all, with Zarathustra also on the hunt, they make up the traditional number of three.) In addition to any biblical allusions, that there should be *two* travelling together (and with so little accompanying ceremony) reinforces the sincerity of their disgust that no one, not even the kings, is 'first' among human beings. In the absence of any true nobility among those who command, the rabble is on the ascendency. Nevertheless, Zarathustra's joke is that there are two kings but only one (of them is an) ass. Obviously, 'nobility' does not just mean aristocracy; that the kings are designated as 'on the left' and 'on the right' means that they come from across the political spectrum. (Nietzsche might intend them as parodies of the French and German monarchs.) They search for the 'superior human' whom they can, properly, call 'king'. Zarathustra invites them to his cave, where he will join them later after he has found and rescued the superior human whose cry he believes he has heard. Note that Zarathustra is sorely tempted to mock them, these old men talking so enthusiastically about war, struggle and overcoming, but he restrains himself, and perhaps then exemplifies the very 'politeness' they reject. As with all the characters Zarathustra encounters over the next few sections, while these 'kings' might be portraits of contemporaries of Nietzsche, they are *also* portraits of aspects of Nietzsche himself – here, for example, the King 'on the right' gives voice to Zarathustra's/Nietzsche's own critique of modern, democratic society, and his becoming stateless. Finally, note that the last lines about a type that is 'capable of waiting' returns us to the idolisation of the present time that is criticised in, for example, Prologue, Section 5 and Part I, Section 9.

Section 4, 'The Leech'

In this rather strained allegorical portrait Zarathustra steps on a man who is lying in marshy land. The man represents a severe version of a kind of intellectual conscience, for which, as the action and the section's ending demonstrate, Zarathustra does not have much time. He quickly leaves the scene extending his customary hospitality to 'the conscientious in spirit'. The conscientious man has the life-blood sucked out of him by the object he is studying. In his blinkered search for the leech he has lost all sense of priorities and proportion: this is a portrayal of modern scientific attitudes characterised by positivistic optimism in which the picture of the whole gets obscured by excessive specialisation (leech's *brain*), obsession with detail, and oblivion to the question of the *value* of the enquiry. In the end the studying subject resembles the object that he studies: the man has himself turned into a mud-parasite. Moreover, the leeches get fatter; practices of study followed by the scientist involve an interpretation of the world but also thereby reinforce the interpretation. The reader should compare the use of the idea of a conscience in *The Gay Science*, especially section 335, although the subject there is moral duties rather than scientific ones. The distinction there between a narrow conscience and a 'conscience behind the conscience' (the meta-virtue of honesty which we have seen often here) helps us to understand

Zarathustra's distaste for the leech. Also, see Part I, Section 12, the only other time Zarathustra speaks of spirit in connection with conscience. There, the 'play-actors' *lack* conscience of the spirit, and they are like a perverse mirror image of the leech. Significantly, the very next section gives us just such a 'play-actor'.

Section 5, 'The Sorcerer'

The sorcerer is, most likely, a satirical portrait of Richard Wagner. (See Chapter 1, introduction, The Text, and note on Nietzsche, Music and Language, with commentary on Part II, Section 17.) Here, Wagner is depicted as a play-actor, able to fool many subtle wits, but not Zarathustra and, ultimately, not himself. Thus, if only for a brief honest moment, the sorcerer becomes 'disenchanted' with his art and with himself, and is thus a 'penitent of the spirit' (see Part II, Section 17, which is indeed followed by 'On Great Events'). (Nietzsche, and Northern – especially German – philosophers, poets and composers seem to specialise in *moments*: insight, transformation, ecstasy. See the references cited and discussed in the commentary on Part III, Section 12.)

The long, play-acted poem is the first of several poems from the privately printed Part IV of *Zarathustra* that Nietzsche planned to issue as the *Dionysus Dithyrambs*, a collection he prepared for publication shortly before his insanity. There the poem bears the title 'Ariadne's Lament', and it is made clear that the 'God' is Dionysus. The poet is tormented by an unknown God who, when a demand is made, slips away. The gaze of the God forces brutal introspection and striving. We should, however, note the parallel with Part III, Section 15, 'The Other Dance-Song'. The mood is quite different, but in both cases the poet loves, but is 'tortured' by an ambiguous figure characterised as elusive, cruel, alternately near and far, barbed and jealous. The kidnapping image reverses an element of the Dionysus myth. The section ends with Zarathustra's suspicion that the sorcerer was in some way 'tempting' or 'testing' him, and not just playing a game – the verb *versuchen* and associated constructions are frequently used in the text, but have to be translated variously: to tempt, to test, to experiment and, just as *suchen*, to seek (see, for example, Part III, Section 2.1 at the point where Zarathustra is addressing the sailors).

Section 6, 'Retired from Service'

This section adds to the book's discussion of the end of Christianity and provides a more differentiated picture of the problem of priestly devotion than Part II, Section 4. Zarathustra meets the last pope. The last pope represents piety as a residual attitude long after the instigator of this 'virtue' has abdicated: piety as an ingrained moral value after the death of God, a kind of repetitive strain injury of the religious psyche, similar to the ingrained feudal demeanour of the two kings, long since displaced in a 'democratic' social context. The pope is blind in one eye. This is a reference to the *Theologia Germanica*, an anonymous religious text sometimes attributed to Meister Eckhart and championed by Luther.[81] Christ has two eyes: the right views eternity, the left time, earthly matters, human beings. The human has the same two eyes, but can only use one at once: 'if the soul shall see with the right eye into eternity, then the left eye must close itself and refrain from working, and be as though it were dead'.[82] The last pope is thus blind in both eyes, for different reasons: he is blind in the left eye because as pope he had no time for worldly affairs – no understanding of the earth, life or of the human; he is blind in the right eye because there is *nothing to see*. Nietzsche is thus, briefly, trying out a new trope to describe the wholeness of overhuman: two eyes. Neither is focused on eternity as such, to be sure, but one on becoming, overcoming and the ideal of overcoming, on the dimensions of depth and height (the masculine principle), the other focused on achievements of form or moments of beautiful stillness (the feminine principle). Metaphorically, the use of both such eyes allows insight into deep perspective (see Part III, Section 10). See also 'The Drunken Song', section 19, where we discuss related ideas further.

Both the pope and Zarathustra are godless: the former *suffers* from godlessness whilst the latter *rejoices* in it. Zarathustra urges the pope to let go of the dead God, whose dying the pope nostalgically reminisces about instead of heeding Zarathustra's advice. The highest homeless representative of God on earth has in addition something in common with the most radical of atheists: they are both pious. Zarathustra's atheism is a negative, secularised form of religious piety: a religious attitude that hallows this world and sees manifold natural processes and ascending life as Gods. The overhuman offers a new type of value-creating religion, both worshipper and worshipped. The pope figure has not yet managed to take the step of re-channelling his piety in this secular direction.

Section 7, 'The Ugliest Man'

The section begins with Zarathustra reflecting on the good fortune of meeting such thought-provoking characters, but the mood changes rapidly as he enters a dead landscape; by the end of this section he is chilled to the bone and desirous of further solitude. He believes he remembers this valley; some of the imagery repeats the valley of 'wild cliffs' in Part II, Section 2, 'On the Vision and the Riddle'. Here he finds the ugliest man, the murderer of God. This is the personification of all that is ugly, wretched, debased and pitiable in human beings, the living refutation that God's creation is *perfect* and that God is *good*. Moreover, with his 'heaviest feet' he destroys and kills everything he walks over: this is the human that, as a diseased form of life, has come to reject life itself, thus is also the living refutation that God gives and sustains *life*. Finally, the ugliest man also personifies great misfortune and failure, a living refutation of the idea that creation has a *purpose*. The last pope told us that God, gone old and soft, died of pity for the human. Here the outcome is the same but rather than a kind of suicide we have murder, and murder from out of the spirit of revenge no less. The human murdered God as revenge for His omniscience, which saw to the bottom of its ugliness. This idea refers back to the the role of pity in the cycle of revenge, discussed in Part II, Section 3 – in other words, not only the outcome is the same as the last pope's version of events, but also the ultimate cause: pity. As the destroyer of God, the ugliest man will also remind us of the 'sublime' one in Part II, Section 13 and Part I, Section 10: the sublime is the 'mantle' of the ugly. Thus, Zarathustra can admire the ugliest man at least for his rejection of pity and for his 'great despising' and destruction of values. Nevertheless, the murdering of God is not a redemption of the ugliest man, but the summation of his ugliness.

Notice, near the end, Zarathustra says 'only the one who does, learns'. Our translator directs us to an unpublished note that reads 'Not to your ears, but to your hands do I direct by teaching' (*Werke* 10: 17 [54]). In this book, the hand may be a welcoming or a bestowing hand, but it stands for activity (see especially Part I, Section 4; Part III, Section 10.2; Part III, Section 12.29). The idea here is that wisdom or understanding are impotent unless they are realised as a form of activity, which is both to say exteriorisations of the will back on to the social or natural domain, and through practices of internalisation a transformation on the level of the living body. See the discussion above under Part III, Section 9 and Part III, Section 7.

Section 8, 'The Voluntary Beggar'

Another attendant of the evening feast will be the voluntary beggar. This figure exemplifies Nietzsche's critical double-thrust directed partly against utilitarian and Marxist social philosophising and partly against the religious egalitarianism of the Strauss and Feuerbach kind, based (as he sees it) on moral laziness and simplistic good and evil-dichotomy. Both are related to *ressentiment* (ultimately reactive will to power) as motivation for slave-revolt. In the figure of the ascetic beggar we have the Jesus of the Sermon on the Mount (the passage is full of jesting references to the Gospels; this is Jesus as social egalitarian). Such Christianity has in common with the contemporary socialist in this late modern age that their egalitarianism is derived from a wrong interpretation of 'social realities'. The revolutionary rhetoric in these types masks a lack of understanding of the world and of the nature of life, and a completely anti-revolutionary drive to preserve forms of life, at all costs. There may be a gesture towards Buddhism here also, and the herd of cows would be a joke at the expense of the idea of reincarnation.

The voluntary beggar has left behind all earthly riches to live with the poor; however, he also has a view to a world beyond, thus the reference to the Kingdom of Heaven. In Jesus's teaching (Matthew 18: 3), we have to convert back into children to be able to enter the heavenly kingdom; for comical satirical effect, 'children' are replaced here by cows. But this means a commitment to a certain form of life. The image of the advancement of the human the beggar sought to bestow was founded on a completely delusional (other-worldly) account of life – he thus seems to have one blind eye, just like the last pope. Zarathustra plays devil's advocate when he asks the beggar to state his position regarding the rich. All he gets by way of an answer is a tirade against both rich *and* poor. There is no real concern for the human of whatever class. Zarathustra can agree with the diagnosis of the 'mob- and slave-insurrection', but the voluntary beggar's disgust does not lead to a sense of nobility, but rather to a desire to learn a new mode of life (cow-life) that will both preserve itself and also be happy because unconscious of disgust, and will finally thus be conducive to the other-worldly. Notice that Zarathustra is not above being affected by the warm benevolence of the cows, although he knows also that their 'sympathy' will not ever actually 'heal' anything.

Section 9, 'The Shadow'

This book is rich in imagery of 'shadow'. In Part II especially, the Shadow was an image of Zarathustra's future – it was the object of the sculptor's yearning in 'On the Isles of the Blest', it chided him for delay in 'On Great Events', and he was meant to be the 'shadow' of the coming overhuman in 'The Stillest Hour'. The shadow was cast in front of him, showing the path. Throughout, though, 'shadow' also carries a different meaning – see, for example, Part II, Section 13, which contains the famous image of leaping over one's own shadow. Here in Part IV, the symbolism of the shadow has turned much more to that negative meaning. We had the ominous shadow of the soothsayer, coming to tempt Zarathustra. Here, in this section, the allegorical portrait of the shadow has at least four meanings. First, it is imaged as trailing always *behind*, and is thus the past – both in the sense of Zarathustra's/Nietzsche's own individual past, things left behind or taken from them, also their misunderstandings and overcomings (see Part II, Section 11, for example); and also in the sense of a cultural or even physiological inheritance against which we have seen Zarathustra struggle (see our discussion of Part II, Section 5). Nietzsche might be referring to an earlier stage of his own work, such as the middle years of the 1870s, when he had not yet replaced his faded enthusiasm for the cultural project of Wagner with some other 'goal' (the overhuman). Secondly, the shadow stands for what remains to be overcome, or lies ahead as a dangerous temptation; here, 'some narrow belief, a harsh, severe illusion'. Thirdly, the shadow is that part of one's spirit that does not face into the light, does not give to itself direction, does not desire but merely follows behind, and even its following behind is aimless (that is, it 'wanders'). In other words, it is the negating, even nihilistic dimension of Zarathustra's/Nietzsche's own thought when separated from both the creative or affirmative (this is also the meaning of the extensive shadow imagery in Part II, Section 13) and the nurturing, protecting and beautiful (here, the 'noble lies' of innocence, or the 'haven' of a goal). In this respect, the figure of the shadow is also a summary of the other 'superior humans' we have met.

Above we referred briefly to Part II, Section 13, 'On Those Who Are Sublime'. There, the sublime one is called upon to jump over his shadow and become still, perfect and beautiful. Thus, it is no surprise here that this section on the shadow is followed by 'midday' – the time of the least shadow, of course, and also a moment of blissful perfection experienced by Zarathustra. As we shall see, 'At Midday' is a depiction of the quasi-mystical state of beauty and stillness, but again it is an interlude and not an end, for Zarathustra forces himself to wake and rise and continue with his seeking. (On the shadow as guide, see Dante, *Inferno*, Canto I, 64–120.)

Section 10, 'At Midday'

This section continues in the high visionary style of Part II, Section 22: 'The Stillest Hour'; Part III, Section 4, 'Before Sunrise'; and Part

III, Section 14, 'On the Great Yearning'. It is another Dionysian vision of transformation, the final one, in fact, here interspersed between Zarathustra's roaming in the hills and woods and the oncoming bacchanalia of sections 12 to 19. It follows on directly from Part III, Section 14 in the sense that what is experienced here as dream-evoked epiphany is related to the great yearning leading up to the moment of Ariadne's song to Dionysus and the overhuman: the fusion of Self and soul, masculine and feminine, Dionysus and Ariadne. Here, though, this moment apparently *has arrived*: this is not the 'stillest hour', but the 'stillest moment' of fulfilment where the world has 'just become perfect'. The phrase about the world becoming perfect occurs in only three sections of the text: here; back in Part I, Section 18; and in Part IV, Section 19. In the earliest section, it occurs as one of the clichés that the sexually addled Zarathustra comes out with concerning women. As we saw, interpreted as a claim about women it is just offensive; interpreted as a claim about the symbolic structure of human psychology, however, it is one of the emblems of the cyclical relationship between the masculine virtues of critique, destruction and struggle ('warrior') and the feminine virtues of giving birth and nurturing or preserving.[83] Every mode of life (whether in the individual or across a people) is a form, something that is 'still' compared to the 'river of becoming' and the seething of the will to power. Here, we have the image of the soul 'nestling' against the land in the 'stillest cove' of life. This stillest moment is the moment of perfect happiness, where beauty has been attained that is consummate to the whole of being. Here, in line with the myth of Pan, no mythological pastorals (fluting shepherds), no poetry, indeed not even music is desired – poetry and music have become redundant. All striving has ceased. Zarathustra does not consume the perfectly ripe grapes (slake his thirst and carry on), he leaves them be and lies down. Thus the transformation is accomplished in the moment of timeless time, Eckhart's *Aeternitas* or 'nu'.

The overall health of a mode of life depends, however, not only on the momentary alignment of its constituent drives with the nature of life more generally and the achievements of form thereby arrived at, but also with its devotion to going under, its yearning for a yet higher state – which is, of course, *also* part of this alignment. (See how Nietzsche uses the image of the soul stretching out at *Twilight of the Idols*, 'Morality as Anti-Nature', section 3.) The metaphysics of the moment, as we discussed it in Part III, Section 2, already suggests this: for the moment may be compressed eternity, timeless time, but it is also the nuclear difference of past and future, becoming itself. Now, the 'sublime one' (Part II, Section 14) is the masculine drive separated from the feminine; the moments of beauty and perfection are the feminine separated from the masculine (here, for example, the land as haven from the sea). Only rarely do we see them isolated like this, since precisely such artificial separation is a kind of spiritual illness (or opportunity for comedy and satire). Only in the combination of masculine and feminine does insight and, more importantly, creativity (symbolised as sexual ecstasy, and then as pregnancy and song) happen. Even here in this section the perfect world is struck through with a 'golden mournfulness', and the moment begins to end when the speaker is 'stung . . . in the heart'. The beauty and perfection of the moment is a kind of Apollonian consolation for, or shield from, the double woe that is both the thought of eternal recurrence (the adjective 'ripe' [*reif*] is the opportunity for a pun, for in noun form it also means 'loop' or 'hoop' – thus the 'golden round hoop') and also the requirement that overcoming happen all over again (thus, for example, the pain of birth, the vintner's knife). This moment is thus a moment temporally (taking up, in fact, no time at all) and a moment also in the sense of a constituent part, one side of a whole and healthy human life.

Thus the parts of Zarathustra's psyche struggle: the 'ego' wants to wake and carry on ('many a good stretch of the way is still left for you'), his 'soul' wants to sleep and remain in the perfect, golden moment. Only the ray of sunlight on his face finally wakes Zarahustra: the sun and sky as images of the demands for self-overcoming and the advancement of life, and Zarathustra's continuing 'work'. This leaves Zarathustra desiring for what is elsewhere called the 'Great Midday', the Dionysian new phase when feminine and masculine do not struggle against one another, or alternate cyclically, but form the mode of life whose beauty *is* overcoming: 'when will you drink my soul back into you?'. 'Get up . . . you little thief, you lazybones (*Tagediebin*),' he says. Nietzsche has coined a feminine noun here, suited to the 'soul'. The noun *Tagedieb* (literally, thief of the day – a waster of time) occurs only three times in the text: in Part II, Section 10; Part IV, Section 8; and here. On the first occasion it appeared to be a sexual metaphor. In 'The Voluntary Beggar' things are less clear, but to interpret the voluntary beggar as in some way also voluntarily emasculated or impotent makes a great deal of sense within the symbolic vocabulary of the book. Here in this section (which also repeats the adjective 'little'), Zarathustra is urging his feminine soul, blissfully attuned to the world become perfect, to 'be a man' (this phrase occurs in the shadow's poem in section 16) and get up. In such subtle ways – and some, as we have seen, far less subtle ways – Nietzsche plays gleefully with his carefully constructed symbols of gender.

Section 11, 'The Welcome'

Zarathustra returns to his cave only to hear the same cry of distress – now that Zarathustra is closer, it is clearly composed of many voices. This last point reinforces the allegorical and also autobiographical significance of the superior humans, since they represent the many voices and drives that can make up a 'single' soul (see note on the Comprehensive Soul, with the commentary on Part III, Section 7). Zarathustra, it turns out, had already found the superior humans, they are his guests, meaning also that the 'bait' of Part IV, Section 1 had worked. The last eight sections have been an elaborate riddle, drawn out to ridiculous lengths for comic effect, like a French farce or Shakespearean comedy of mistaken identity. Zarathustra welcomes them, accepting the 'gift' they offer which is the strength and courage to protect and encourage them, offering them in return security in his domain, and also his heart. What we will need to ask ourselves near the end of the book, however, is how this notion of the protecting sovereign relates to the temptation to pity, and to Zarathustra's continuing work.

Notice, though, that the superior humans are only in distress when Zarathustra is not nearby: as the king on the right says, 'at the sight of you' many are refreshed and healed. It is this fact – their dependency upon him, and that these might be only the first few of those who will be dependent – that Zarathustra realises when, in the middle of the passage, he briefly withdraws 'in fright'. This leads him to frankly admit in the second half of the section that this superior mob are *not* those for whom he was waiting, those of the 'great yearning'. The men he has encountered only want to be 'spared' – that is, they represent at bottom a mode of life that lacks courage (thus the reference to 'laughing lions') and reactively wishes to protect itself. The theme of fear and courage is an important one throughout this part; see also Part IV, Section 15. Moreover, they are 'signs' that properly 'superior ones are on their way to me'. We should note that the interpretation of signs, and the interpretation of things as signs, occupies Zarathustra for much of the rest of the book. These observations leave his guests in 'dismay' – although they themselves had said (in the voice of the king on the right) that 'better men are on their way to you'. In any case, these 'superior humans' are poor company for themselves (thus the cry), and for Zarathustra's poor eagle assaulted by needy questions. Thus, 'someone else must come' to lighten the tone – at this point we do not know if this 'someone else' is Zarathustra himself, or the 'others' for whom Zarathustra is waiting.

Section 12, 'The Last Supper'

This section starts the extended satire of the Last Supper as critique of late modernity. The introduction is made here by way of a debate about food and drink, especially bread. Zarathustra lampoons the ascetic core of Christian teaching that puts spiritual above physical nourishment. Zarathustra's 'materialism' comes to the fore again, akin to Brecht's in this point: 'food comes first, morals follow on . . .!' 'The spirit is a stomach' (Part III, Section 12.16). His holistic approach to the body includes diet as part of the practices of internalisation. Bread alludes at least thrice to the Bible. First, 'one cannot live on bread alone' (Deuteronomy 8:3, Matthew 4: 4) but also requires spiritual 'nourishment'; secondly, bread as the symbolic body of Christ in the Last Supper and the sacrament of the Eucharist; thirdly, the 'manna' that feeds the Israelites in the wilderness (Exodus 16: 4ff).[84] Bread (the product of an agrarian, settled culture) is out of tune with a solitary's life so man will have to adapt and make do, but not with spiritual doctrine, but with other, far superior foods. For bread, Zarathustra substitutes the lamb (of Christ), a more carnivorous image (see the sorcerer's song in section 14). The kings have wine (like bread, the product of a relatively advanced social organisation, but Zarathustra does not object), but then they are also the ones that expect bread. The voluntary beggar exhibits an artificial asceticism expressed here in terms of his veganism. To be sure, as with the message of Part III, Section 6 ('Upon the Mount of Olives'), the devising of a successful life-practice and philosophical practice commences with inherited, environmental and acquired dispositions. There is no 'the way'. Thus, the specifics of diet should give way to the meta-virtues of 'strong bones' and 'light feet'. To the voluntary beggar Zarathustra replies, 'as long as it makes you happy'. But this is ironic, for happiness as such is not the point. Modern humanity has forgotten that its habits of nourishment are formed as an immediate consequence of an exchange between man and nature. Nature gives, man receives. The soothsayer is a glutton, overburdening nature (here, Zarathustra's animals); the voluntary beggar may be artificially ascetic; the kings want bread.

Zarathustra's culinary practice is a communal one; Zarathustra envisages the community of the overhuman to be equality among equals – regardless of wider social and political class. (Compare Part III, Section 12.12.) This vision of non-specialised proximity between man and nature comes close to one of the few utopian projections in Marx's *German Ideology* (1845) where it is suggested that non-alienated labour frees up human beings to 'do one thing today and another tomorrow, to hunt in the morning, fish in the afternoon, rear cattle in the evening, criticise after dinner, just as I have a mind, without ever becoming hunter, fisherman, herdsman or critic',[85] a variety of delightful epicurean activities emanating from a well rounded person that might have found Zarathustra's acclamation.

Section 13, 'On the Superior Human'

This section represents the conversation at the table of the Last Supper. It consists of twenty short passages, many of which echo previous sections; the whole is in large part a compressed recapitulation of Zarathustra's description of the superior human for which he seeks and yearns. We find, for example, a repetition of the critique of modern democratic equality and its relation to theism in subsections 1 to 3. More specifically, though, this section provides a portrait of the superior human as that select group who will be able to take charge of the development of the human, and thus be a bridge or step towards the overhuman. With respect to human life as a whole, the superior human has value as a transition.

Let us here note a few important ideas. First, at the end of section 13.3, there is 'I love you for not knowing how to live today'. This is a nice expression of the notion of untimeliness, employed by Nietzsche in the title of an earlier collection of studies (*Untimely Meditations*), and a section in *Twilight of the Idols*. Here, though, it is cast in terms of 'how to live' (a theme anticipated in section 12): the superior humans are fragments of a mode of life that has not yet arrived (see also Part III, Section 20). And yet this mode of life is already at odds with the dominant modes of life it finds around it (see section 13.9, 'this today belongs to the mob'). Thus, section 13.6: 'you shall have it worse and worse'. This latter addition, though, turns swiftly into a rebuke: 'For you suffer from yourselves, and have not yet suffered from *the human*'. In other words, these superior humans' primary motivation remains self-loathing (compare, for example, Part I, Section 16; Part II, Section 5; or Part III, Section 8), an internal struggle of drives and values not yet overcome. Although the individual superior humans, as we saw, echo many of Zarathustra's critiques of modernity, their suffering is still one-dimensional. Such overcoming would not mean the end of suffering, but its intensification, for one suffers from *all* the many varieties of the small, weak or sick, those whose mode of life is a testament to the unrealised possibilities of the human.

Section 13.8 and 9 briefly introduce the themes of truth and lies. The 'mob' is 'innocently crooked and always lies', in the market one only convinces through 'gestures' (play-acting – precisely the sorcerer's strategy), nor should one trust scholars with their 'cold and dried-up eyes' who are unable to lie. The key idea here is that claims of truth or falsehood are always expressions of a will to power. The question to ask is whether such claims are cunning in the service of a reactive mode of life, or rather 'honest' in being the expression of a spirit aligned to the nature of things as will to power. Because of the former, even the victory of a 'truth' (here, for example, a proposition that the free spirit might agree with, superficially) might be in the service of a 'mighty error', in which case a genealogical analysis is called for that will peel back the grounds of a certain claim, disposition or mode of life. However, honesty is not above itself being cunning (the ruse of the honey), and thus 'whoever cannot lie does not know what truth is'. Such honest cunning is not unrelated to what led us, in reference to the end of the Prologue, to call Zarathustra the serious prankster. All this ties into the account of the function of language as bestowing, as in the service of healthy life and its desire for higher forms of life (see Part I, Section 7; and Part III, Section 9).

The notion of honesty takes a different direction in section 13.10 to 13: honesty is now the honesty of one's desire for overcoming. This overcoming must be on 'your own legs'. This being on 'your own legs' reflects the dilemma Zarathustra faces: at what point does his help for the superior humans become a 'crutch'? Similarly, 'one is pregnant only for one's own child'. The grammatical 'for' in this last phrase means something quite different from, for example, 'for one's neighbour' or 'for the sake of justice'. These latter are supposed expressions of an abstract purpose, law or principle which stands behind willing, as if the ground or motivation of will could be distinguished from the act of will. But such a type of willing is indeed beyond the 'capacity' of will. One must be liberated from 'for', 'in order to' and 'because' for two reasons then: first, so that one's work is not in servitude to some other will. The second reason is more general in character: because avoiding this key misrepresentation of the nature of willing is part of the wisdom that is the spiritualisation of such an aligning of the spirit to the nature of will to power. Note that one's overcoming is not owned by and unique to some individual, but is part of the cultural and physiological inheritance of which any individual is a continuation (thus, 'the virtue of your fathers'). In *The Gray Science*, Nietzsche talks about this under the heading of 'atavism' – the appearance in a later generation of a virtue (or vice) originating earlier (see *The Gray Science*, sections 10–11).

Section 13.14 to 20 is a staccato meditation on the theme of laughter at oneself. The superior human as bridge or transition will make attempts or experiments, and will most often fail: they will, for example, make miscalculations in their teaching (as Zarathustra did, he reminds us in the first passage of this section) or fall back into their cries of need or melancholic self-doubt (see, for example, the very next section). Liberated from both a cosmic sense of purpose (God's plan) and also a more human level of historical necessity (such as the progress towards the perfectibility of the human posited by the Enlightenment), we now play at the great 'mocking- and gaming-table' of the Gods. What does it matter, Zarathustra tells us, for so much remains possible and indeed (despite its accidental character) so many small things have worked out perfectly. The lightness of laughter contrasts with Zarathustra's Devil who, now named the spirit of melancholy, features in the next section. Such laughter is what the superior humans finally achieve in the 'ass festival', and yet even then in a fragmentary and fragile form such that they fall back quickly enough.

Section 14, 'The Song of Melancholy'

Throughout the evening, Zarathustra will be exiting and entering; even at home he cannot stop wandering. His guests are putting him out of his home; this is a reflection on the danger of his 'hospitality'. In any case, he goes out for a breath of fresh air – these not-quite-superior-humans are a bit smelly. The theme of good versus bad air runs throughout the next few sections: we have the 'cleared' evening air of the sorcerer's poem, the 'sultry and poisonous' air decried by the conscientious in spirit, the 'muggy air' feared by the shadow and his keen nose, the 'clear Oriental air' of his poem, and so forth. Air, clearly enough, symbolises health, nobility and honesty (see also, for example, Part I, Section 7; also, among many such passages, *Twilight of the Idols*, 'Reason in Philosophy', section 3). Zarathustra here realises by comparison how fond he is of his animals, pure expressions of life's natural virtues. As soon as he leaves, though, the sorcerer stages a philosophical putsch.

In allegorical form Nietzsche here perpetuates the discussion of the differences in spirit, philosophical position and artistic outlook that separate him from Wagner. The sorcerer delivers a speech from out of pure melancholy, another manifestation of nihilism and a form of renouncing the world. He is philosophically stuck in a rut because 'the old God has died and no new God lies as yet in cradles'. Nietzsche portrays here Wagner as a calculating seducer of the senses through fake – but extraordinarily effective – musical conjuring. He also analyses the course of that most modern of mental illnesses since Dürer first drew attention to it in his 1512 etching *Melencolia I.* The depiction of melancholy becomes a major trope in the history of modern Western literature, painting and music – to name but two examples in the area of literature: Robert Burton's (1577–1640) seminal work *Anatomy of Melancholy*, and James Thomson's (1834–82) long Victorian poem *The City of Dreadful Night* (1874). The poem that follows, though, will not be disowned by Zarathustra/Nietzsche; Nietzsche uses it as the very first of the *Dionysian Dithyrambs.* This is an example of a 'truth' on whose behalf a 'mighty error' has fought (section 13.9). Wagner simply cannot help it: he uses an authentic experience of melancholy as a pretext to show off his conjuring tricks. But, clearly, it is he who has become bewitched by Nietzsche, not the other way round![86]

The sorcerer presents us with a more substantial form of this paradoxical state of melancholy than he claims. The sorcerer's 'God is dead' is the state of nihilism, but Zarathustra's thought must be an overcoming of nihilism. As a striving philosophical critic and free spirit, Zarathustra has to justify himself constantly for the poetic means of communication. The poem presents the goal of reaching philosophical truths under conditions of the absence of any transcendent guarantees, as an elusive ideal that can only be realised through constant invention. The Promethean day-work of truth-seeking is followed by night-time despair. And there is doubt – both public and internal – that the narrator who is 'only fool, only poet' (who cannot be taken seriously as philosopher of the conventional type) could ever come into the possession of truths: he is neither scientist, scholar nor priest. So, the poem must also build a metaphor for the nature of truth. It is in the nature of truths themselves and the flux of natural processes within which they are embedded that a form must be found to grasp and express them in such a way that they can have an *effect*. The philosopher can therefore of necessity only express his philosophy in poetic form, because *truth can only be communicated poetically*: Nietzsche's radical anti-Platonic epistemological stance is articulated here. (The reference to Plato is cemented with the word 'banished' at the end.) The poet ensnares truth, by attracting or seducing it, or hunting it like prey. The poem is in the style of a free verse ode. A main feature of Nietzsche's late poetry is its deliberate thematic and stylistic 'hybridity' where the sublime is followed abruptly by the parodistic and the ridiculous. As in *Zarathustra* as a whole, buffoonery and epiphany enter into an uneasy balance in this poetry, which accounts for the strange attractiveness of both.

The first stanza refers directly to Hölderlin's first Pindar-style free verse ode: '*Wie wenn am Feiertage* . . .' ('As when on a holiday . . .)' with its many references of 'recently cleared air' after a night of thunderstorms. The 'heated heart' is asked to remember its thirst of the evening before. This thirst is, as the end of the poem tells us, the result of a day's scorching 'truth-madness', relieved now by night's consoling dew. The poet longs to leave this 'day-yearning' which arrived at 'a single truth' which is '*That I be banished/ From every truth*'. The second stanza asks with those who scoff: how can a mere poet be 'a suitor to truth'? The idea of a 'suitor' (*Freier*, the word is related to 'free', so Nietzsche may intend us to hear 'free to seek marriage' or 'to make free with' – that is, seduce) calls to mind again the gender symbolism; also, see the opening of *Beyond Good and Evil* where, famously, 'truth is a woman'. The qualities in a poet, the demands made by his craft, his aesthetic ('colourfully masked, to itself a mask, speaking mere motley') – do these not turn him into a mere lying fool, as Plato suggested in the *Republic*, preventing him from getting at truths?

In stanza 3, the ground is shifting and the negative qualities of the conventional truth-seekers are being insinuated ('still, stiff, smooth, cold'; 'posted up before temples'; 'the gate-guard of God', and so forth); the Sorcerer cheekily garners several of these images from the dinner conversation (section 13.17). The poet is indeed not a suitor to truth, but only if 'truth' is the kind of thing sterile, sexless, bloodless scholars and scientists are concerned with. This is contrasted with the characteristics of the poet more adequate to captivate elusive truths ('Quick! Into every coincidence', and so forth). The attention to smell is attention to the most bodily of senses, the one linked to primeval hunting. It also reminds us that Zarathustra is not listening because *he* wanted some fresh air – getting away from a smell that the others had not noticed. The image of the cat comes from the previous section too (13.17) and is designated later a 'panther', one of the conventional symbols of Dionysus. Stanza 4 gives us an alternative hunting image of eagle and lamb, taken from Part III, Section 11 and recalling also the dinner that they have all just eaten. (There is also in this, of course, a reference to the hunting down of the herd animal, which anticipates the next image.) The human is God and sheep, not so much a hybrid as a incomplete, stunted fragment. One of the myths concerning Dionysus as God of life and life-cycles is that he was torn apart and returned to life. (Likewise, the ecstatic revellers of Dionysus supposedly tore animals limb from limb.) The poem here suggests that the truth of the human is not a scientific observation, proposition or description. Rather, the truth of the human is an activity or practice of refashioning (ripping apart) the human, constructing the whole, and an activity that in its alignment with the innermost urges of all life for overcoming, does so laughing and blissful.

After this crescendo, there is a much quieter meditation. We return to evening, and the scorched thirst. This time, though, rather than the consoling dew, we have the jealous, green moon, 'hostile towards day', reaping roses that 'sink down' into the night. (The moon is a persistent image in the book, but carries a number of conflicting meanings. See Part III, Section 2.2; and Part II, Section 15.) The rose is the emblem of day-time achievement: not truth, but beauty, perhaps. The poet 'once' suffered from 'truth-madness' and laboured in the day for 'roses'. But, scorched and thirsty, he sank away from his 'day-yearnings' just as these roses do. He is finally 'sick from the light'. Again, we have the devastating thirst that nearly destroyed the poet, and this thirst is now a single truth, couched as an imperative: 'That I be banished/ from every truth'. Before being pronounced derisively by others, 'only fool only poet' had to be pronounced proudly by the poet as his transformation into poet. The end of the poem is thus more bitter triumph than melancholy.

Section 15, 'On Science'

Only the conscientious in spirit is unmoved by the sorcerer's song. The superior humans are articulated by contrasts such as this one, or between soothsayer and voluntary beggar on the subject of food. The sorcerer, whose spirit has no conscience, does not really know or care what he is saying, as long as it has an effect; the conscientious in spirit is too narrow for truth. This fool and poet business is too insecure a position for him, for he has come to Zarathustra seeking the opposite: security. For the seeking of security is the essence of science, he says: science is fear made 'spiritual' (that is, made so as to be active within consciousness and in discourse as a set of principles and virtues). It is a condition of science that it understands its world as one intrinsically understandable and above all controllable. In this way existence can be improved and specific grounds of fear removed (for example, fear of hunger can be removed by technological innovation in farming). But there is a more profound fear also: fear that the world is *not* as science must project it, thus not understandable and not controllable (compare, for example, Part III, Section 12.7–8). As far as it goes, this agrees with Nietzsche's analysis that the conditions of knowledge of the world lie in errors, and serve the preservation of a mode of life (see our discussion and citations in Part I, Section 4).

It is the more profound fear that Zarathustra picks up on when he returns into the cave: the superior human should be courage spiritualised, and courage (not fear) is the whole prehistory of the human; were it not for courage, there would be no history. (Notice in 'prehistory' something of the primeval scenes evoked by the sorcerer's poem.) It is clear that Zarathustra has in mind not just courage in the face of this or that misfortune (something like this was the topic of the last few sections of Part IV, Section 13) but rather a courage that is positive 'pleasure in uncertainty' and which is aligned to the Dionysian nature of things as continuous becoming. Such courage is important because, in the interest of knowledge and enhancement it is willing to risk itself. What is being outlined here – although not fully developed – is a 'gay' or 'joyful science' of seeking and experimenting as presented in *The Gay Science* (see, for example, section 327). At this the sorcerer (always *too* ready to agree, and he thus catches an angry look from Zarathustra) claims his melancholic evil spirit has been overthrown.

Section 16, 'Among the Daughters of the Desert'

The character who is now named as both wanderer and shadow urges Zarathustra not to leave the cave, lest 'the old gloomy misery' might return. It seems that without Zarathustra's presence, the superior humans are still prone to relapse – and indeed, it is relapse that the poem, though good-humouredly, dramatises.

The Last Supper is already at the dessert stage: time for a morsel of fruity poetry. This is another of Nietzsche's late *Dionysus Dithyrambs*. It follows in the footsteps of Goethe's last monumental collection of poetry, the *West-Eastern Divan* ('West-Östlicher Divan') first published 1819 and then in an expanded version in 1827. The idea is that of an intermingling of Western and Eastern cultural perspectives by means of a complex poetic charade or role-play. The wise old Western poet assumes the identity of Hafiz, the foremost poet of the Orient. Western poetry and cultural values reflect on themselves by looking at the contrasting Eastern mirror image, a predecessor of Nietzsche's methodological perspectivism with its continual re-framing according to images of forms of life.[87] Nietzsche follows Goethe's example in using the Orient as a critical lever to prise open encrusted European cultural habits. The metaphoric imagery of the shadow's poem sets up a contrast between European nihilism and Asiatic enclaves of existential balance (which includes here again a rapprochement between the sexes). This poem also provides a commentary on the Asiatic (and Southern) perspective applied throughout the book in making Zarathustra Nietzsche's mouthpiece.

This poem works partly with metaphorical material from earlier, such as in Part II, Section 8, 'On the Famous Wise Men'. The contrast is set up there between the free spirit who 'goes into Godless deserts and has broken his reverential heart', and the 'well-nourished famous wise men', city-dwellers and draught animals who 'draw, as asses – the people's cart'. The poem also picks up on the themes debated earlier in connection with elevation of the body in the moment of sexual release, which dissolves it into the Dionysiac (Part II, Section 10; and Part IV, Section 10, for example). Envisaged is the integration of antagonistic opposites – North and South, Europe and Orient – and these are the symbolic setting for profiling antagonisms such as moral mindedness ('moral roaring-ape') versus easy eroticism, and of course the anthropologically determined frictions between the inner masculine and feminine sides in human beings (desert and oasis). The poem's vision seems to promote a kind of sexually integrated, unified state of being where male and female elements come together forming a harmonious balance in the person ('little date', swaying like the palm, 'be a man, Suleika!').

We enter a harem in an oasis.[88] Again, of course, it is a *ménage à trois*. The solemn European (from the North) barges in 'roaring' with morality, only to find himself transposed into a state of paradisical being where the dichotomies of good and evil have already been eradicated ('nothing for you'), but not completely transposed, since the European pompously alludes continually to his culture and its values: 'very learned allusion', 'linguistic sin', 'as the ancient poets relate' and so forth. At the end of the poem, indeed, he confesses that he cannot quite give up the moral habit either. The palm-tree image in stanza 6 (the only stanza, it should be noted, relatively free of the poet's highly Westernised asides) is either a patently and deliberately ridiculous swooning fantasy, or a (no less ridiculous) trans-gender ('Be a man, Suleika!') image of the female palm tree becoming phallus and ending with fellatio (anticipated already by the biting of the date). This 'climax' gives way to the poem's concluding stanzas where we see the sarcastic reassertion of European moral bathos. There is a clear reference to Luther's peasant-stubbornness: 'I can do no other, so help me God', together with what in the context must be the sexual innuendo of Luther's famous adage 'Here I stand . . .' All this causes hilarity in the deranged 'superior humans'. The Last Supper now deteriorates into complete drunken bedlam.

Sections 17–18, 'The Awakening' and 'The Ass Festival'

Section 17 is rather odd, containing disparate materials. Amid the laughter that greets the wanderer and shadow's song, Zarathustra retreats outside once more to be with his animals. There he expresses a somewhat irritated but still positive appraisal of his guest's 'convalescence' – irritated, because these are 'old people', by which is not only meant 'elderly' but also people who belong to a time that Zarathustra has put behind him, who are thus untimely everywhere. They could never be his 'children'. They may turn out to be valuable fellow workers for human advancement, but they are not this advancement itself. Thus, they convalesce and laugh 'in their own way'. The notion of convalescence, of course, echoes his own recovery from the great weight of the thought of eternal recurrence (Part III, Section 13). Is the spirit of heaviness, which dogged Zarathustra till the end of Part III, now departing from these superior humans? The most hopeful sign is that they are becoming 'thankful' – this is a reference to the overcoming of eternal recurrence, and especially as it is discussed in Part II, Section 20. Their thankfulness, that is, is the ability to 'will backwards' and to make the contingent welcome. Zarathustra anticipates that the Superior Humans will soon be 'planning festivals' – that is to say, making sacred their thanks to life and earth. And, indeed, very shortly the noise abates, and the scent of incense wafts from the cave. Going to investigate, Zarathustra finds the company mock-worshipping the ass, praising the ass's virtues as if they were those of a wise, beneficent and creating God – and using mock-biblical rhetoric, including slightly altered quotations from Luther's translation of the Bible.[89]

Since Aesop's Fables, the ass is one of the key creatures in the European allegorical arsenal of *bestiarium humanum.* In *The Birth of Tragedy* Nietzsche links the rise of these secular morality parables with the end of the tragic age and the rise of modernity; in fact, he links the fable with the origins of the novel as a modern hybrid form. The donkey as a fable type is 'stubborn and clever' (Part II, Section 8 – where clever is used to mean, as it generally does in Nietzsche, 'able to manipulate in small and petty ways', and thus is never that far from 'stupid'), filled with 'ill-will', and the object of ridicule. In *Ecce Homo*, Nietzsche identifies the ass with Germans in particular; Nietzsche is thus the '*anti-ass par excellence*' ('Why I Write Such Good Books', section 2). Particularly here in Part IV the long ears are an important image: they indicate a type who cannot hear Zarathustra and, in general, whose senses are detuned from life and health.

The praise of the ass is the satirical peak where the solemn doctrine of overhuman transformation is mocked, fulfilling the book's oft-said injunction to laugh. The old world of decadence is dying in the helpless laughter, and its representatives can no longer maintain the dignity of their ridiculed positions. As in the prose of Nietzsche's revered role models, Jean Paul, for instance, or Heine, the high epiphany of vision and the irreverent ribaldry and satire are the two equally weighted stylistic faces of this book. The reader should also see the comments in *The Gay Science* on nobility and sacrilege, section 135. Also, notice the notion developed there that nobility consists in having 'no fear of oneself, to expect nothing contemptible from oneself'; this develops into not being ashamed of oneself (here in *Zarathustra* we have seen bad love of oneself; (see also our discussion of Part II, Section 15) and thus the ability to laugh at oneself (*The Gray Science*, sections 294 and 107). Self-mockery would indicate a self that has nothing to hide from itself – it is ontologically honest and has spiritualised that honesty both as 'serious' philosophy and, without contradiction, as self-parody – and which has the lightness of approach (has overcome nihilism and the great burden of eternal recurrence in order to affirm existence) also indicated by the images of dancing or flying.

The section entitled 'The Ass Festival' begins after the festival itself has finished. The asses being celebrated, it would thus appear, are the superior humans themselves. Zarathustra gives us three different interpretations of the festival (the three subsections of 18): in such chaos, the precipitation of order is fragile and may go off in several directions. In the first subsection, each higher human defends himself in his own way, often using little quotations from earlier in the book. The pope claims that it is better to worship God as *any* form, rather than as spirit ('no form', meaning transcendent to the earth); the conscientious in spirit claims that the ass, as embodying the ideal of slowness and stupidity – a kind of paragon of scientific method (see *The Gray Science*, section 231, and compare also section 293) – is 'worthy of belief'; the Ugliest Man argues that one must be an 'annihilator without wrath' and laugh while killing. All these justifications capture something of Zarathustra's teaching, in a way that also extends each of the superior human's own character.

In subsection 2, Zarathustra pronounces all these justifications to be 'disguises', rationalisations after the fact. The excuses they give are elaborate parodies of the knots into which the reasoning of Nietzsche's contemporaries ties itself when trying to deal with the situation of modernity. Behind the disguise, the superior humans had simply become children again – this is, of course, the key symbol of transformation, from Part I, Section 1. Their invented festival is 'a little brave nonsense . . . a rushing wind to blow your souls clear'. Remember this festival, and thereby remember me, he tells them, in an echo of Jesus at the Last Supper. Such ridiculous, parodic festivals are fit to be the sacred institutions of a future community. Zarathustra seems very pleased with these superior humans who have all 'blossomed'. The superior humans, whom Zarathustra at first greeted as not the ones that he sought, and then kept having to leave for better air, are becoming something admirable. But there is still something naggingly fragmentary about their convalescence and transformation. They have become as children, to be sure. However, to become the spirit-child does not mean simply to act like a pious child. Rather, 'we have become men – and *so we want the Kingdom of Earth*,' Zarathustra says. That is why he invites them outside to the night air to cool down. The superior humans still depend too heavily on Zarathustra for stability, security and direction; they may never be capable of the critical distance and autonomy that Zarathustra demanded of his disciples at the end of Part I.

Section 19, 'The Drunken Song'

This section creates a beautiful construction out of many of the book's most potent symbols and ideas: the still moment, death at the right time, the dog howling in the moonlight from 'Part II, Section 2, 'On the Vision and the Riddle', the world becoming perfect, and so forth. It begins with the company invited outside by Zarathustra (itself a sign of both a measure of disapproval at their overheated childishness, but also just how newly 'pleasing' they are to him, since hitherto the cave entrance and night air have been Zarathustra's refuge from his guests) to see his 'night-world'. These 'old people' are 'amazed that on earth they felt so well'. Just before midnight the ugliest man speaks of even *his* being contented (*zufrieden*) with his life and thus his acceptance of eternal recurrence. That he could welcome his life again, without satisfied consciousness of its return, without knowing it or learning from it, and without modification, is an extraordinary overcoming of the despising of self and life, and of the thought of death as escape.

However, Zarathustra is briefly struck dumb. The ugliest man's evocation of the eternal recurrence – the first explicit mention of the idea in Part IV – has set off in Zarathustra an ecstatic reverie, he even speaks in tongues (the symptoms are also strikingly reminiscent of stroke). The narrative repeats lines from 'The Seven Seals' (Part III, Section 16.1). The repeated passage is shortly afterwards followed there by 'verily, long must one hang as heavy weather on the mountains if one is some day to kindle the light of the future'. His vision then has to do with the approaching fulfilment of prophecies, and perhaps also the sign that his true children approach and it is time for his returning to the human (see the next section). That Zarathustra should be prompted to a sustained and poetic reverie on eternal recurrence after the ugliest man's 'one more time', as if reminded of a thought that they had all put aside, may also suggest that (like the *précis* of eternal recurrence that his animals give in Part III, Section 13) the ugliest man's was rather a hurdy-gurdy version – the ugliest man still has not seen and adapted himself to the core of this thought. His use of the verb 'contented', a less than overwhelming choice, reinforces this interpretation (although the German word is different from that used in Prologue, Section 3; the word used here, *zufrieden*, is used at only one other point, in a negative modification, at the beginning of Part I, Section 3); likewise, the use of 'buffoons' and 'jesters' in Part IV, Section 18.2. In contrast to 'contented', the key word in what follows is 'joy' (*Lust*). It is not that one should doubt the sincerity of the ugliest man, or the new-found health and thankfulness of the rest of Zarathustra's guests. However, upon recovering somewhat, Zarathustra does push away their hands and, moreover, the section that follows makes clear that (as Zarathustra said already in the Welcome) they are not the ones whose spirits are fully realigned and consummate with the will to power and the thought of eternal recurrence; they are not his children.

As a soothsayer himself, Zarathustra anticipates by a few moments the tolling of the bell at midnight. The bell is the voice of Deep Midnight which speaks 'secretly', 'terribly' and 'heartily (*herzlich*, thus literally of or with the heart: warm, heartfelt)' to Zarathustra. Midnight is the darkest hour, the hour of least light, where the contours of things melt into one another, the time of penetration to the ground of things. Reciprocally, midday is the hour of least shadow, it is the moment of neither burden of the past nor struggle towards the future (thus the Great Midday is the very arrival of the future). In the text, midnight is thus also a place of melancholic thoughts or dreams (Part IV, Section 14.3; and here, 'already counted out the heart and pain beats of your fathers'). It is most obviously associated with death (as at Part II, Section 19, 'the mountain-castle of death'; Part III, Section 2, 'when even dogs believe in ghosts'; and Part III, Section 15, 'you want to leave me soon'). More importantly, though, midnight *like* midday is also a moment of transition, when one phase of the day passes over to another. Thus, the above cited passages are also points of change or overcoming (the storm at the gates of death, the shepherd biting off the snake's head, the overcoming of the desire to leave life, and also see the first sentence of Part III, Section 1 which follows on from 'The Stillest Hour'). What follows here in this section are a series of short passages each of which ends with a line from the midnight bell-tolling poem from Part III, Section 15.3, minus only the first person lines (which thus means that the whole section has exactly twelve parts). The entire poem is then repeated at the end of the section. Notice that the poem comes from the end of the section which is immediately prior to that containing the lines quoted above ('The Seven Seals'). Zarathustra is thus repeating for his guests, speaking on behalf of Deep Midnight, moments from his own convalescence at the end of Part III: the midnight bells are the moment of his overcoming of disgust with and desire to flee from life, the 'Seven Seals' are the song of the affirmation of eternal recurrence. As is made clear in the final section of the book, though, this turns out to *also* be a convalescence *from* Zarathustra's period of engagement with the superior humans, and thus a transition to the next (unwritten – though Nietzsche did at one point plan further parts) stage of his teaching.

What is new here is the meditation on woe (*Weh*) and joy (*Lust*), which in the original poem are left without any additional comment. A mode of life that conceives of itself as woe is a despising of life, though even this despising is a product of life and its servant (see Part I, Section 4: 'The creating Self created for itself respecting and despising, it created joy and woe'). But let us compare that earlier passage and this one. There, such self-despising life serves life in the merely negative sense that, because it can no longer 'create beyond itself', it 'wants to die'. Here, though, we have something quite different: 'all that suffers wants to live, that it may become ripe . . . yearning for what is farther, higher, brighter'. When suffering says here 'I do not want me', this is not simple self-loathing and thus not an appeal for death or for escape. Rather, what is being described here is a mode of suffering that is healthy and *productive*, akin to Zarathustra's remark in Part IV, Section 16.6 – 'you . . . have not yet suffered from *the human*' – or to the urgent need of the vintner's knife in Part III, Section 14.

But, deeper even than such productive woe is joy. Joy does not want children, it wants itself. However, this too must not be misinterpreted: it is not that joy is unproductive or without relation to the 'work'. For joy *also* wants woe, and thus *also* wants the yearning for ripeness and children. Joy wants itself: this means joy wants the world as it is, was and will be. Joy is thus the redemption of the moment through eternal recurrence. In addition to the metaphysical account in Part III, Section 2, 'Moment (*Augenblick*)' is used symbolically in two contrasting ways. First, it is used as the ephemeral moment (for example, in Part I, Section 9, 'you would throw yourselves away less on the moment'; or Part II, Section 11, 'you divine moments! How quickly you died away!'; likewise as an achievement to which one is no longer adequate: Part I, Section 9; and Part IV, Section 5.2). Secondly, it is used as the ecstatic, somehow timeless vision in all the songs of epiphany. We can finally see now how the notion of eternal recurrence removes the contradiction between these two. As we saw already in the gateway of the 'moment' (Part III, Section 2) – which occurs precisely within a vision – the moment is both fleeting, what we called there the nuclear difference of past and future, but it is also the point from which the two opposing lanes of past and future can be inspected precisely in their continuity, their being 'all chained together, entwined, in love'. Joy is the only state of spirit that is not, intrinsically and in its being, a denial of eternal recurrence. Joy has overcome woe without simply leaving it behind. That is, joy is the affect belonging to that mode of life that has aligned itself to the will to power and the thought of eternal recurrence, and done so in such a way as to not *also* abandon its 'work' for the overhuman. Joy is feminine and masculine. (See *The Gray Science*, section 288 where an 'elevated mood' embodied is described as 'a continual sense of ascending stairs and at the same time of resting on clouds'.)

Section 20, 'The Sign'

It is confirmed here that Zarathustra is leaving the superior humans behind, still asleep and severely intoxicated. (There is an allusion here to Socrates, having drunk everyone under the table, leaving the *Symposium* at dawn, clear-headed.) Zarathustra emerges to greet the sun – just like in Prologue, Section 1, the book having come full circle. He exclaims: 'They are not my rightful companions!' For the last time Zarathustra is struck down in a timeless-time reverie induced by his animals and the arrival of the 'sign'. A flurry of dove circles him, along with a lion (who, when a bird's wing tickles his nose, laughs). This fulfils the prophecy of Part III, Section 12.1. As we noted earlier, the laughing lion is a modified version of the final, child-spirit transformation of Part I, Section 1. The superior humans, presumably, can be the child and 'invent' a new festival (but not perhaps with the quality of innocence, since they put on disguises immediately after), *or* they can be the lion. As we shall see in a moment, they cannot yet be both; they are still fragments of human overcoming. The superior humans finally arise and come outside, startling the lion who leaps at them – they cry out 'as if from a single voice' and scamper. This is the cry of need again, and it sparks a recollection and realisation from Zarathustra (as if the whole of Part IV after section 2 was a dream from which he is awaking). The soothsayer's temptation to pity was for just these superior humans – and that pity was what sought out their cry, invited them to his cave and served them as crutch through their melancholic moods and fragmented convalescence. Zarathustra stands, '*That* – has had its time!'. He will now leave them to it. He is going down for the last time, his children await. But of course they are not represented in the text – they are represented in the *future readers* of the text.

3. Study Aids

Types of Question You Will Encounter

There are five broad types of assignment you are likely to encounter. These are:

1. *Explanation*: the assignment is typically to take a short passage from *Zarathustra* and explicate it. This means (1) to lay out in detail the structure, meaning of key terms or symbols, and overall sense of the passage; (2) to put it into context with respect to what Nietzsche is up to in surrounding passages; (3) possibly also to contextualise it with respect to Nietzsche's work as a whole, and other philosophies (for example, Schopenhauer); (4) possibly also to bring to bear on the passage the varying interpretations from the secondary literature, and reasons behind these interpretations. You may also be asked to assess the *validity* of Nietzsche's views here.

2. *Philosophy and literature questions*: *Zarathustra* is a great work of philosophy but also a great work of literature, and the two aspects cannot be separated. Questions of this type are asking you to explore how the one goal is achieved through the other. For example, 'What is the significance of the food and drink imagery in the text?' This begins as a literary question, asking you to assemble and discuss the relevant images, and then look behind them, so to speak, for the philosophical ideas or analyses (for example, health or nature) that might be represented through these images.

3. *Issues in Nietzsche interpretation*: Few philosophers have excited such a wide variety of interpretations, which are so energetic in their disagreement. There are many different 'Nietzsches' around. This type of question is asking you to compare a few of these, usually on a specific topic (for example, eternal recurrence), giving each a fair, detailed and well researched representation, and then to critically assess which you have

discovered to be most valid. The methods of critical assessment should vary from the internal logic of the positions ('X seems to contradict himself in saying . . .'), and the evidence in Nietzsche ('To agree with this position, we would have to ignore what Nietzsche writes in . . .'), to the implications for other issues ('Y's interpretation seems plausible on its own terms, but becomes less so when we extend it to Nietzsche's account of . . .').

4. *Contemporary philosophy problems*: Here the focus is on a debate characteristic of Nietzsche's historical period. An example would be 'Does Nietzsche have a theory that corresponds to Marx's account of ideology?' Again, you will probably be expected to bring to bear and assess the interpretations of commentators. Notice that such questions are often comparative in nature. The important things to remember with comparative assignments are, first, to do a thorough and balanced job on *both* sides, and, secondly, to not just leave these accounts side by side but to actually do the work of comparing and evaluating them, point by point.

5. *Philosophical problems*: The task is to use a Nietzschean analysis to try to illuminate a philosophical problem that is not historically specific, or which is 'of today'. An example is 'What if anything does Nietzsche add to our understanding of evolution?'

Tips for Writing about Nietzsche

1. It is easy to get lost in Nietzsche. 'I know he says X somewhere, but where, and even in which book?' When you take notes, therefore, it is even more important than usual to write down page references.

2. Different translators render terms differently, and you do not want to be making a point in your essay based upon a difference in translation, rather than a real point in Nietzsche's German. Most English translations provide many helpful footnotes about the translations of terms (always read the notes!), as well as bilingual glossaries or indexes. The Project Gutenberg ebook website has the German text available for download.

3. Avoid the temptation to write like Nietzsche. The result is unlikely to be clearer than the original, so what's the point?

4. Again, Nietzsche does not develop a precise philosophical vocabulary in this book – not in the usual sense, at any rate. But there is an elaborate system of images and symbols, which play a similar role. Treat

this system with the same care, precision and consistency as you would the technical vocabulary in a very different philosopher.

5. Do not quote Nietzsche and then move on, as if the quotation were self-explanatory. If it were, you would not need to write an essay! Instead, write a sentence like 'What Nietzsche means is this . . .', or even 'There are two ways of interpreting what Nietzsche means here . . .' Your job is to explain and make things clearer, not just to assemble quotations.

Notes

1. Introduction and Historical Context

1. See the section on 'The Swiss Nietzsche' in Guide to Further Reading.
2. Gründer, Karlfried (1989).
3. See section on 'Nietzsche and His Impact on German Culture and Politics' in Guide to Further Reading.
4. Compare *Ecce Homo*, 'Why I am a Destiny', 3.
5. *Ecce Homo*, 'Thus Spoke Zarathuatra', 1.
6. *Twilight of the Idols*, 'What I Owe the Ancients', 4–5.
7. The Herzogin Anna Amalia Bibliothek, Weimar, Germany, holds the remainder of Nietzsche's library. Shelf mark C701.
8. And see Martina Lauster (1995)
9. It is always possible to consult the notebooks to glean further clarification. We agree, however, with the critical voices warning against elevating the notebooks to the status of final pronouncements. There is a contrary view, though, which is that Nietzsche was cautious in his publications and hid his most far-reaching ideas in the notebooks. See Guide to Further Reading.
10. See especially Michel Foucault (1991), pp. 76–100.
11. Cf. 'On the Uses and Disadvantages of History for Life', in *Untimely Meditations* (1997), pp. 57–124.
12. See sections on '*Zarathustra*: Contexts and Origins' and 'Nietzsche, Greek and Asian Cultures, Tragedy and Mythology' in Guide to Further Reading.
13. Robert Hollander draws attention to the fact that Dante was involved in a dispute about the two cardinal ways of symbolising meaning in allegory. See Introduction to Dante *The Inferno* (2000), pp. xxx–xxxi.
14. In ancient times allegory was defined as "otherspeech", in which a speaker or writer said one thing but meant something else by it . . . If

I say "Beatrice" I do not mean her, but what she means, . . . We can discard the literal for its significance, or in more modern terms, the signifier for the signified': Hollander's Introduction to Dante *The Inferno* (2000), p. xxx. Here, we claim that Nietzsche's use of allegory is more complex than this: the signifier and its context in the text is not simply transparent.

15. On allegory and modernity see Walter Benjamin (2009).
16. Cf. Nietzsche, *Der Musikalische Nachlass* (1976).
17. See section on '*Zarathustra* and Nietzsche's New Style' in Guide to Further Reading.
18. On *Parsifal*, see Paul Schofield (2007).
19. Curt Paul Janz (2007), pp. 22–8.
20. Richard Wagner (1899), vol. 3 p. 74.
21. See also Hermann Hesse (1971).
22. See section on 'Aesthetics of Modernism' in Guide to Further Reading.
23. See commentary on Part III, Section 4, and a note on Epiphany.
24. Joyce (1978), pp. 188–89.
25. See section on 'Nietzsche's Impact on Twentieth-Century Philosophy and Theory' in Guide to Further Reading.
26. For example, Adorno and Horkheimer (2002), which shows strong echoes of Nietzsche's psychology of culture in its juxtaposition of 'primeval' Greek and post-Homeric Enlightenment culture.
27. Cf. Jung (1988) and other entries in 'Twentieth-Century Psychology and Cultural Anthropology' in Guide to Further Reading.
28. Martin Heidegger (1991).
29. Gilles Deleuze (2006)
30. See Foucault entries in Guide to Further Reading. Also see Clayton Koelb (1990) and Paul de Man (1979).
31. Gilles Deleuze and Félix Guattari (2004).
32. Jacques Derrida (1991).
33. Gianni Vattimo (2008).
34. See 'Commentary' in Guide to Further Reading.

2. A Guide to the Text

1. Plato, *The Republic* 507bff.
2. The market place stands for the centre of the town or city and also its essence as a mode of social living (see *Republic* II 371b). It is also the place where Socrates did much of his teaching (see *Apology* 17c), and the

contrast between Socrates' relative success and Zarathustra's failure in the market tells us much about Nietzsche's conception of the former.

3. This is satire also at the expense of the Hegelian absolute end of history when human progress has reached its destination. Such a progress has transcended history. What Nietzsche/Zarathustra requires is a conception of time such that transcendence of this (or any other) type is rigorously impossible. This conception is provided by eternal recurrence (see Part III, Section 2).
4. See *Ecce Homo*. 'Why I Write Such Good Books', 1.
5. See Robert Gooding-Williams (2001), especially pages 23 ff. Also, see 'Bartleby; or, the Formula' in Deleuze (1997).
6. See also *Beyond Good and Evil*, 230.
7. Spiritualisation is thus one manner in which life changes itself. It is the first element in a whole taxonomy of the mechanisms or processes by which new forms develop. Other obvious elements found in *Zarathustra* include creation, revenge, or degeneration. Thus, Nietzsche names a chapter in *Beyond Good and Evil* 'The Natural History of Morals'; and the book that follows gives us in its title the famous concept of genealogy.
8. See *Kritische Studienausgabe* 11, 28 [47].
9. Simon William (2004), pp. 5–19.
10. See Frazer S. Clark (2006); Hugh Ridley (1980), pp. 338–55.
11. Nietzsche's conception of Self influences what Freud later calls 'superego'.
12. Freud's 'death drive' or *thanatos* seems anticipated here. See Sigmund Freud (1955 and 1961), Volume XVIII, pp. 7–64, and Volume XIX.
13. For one of many alternative views, see Sarah Kofman (1993).
14. For Schopenhauer, insofar as it is not appearance and thus not subject to the forms of appearance, the Will cannot be 'many'. However, it also cannot be 'one'. Nietzsche's account of will to power as relationality is thus an attempt to think without constitutive reference to number. (See also Plato's *Parmenides*.)
15. It is a materialism, of course, that does not commence with the positing of a basic matter, such as the atom.
16. Gilles Deleuze and Félix Guattari (2004).
17. Wilhelm Reich (1973).
18. See Stephen J. Costello (2002).
19. Cf. *The Genealogy of Morality*, particularly Second Treatise, sections 4, 13 and 14. And see *Twilight of the Idols*, 'Skirmishes of an Untimely Man', 45.
20. See *Ecce Homo*. 'Why I am So Clever', 1.

21. This is an interesting hypothesis for the understanding of Fascism, broadly similar to Adorno and Horkheimer (2002).
22. See *The Gay Science*, section 107, for a discussion of roles of art, the fool and laughter.
23. Bertolt Brecht (1994).
24. See Carlyle's critique of 'mechanisation' as outlined in 'Signs of the Times' (1986), p. 67.
25. See Hans-Ulrich Wehler (1993), and 'Nietzsche and His Impact on German Culture and Politics' in Guide to Further Reading.
26. Plato and Aristotle discuss the importance of leisure to philosophy in *The Republic* and *Nicomachean Ethics* respectively.
27. See the essay 'Friendship' in Emerson (1983).
28. Cf. John Richardson (2004).
29. Cf. Max Nordau (1892). See 'Nietzsche and Science' in Guide to Further Reading.
30. Darwin in the *Origin of Species* frequently references the work of Alexander von Humboldt.
31. Cf. Gregory Moore (2002).
32. They are in Darwin (1883) too. (See note on Nietzsche and Evolution, with the commentary on Part I, Section 15.)
33. See Ludwig Tieck's novella *The Fair-Haired Eckbert* (1863) where the old woman is a synthetic metaphor, part Greek moirae (spinning the thread of fate), Northern norn, the holy mother of God, nun and witch.
34. Curt Paul Janz (2007), p. 15.
35. Karl Marx (1974), pp. 74 and 92–93.
36. *The Genealogy of Morality*, Second Treatise, sections 4, 5 and 6.
37. There is a sophisticated link to Plato here (*Republic* 507b ff), where there is the image of the sun bestowing like an overfull treasury, and where this is symbolic not of a specific idea but rather of the Good, the condition of any idea.
38. Nietzsche writes 'this turning of all need' – see Parkes' note on page 296 of the Oxford edition. We will only add that there is a clear connection between this idea of a 'turning' and both the notions of moment and redemption of contingency as Nietzsche develops them at the beginning of Part III. Please also see our discussions throughout concerning what we have called the 'alignment' of body or spirit with the nature of will to power. At the level of the whole of human life, the Great Midday is a key image of such a moment of turning; see Part IV, Section 10, and *Kritische*

Studienausgabe 10, 21 [3], 22: 'The great Midday as turning point – the two paths.' (Our translation).

39. For a brief discussion, see Douglas Burnham (2005).
40. Sonneto XIV. A VITTORIA COLONNA. [1550.]

    When divine Art conceives a form and face,/ She bids the craftsman for his first essay/ To shape a simple model in mere clay :
    This is the earliest birth of Art's embrace.
    From the live marble in the second place/ His mallet brings into the light of day/A thing so beautiful that who can say
    When time shall conquer that immortal grace ?

41. A principle that is at the core of all Nietzsche's writings right from the beginning (*The Birth of Tragedy*, his first book). See note on Nietzsche, Music and Language, with the commentary on Part II, Section 17.
42. This ontological point is often spoken of epistemologically, for example in terms of 'honesty' or 'understanding', and here even in terms of a *lack* of awareness by 'you virtuous ones'.
43. Emerson (1983) pp. 563 and 560.
44. Thomas Carlyle (1986), pp. 149-282. But see *Ecce Homo*, 'Why I Write Such Good Books', 1.
45. Imaginary conversations are a popular genre in European nineteenth-century writing, cf. for example the English post-Romantic Walter Savage Landor (2006).
46. The reader should notice the interesting parallels of grammar and sentence structure with *Beyond Good and Evil*, section 56.
47. Eliot (2002), Part V, 431.
48. All three of these are collected in the Cambridge edition of *The Birth of Tragedy*.
49. Accordingly, at several points Zarathustra clearly considers style more important than content (e.g., Part III, Sections 7 and 13). One reason is that style reveals more, for it is a more immediate expression of the underlying will to power. Thus also Joyce chose Carlyle and Nietzsche's *Zarathustra* in his parodic history of style in 'The Oxen of the Sun' in *Ulysses*.
50. The verb 'express' is here '*darstellen*', with its theatrical connotations, and elsewhere 'expressions' is '*Ausdrücke*'; it is definitely not to be translated as 'represents' or 'representations', for reasons obvious enough.
51. See 'Nietzsche, Music and Wagner' in Guide to Further Reading.
52. Curt Paul Janz (2007).

53. See Graham Parkes (2008).
54. Notice the 'glass coffins'; they are like display cases and thus the castle is a kind of museum (Nietzsche may have had an institution like the British Museum in mind). The point being made is that there is a relation between the urge to collect the past and the cultural exhaustion of which the Soothsayer is a symptom (see also Part II, Section 14).
55. The beautifully comic evocation of 'an ear as large as a human being' is probably a reference to Wagner, although *not* to the 1869 *L'Eclipse* cartoon, which is of an ordinary-eared Wagner driving the stake of his music into a giant ear.
56. On the mask, see especially *Beyond Good and Evil* section 40, not forgetting that the section is partly autobiographical! We must keep in mind that the mask is not something voluntarily put on or taken off, nor rigorously separable from what it masks. Rather, the mask is a way of pointing to the fundamental importance of relations: between social strata, between individuals, and indeed within individuals.
57. The dog also refers to Tieck (1927).
58. See Walter Benjamin (1992), p. 249. There may be a link here also to Nietzsche's advocacy of small-scale, compressed musical works, in contrast to the epic scale of Wagner. See Janz (2007), p. 25.
59. Klossowski (2000), especially pp. 93–120.
60. Part, then, of Nietzsche's comprehensive immanence is the dismissal not only of transcendence in the sense of a God or the Platonic forms, but also transcendence within the nature of time. This would include any 'law' of time that was not merely an abstraction from time; also, there could be no Hegelian absolute at the end of history. Note that in Aristotle circular motion (described in the *Physics*) might be seen as a kind of prototype for his thinking (in the *Nicomachean Ethics*) of an act that is its own end.
61. See the Nietzsche's Notebooks: Kaufmann (1968) and Bittner (ed.) (2003).
62. On such a conception, *every* moment is a decisive moment in which the whole of history and the realisation of human possibilities is wrapped. This was no doubt hugely influential for Heidegger's notion of the moment of insight – although Heidegger tends to gesture back towards Aristotle's treatment of *kairos*, the decisive (or correct) moment (see *Nicomachean Ethics* Books II and IV and Heidegger [1988] p. 288).
63. *The Birth of Tragedy*, 'Attempt', section 3.
64. In the Surrealist Manifesto of 1924.
65. Jean Paul (2004), pp. 66–7.

66. The correspondence of landscape and states of mind is a well established Romantic and Gothic trope: e.g. Caspar David Friedrich's painting *Lost Hope*, the work of Tieck and the ground-breaking novella *Lenz* by Georg Büchner (2004).
67. By 'exterior' here we mean the essential relationality of will to power, such that every 'thing' has no metaphysically original 'interior' but appears as what it is from out of a field of relations that lies 'outside' of it. (See Burnham 2004, especially chapters one and two.) This exterior is thus physiological (referring to the set of drives that make 'me' up), spatial (referring, for example, to the set of material or soical relations within which I find myself) and temporal (thus the problems of the redemption of the past in a 'whole' human being of the future). Nietzsche's thought here owes much to Emerson. Emerson (1983), 'The Poet', p. 448. See also Emerson's sustained work on 'representative men'.
68. Nietzsche's position seems to rely upon the inheritance of acquired characteristics, an idea now long abandoned by genetics, but still defensible in the context of culture (as in contemporary dual inheritance theory).
69. See Part I, Section 2; and Part II, Section 14.
70. Moreover, they roughly coincide with the subdivisions of Freud's later model in subconscious, the ego and the superego.
71. 'Stutter' and 'stammer' translate the same German word.
72. For a discussion of this idea, see Burnham (2007), pp. 83 ff.
73. See *Writings from the Late Notebooks* 37 [4]. The end of this passage is a fine moment of self-mockery between Nietzsche's voice and Ariadne. Ariadne is 2,000 years behind – and ahead.
74. On Nietzsche, women and the sea, see Irigiray (1991.
75. Cf. George Lièbert (2004), pp. 30–49.
76. Nietzsche worked on other sections of *Zarathustra*, and intermittently on a drama based on Zarathustra, both of which included a female character usually called 'Pana'. (This is a feminine version of the name Pan, the Greek god associated with Dionysus. It also, though, suggests Pandora.) This material sheds light on Nietzsche's struggle to arrive at an adequate gender-symbolism. See especially David B. Allison (2001) pp. 159ff., and Krell (1986).
77. See Roger Hollinrake (1982), p. 47.
78. Cf. Joachim Lutacz (1994).
79. Flaubert (2000), pp. 460–4.
80. Johann Wolfgang von Goethe (1824, 1827).

81. Also see *Untimely Meditations* I, p. 54
82. A similar idea is found in Boehme, and has entered popular religious discourse ('one eye on eternity . . .').
83. The masculine and feminine are thus basic modes in which the will to power realises itself in appearance. The third mode is the Dionysian, the creative, which is both masculine and feminine. The first two modes, if considered in themselves as *ends*, would be a falsification of the nature of will to power.
84. The reader should note many parallels to the Exodus passage: flesh in the evening, dew, honey, and even Moses's 'Who am I?' is a mirror image of Zarathustra's 'What do I matter?'.
85. Marx and Engels (1970).
86. See Roger Hollinrake (1982), p. 78.
87. Goethe (1998). And see Edward Said (1979), although Goethe's East is by no means as naive or self-serving as attitudes towards the Orient as paraded in Oriental Gothic: Beckford's *Vathek, An Arabian Tale* (1886), for example, or Coleridge's *Kubla Khan* (1797).
88. If we step outside the image, the 'daughters of the desert' might as well be connected autobiographically, referring to Nietzsche's legendary brothel experience. See Frances Nebitt Oppel (2005) and Philip Grundlehner (1986).
89. Nietzsche in these sections creates a hybrid of two festivals common across Europe in the Medieval period up to the sixteenth century: the Feast of Fools and the Feast of the Ass. The former involved a comic social inversion, with young people of low social station being named 'Pope' or 'Bishop'. The latter celebrated the ass that took the holy family on the flight to Egypt. The assembly would 'hee-haw' their responses to the Priets's words. Nietzsche takes such events as evidence of an irrepressible spiritualisation of the Dionysiac and of the 'chaos within' (Prologue, Section 5) even cultures that otherwise looked stagnant.

Bibliography and Guide to Further Reading

The Texts

As our 'baseline' translation, we use Graham Parkes's new translation, Friedrich Nietzsche, *Thus Spoke Zarathustra* (Oxford: World's Classics, 2005) – both because it is an excellent translation and especially musical, and also because it includes more than the usual quantity of helpful notes. The standard German text is volume 4 of the *Kritische Studienausgabe*, ed. Giorgio Colli and Mazzino Montinari, (Berlin: Walter de Gruyter, 1988 [inexpensively reissued in 1999 by dtv]). See also William H. Schaberg, *The Nietzsche Canon. A Publication History and Bibliography* (Chicago: University of Chicago Press, 1995).

Nietzsche's other publications are quoted by part and section (for example, *Ecce Homo*, 'Zarathustra', section 3)

Beyond Good and Evil (BGE), ed. Rolf-Peter Horstmann and Judith Norman, trans. Judith Norman (Cambridge: Cambridge University Press, 2002).

The Birth of Tragedy (BoT), trans. Ronald Speirs (Cambridge: Cambridge University Press, 1999).

The Anti-Christ (AC), Ecce Homo (EH), Twilight of the Idols (TI), ed Asron Ridley and Judith Norman, trans. Judith Norman (Cambridge: Cambridge University Press, 2005).

The Genealogy of Morality (GM), ed. and trans. Maudemarie Clark and Alan J. Swensen (Indianapolis: Hackett, 1998).

The Gay Science (GS), ed. Bernard Williams, trans. Josefine Nauckhoff and Adrian Del Caro (Cambridge: Cambridge University Press, 2001).

Der Musikalische Nachlass, ed. Curt Paul Janz (Basel: Bärenreiter, 1976).

Untimely Meditations, ed. Daniel Breazeale, trans. R. J. Hollingdale (Cambridge: Cambridge University Press, 1997).

Nietzsche's Notebooks

Bittner, Rüdiger (ed.) and Kate Sturge (trans.), *Writings from the Late Notebooks* (Cambridge: Cambridge University Press, 2003).

Breazeale, Daniel (ed. and trans.), *Philosophy and Truth: Selections from Nietzsche's Notebooks of the Early 1870's* (Amherst: Humanity Books, 1979).

Gray, Richard T. (trans.), *Unpublished Writings from the Period of* 'Unfashionable Observations', (Stanford: Stanford University Press, 1999).

Kaufmann, Walter, *Will to Power* (London: Vintage, 1968).

(*The Will to Power* is a collection of Nietzsche's notebook entries, severely edited and given a dubious structure by Nietzsche's sister, in an apparent attempt to make Nietzsche look friendly to far-right political movements. It worked. Kaufmann's edition helps the reader to make more balanced judgements).

Commentary

Lampert, Laurence, *Nietzsche's Teaching: An Interpretation of 'Thus Spoke Zarathustra* (New Haven: Yale University Press, 1986).

Rosen Stanley, *The Mask of Enlightenment: Nietzsche's Zarathustra* (Cambridge: Cambridge University Press, 1995).

Whitlock, Greg, *Returning to Sils Maria - Commentary to Nietzsche's Also Sprach Zarathustra* (New York: Peter Lang, 1990).

Biography and General Commentary

Allison, David B. *Reading the New Nietzsche* (Lanham, Maryland: Rowan & Littlefield, 2001).

Ansell-Pearson, Keith (ed.), *A Companion to Nietzsche* (Oxford: Blackwell, 2006).

Danto, Arthur C., *Nietzsche as Philosopher* (Chichester: Macmillan, 1965).

Grundlehner, Philip, *The Poetry of Friedrich Nietzsche* (Oxford: Oxford University Press, 1986).

Hollingdale, R. J, *Nietzsche. The Man and his Philosophy* (Cambridge: Cambridge University Press, 1999).

Irigiray, Luce, *Marine Lover of Friedrich Nietzsche.* Trans. Gillian C. Gill. (New York: Columbia University Press, 1991).

Janz, Curt Paul, *Nietzsche Biographie*, 3 vols (Munich: Hanser, 1978).

Janz, Curt Paul *Zugänge zu Nietzsche. Ein persönlicher Bericht* ('Approaches to Nietzsche.

A Personal Report') (Basel: Schriftenreihe der Stiftung Basler Orchester-Gesellschaft [Proceedings of the Foundation Orchestra Society Basel], 2007).

Kaufmann, Walter A., *Nietzsche: Philosopher, Psychologist, Antichrist* (Princeton: Princeton University Press, 1974).

Klossowski, Pierre. *Nietzsche and the Vicious Circle* [1969], trans. by Daniel W. Smith (London, Athlone, 2000).

Krell, David Farrell. *Postponements: Woman, Sensuality and Death in Nietzsche.* (Indiana University Press, 1986).

Luchte, James (ed.), *Nietzsche's Thus Spoke Zarathustra: Before Sunrise* (London: Continuum, 2008).

Marsden, Jill, *After Nietzsche* (Basingstoke: Palgrave, 2002).

Safranski, Rüdiger, *Nietzsche. A Philosophical Biography* (London: Granta 2003).

Salomé, Lou Andreas, *Nietzsche* [1892], trans. and ed. by Siegfried Mandel (Chicago: University of Illinois Press, 2001).

Sedgwick, Peter R., *Nietzsche: A Critical Reader* (Oxford: Blackwell, 1995).

Tanner, Michael, *Nietzsche* Oxford: Oxford University Press 1994;

Vattimo, Gianni, *Nietzsche: An Introduction*, trans. Nicholas Martin (London: Continuum, 2002).

Zarathustra: Contexts and Origins

Anonymous, *Theologica Germanica*, trans. Susanna Winkworth (London W. F. Draper, 1857).

Ansell-Pearson, Keith *An Introduction to Nietzsche as Political Thinker* (Cambridge: Cambridge University Press, 1994).

Ansell-Pearson Keith, *Nietzsche and Modern German Thought* (London: Routledge, 1991).

Baudelaire, Charles, *Les fleurs du mal* (The Flowers of Evil) (Oxford: World's Classsics, 1993.)

Baudelaire, Charles, *The Painter of Modern Life and other Essays* (London: Phaidon, 1970).

Benjamin, Walter, *Theses on the Philosophy of History*, *Illuminations*, with an Introduction by Hannah Arendt (London: Fontana, 1992).

Brobjer, Thomas H., 'Nietzsche as German Philosopher', in *Nietzsche and the German Tradition* (Bern: Lang, 2003), pp. 40-82.

Büchner, Georg, *Lenz*, trans. Richard Sieburth (New York: Archipelago Books, 2004).

Burnham, Douglas, *Kant's Philosophies of Judgement* (Edinburgh: Edinburgh University Press, 2004).

Burnham, Douglas, *Reading Nietzsche An Analysis of Beyond Good and Evil* (Stockfield: Acnmen, 2007).

The Cambridge Companion to Darwin, ed. Jonathan Hodge, Gregory Radick (Cambridge: Cambridge University Press, 2003).

Carlson, Elof Axel, *The Unfit. A History of a Bad Idea* (New York: Cold Spring Harbor Laboratory Press, 2001).

Carlyle, Thomas, 'Signs of the Times' [1829], in *Selected Writings*, (London: Penguin 1986), pp. 59-86.

Carlyle, Thomas, 'Chartism' [1839], in *Selected Writings* (London: Penguin 1986), pp. 149-282.

Darwin, Charles *The Descent of Man, and Selection in Relation to Sex* (London: John Murray, 1883).

Eigen, Sarah et al. (eds), *The German Invention of Race* (Albany: State University of New York Press, 2006).

Emerson, Ralph Waldo, *Essays and Lectures* (New York: Library of America, 1983).

Fichte, J. G., *The Closed Trading State* [1800] and *Addresses to the German Nation* [1808], ed. and trans. Gregory Moore (Cambridge: Cambridge University Press, 2008).

Flaubert, Gustave *Sentimental Education* (Oxford: World's Classics, 2000).

Goethe, Johann Wolfgang von, *Faust*, Parts 1 and 2, trans. David Luke (Oxford: Oxford Worlds Classics, 1998 and 2008).

Goethe, Johann Wolfgang von, *Poems of the West and the East: West-Eastern Divan*, trans. John Whaley (Berne: Peter Lang, 1998).

Goethe, Johann Wolfgang von, *Wilhelm Meister's Apprenticeship*, *Wilhem Meister's Travels*, trans. Thomas Carlyle (Edinburgh: Oliver and Boyd, 1824 and 1827).

Gould, Stephen Jay *The Structure of Evolutionary Theory* (Harvard: Harvard University Press, 2002).

Jean Paul, *Träume* ('Dreams') (Bern: Gachnang & Springer 2004); also in Tieck, Ludwig, 'The Fair-Haired Eckbert', in Thomas Carlyle, *Translations from the German. Musaeus, Tieck, Richter* [1827] (London: Chapman and Hall, 1863).

Kant, Immanuel, Akademie Ausgabe, vol. 4 (Berlin: de Gruyter, 1968).

Krell, David Farrell, *The Tragic Absolute. German Idealism and the Languishing of God* (Bloomington: Indiana University Press, 2005).

Lacoue-Labarthe, Philippe and Nancy Jean-Luc. *The Literary Absolute*, trans. Philip Barnard and Cheryl (Albany: State University of New York Press, 1988).

Landor, Walter Savage, *Selections From The Imaginary Conversations* (London: Kessinger, 2006).

Lauster, Martina, 'Nietzsche's Übermensch und Baudelaires Giganten: Ein Motivischer und Struktureller Vergleich', in *Nietzsche Studien. Internationales Jahrbuch für die Nietzsche Forschung*, vol. 24, 1995, pp. 184-203.

Martin, Nicholas (ed.), *Nietzsche and the German Tradition* (Bern: Lang, 2003).

Martin, Nicholas, *Nietzsche and Schiller. Untimely Aesthetics* (Oxford: Clarendon, 1996).

Marx, Karl, *Capital. A Critical Analysis of Capitalist Production*, vol. 1 (London: Lawrence and Wishart, 1974).

Marx, Karl and Friedrich Engels, *German Ideology*, trans. Christopher John Arthur (New York: International Books, 1970).

Nordau, Max. *Entartung* (Degeneracy) (Berlin: Duncker, 1892).

Pater, Walter, *Studies in the History of The Renaissance* (Oxford: World's Classics, 1998), cf. particularly the 'Conclusion'.

Plato, *The Republic* trans. Robin Waterfield (Oxford: Oxford University Press, 2008).

Plato, *The Symposium* trans. Alexander Nehemas and Paul Woodruff (Indiana: Hackett, 1989).

Said, Edward, *Orientalism* (London: Vintage, 1979).

Schopenhauer, Arthur *World of Will and Representation*, 2 vols, trans. E. F. J. Payne (New York: Dover, 1969).

Tieck, Ludwig, 'The Fair-Haired Eckbert', in Thomas Carlyle, *Translations from the German. Musaeus, Tieck, Richter* [1827] (London: Chapman and Hall, 1863), pp. 145-59.

Wagner, Richard, *Gesammelte Schriften und Dichtungen*, 10 vols (Leipzig: Fritzsch, 1872-83); *Prose Works*, and trans. W. A. Ellis (London: Kegan Paul, 1899).

Wehler, Hans-Ulrich, *The German Empire 1871-1918* (Oxford: Providence/Berg, 1993), particularly sections I and II.

William, Simon, *Wagner and the Romantic Hero* (Cambridge: Cambridge University Press, 2004).

Zarathustra and Nietzsche's New Style

Deleuze, Gilles *Nietzsche and Philosophy* (New York: Columbia University Press, 1983).

Gooding-Williams, Robert, *Nietzsche's Dionysian Modernism* (Stanford: Stanford University Press, 2001).

Kofmann, Sarah, *Nietzsche and Metaphor*, trans. Duncan Large (London: Athlone Press, 1993).

Moore, Gregory, *Nietzsche, Biology and Metaphor* (Cambridge: Cambridge University Press, 2002).

Nehamas, Arthur, *Nietzsche: Life as Literature* (Harvard: Harvard University Press, 1985).

Schlaffer, Heinz, *Das entfesselte Wort. Nietzsche's Stil und seine Folgen* (Munich: Hanser, 2007).

Weineck, Silke-Maria, *The Abyss Above. Philosophy and Poetic Madness in Plato, Hölderlin, and Nietzsche* (New York: State University of New York Press, 2002).

Allegory

Benjamin, Walter, *The Origin of German Tragic Drama*, trans. John Osborne (London: Verso, 2009).

Hollander, Robert, 'Allegory', in Dante, *The Inferno* (New York: Anchor, 2000), pp. xxix-xxxiii.

Satire

Clark, Frazer S., Zeitgeist *and* Zerrbild - *Word Image and Idea in German Satire 1800-1848* (New York: Lang, 2006).

Ridley, Hugh, 'Nietzsche and Wienberg. A Consideration of Parallels between Nietzsche and the Young Germans', in *Nietzsche Studien* 9 (1980), pp. 338–55.

Nietzsche, Music and Wagner

Babich, Babette, E. *Words in Blood, Like Flowers. Philosophy and Poetry, Music and Eros, in Hölderlin, Nietzsche and Heidegger* (Albany: State University of New York Press, 2006).

Brinkmann, Reinhold *Schumann und Eichendorff* (Munich: Text und Kritik, 1997).

Hollinrake, Roger, *Nietzsche, Wagner and the Philosophy of Pessimism* (London: Allen and Unwin, 1982).

Lièbert, Georges, *Nietzsche and Music* (Chicago:University of Chicago Press, 2004).

Mann, Thomas, *Doctor Faustus: The Life of the German Composer Adrian Leverkuhn, as Told by a Friend*, (New York: Modern Library, 1966).

McGee, Bryan, *The Tristan Chord: Wagner and Philosophy* (New York: Holt, 2000).

Parkes, Graham, 'The Symphonic Structure of "Thus Spoke Zarathustra", in Luchte (2008).

Rosen, Charles, *The Classical Style. Haydn, Mozart, Beethoven* (London: Faber and Faber, 1997), p. 348.

Schmidt, James, 'Mephistopheles in Hollywood', in *Cambridge Companion to Adorno* (Cambridge: Cambridge University Press, 2004).

Schofield, Paul, *The Redeemer Reborn*-Parsifal *as the Fifth Opera of Wagner's* Ring (New York: Amadeus Press, 2007).

Wagner, Richard, *Gesammelte Schriften und Dichtungen*, 10 vols, (Leipzig: Fritzsch, 1872-83); *Prose Works*, ed. and trans. W. A. Ellis (London: Kegan Paul, 1899).

Nietzsche, Greek and Asian Cultures, Tragedy and Mythology

Deleuze, Gilles, *Nietzsche and Philosophy*, trans. Hugh Tomlinson (London: Continuum, 2006).

Derrida, Jacques 'White Mythology', in *Margins of Philosophy*, trans. Alan Bass, (New York: Harvester, 1982).

Heidegger, Martin. *Nietzsche*, 2 vols, trans. David Farrell Krell, (San Francisco: Harper & Row, 1991).

Long, A. A. and D. N. Sedley, *The Hellenistic Philosophers*, vol. 1 (Cambridge: Cambridge University Press 1997), pp. 275-80.

Lutacz, Joachim, '"Fruchtbares Ärgernis": Nietzsche's "Geburt der Tragödie" und die gräzistische Tragödienforschung', in David Marc Hoffmann (ed.), *Nietzsche und die Schweiz* (Zürich: Strauhof, 1994).

Mistry, Freny, *Nietzsche and Buddhism, Prolegomenon to a Comparative Study* (Berlin: deGruyter, 1981).

Morrison, Robert G., *Nietzsche and Buddhism, A Study in Nihilism and Ironic Affinities* (Oxford: Oxford University Press, 1999.)

Sallis, John, *Crossings: Nietzsche and the Space of Tragedy* (Chicago: University of Chicago Press, 1991).

Santaniellol, Weaver (ed.), *Nietzsche and the Gods* (Albany: State University of New York Press, 2001), pp. 87-136.

Schelling, Friedrich Wilhelm Joseph, *Historical-Critical Introduction to the Philosophy of Mythology*, trans. Mason Richey and Marcus Zisselsberger (Albany: State University of New York Press, 2008).

Schmidt, Denis, *On Germans and Other Greeks: Tragedy and Ethical Life* (Bloomington: Indiana University Press, 2001).

Sheppard, Darren, *Plato's* Republic (Edinburgh: Edinburgh University Press, 2009).

Weineck, Silke-Maria, *The Abyss Above. Philosophy and Poetic Madness in Plato, Hölderlin, and Nietzsche* (New York: State University of New York Press, 2002).

Wilkerson, Dale, *Nietzsche and the Greeks* (London: Continuum, 2006).

Williamson, George S., *The Longing for Myth in Germany. Religion and Aesthetic Culture from Romanticism to Nietzsche* (Chicago: Chicago University Press, 2004).

Young, Julian, *Nietzsche's Philosophy of Art* (Cambridge: Cambridge University Press, 1992).

Nietzsche and Science

Babich, Babette E. *Nietzsche's Philosophy of Science. Reflecting Science on the Ground of Art and Life* (Albany: State University of New York Press, 1994).

Babich, Babette E. and Robert S. Cohen (eds.), *Nietzsche, Epistemology, and Philosophy of Science. Nietzsche and the Sciences*, 2 vols (Boston: Kluwer, 1999).

Burnham, Douglas, 'Time as Chaos: Nietzsche and Mann in the Mountains', in Dente et al., *Proteus: The Language of Metamorphosis* (Aldershot: Ashgate, 2005).

Darwin, Charles *On the Origin of Species* [1859] (London: Penguin Classics, 2009).

Lange, Friedrich Albert, *Geschichte des Materialismus und Kritik seiner Bedeutung in der Gegenwart* ('History of Materialism and Critique of its Significance for the Present') (Iserlohn: Baedeker, 1866).

Moore, Gregory, *Nietzsche, Biology and Metaphor* (Cambridge: Cambridge University Press, 2002).

Moore, Gregory et al. (eds), *Nietzsche and Science* (Aldershot: Ashgate, 2004), particularly Thomas H. Bobjer, 'Nietzsche's Reading and Knowledge of Natural Science: An Overview', pp. 21-50.

Richardson, John, *Nietzsche's New Darwinism* (Oxford: Oxford University Press, 2004).

Salaquarda, Jörg, 'Nietzsche e Lange', in *La 'Biblioteca Ideale' di Nietzsche*, ed. Giuliano Campioni and Aldo Venturelli (Napoli: Guida Editori, 1992), pp. 19-34.

Sloterdijk, Peter, *Thinkers on Stage: Nietzsche's Materialism* (Minnesota: University of Minnesota Press, 1989).

The Swiss Nietzsche

Bloch, Peter André, et al. (eds), *Friedrich Nietzsche Handschriften, Erstausgaben und Widmungsexemplare. Die Sammlung Rosenthal-Levy im Nietzsche-Haus in Sils Maria* (Basel: Schwabe, 2009).

Bollinger, Andrea and Franziska Trenkle, *Nietzsche in Basel* (Basel: Schwabe, 2000).

Hoffmann, David Marc (ed.), *Nietzsche und die Schweiz* (Zürich: Strauhof, 1994).

Two Swiss writers of great influence on Nietzsche were Bachofen and Burckhardt:

Bachofen, Johann Jacob, *Mutterrecht (Mother Right): A Study of the Religious and Juridical Aspects of Gyneocracy in the Ancient World* [1861], new translation in 5 vols (New York: Edwin Mellen Press, 2009).

Alfred Bäumler, *Bachofen und Nietzsche* (Zürich: Verlag der Neuen Schweizer Rundschau, 1929).

Burckhardt, Jacob, *The Civilisation of Renaissance in Italy* trans. S. G. C. Middlemore (London: Penguin Classics, 1990).

On Nietzsche and Bachofen, cf. most recently:

Frances Nesbitt Oppel, *Nietzsche on Gender, Beyond Man and Woman* (Charlottesville: University of Virginia Press, 2005).

Nietzsche and His Impact on German Culture and Politics

Ansell-Pearson, Keith, *An Introduction to Nietzsche as Political Thinker* (Cambridge: Cambridge University Press, 1994).

Aschheim, Stephen E., *The Nietzsche Legacy in Germany 1890-1990* (Berkeley: University of California Press, 1994).

Chamberlain Houston, Stewart, *The Foundations of the 19th Century*, trans. John Lees (New York: Adamant Media Corporation, 2003).

Furness, Raymond, *Zarathustra's Children: A Study of a Lost Generation of German Writers* (Rochester: Camden House, 2000).

Gründer, Karlfried, *The Quarrel about the Birth of Tragedy.* (Der Streit um Nietzsches *Geburt der Tragödie*, [contributors are Erwin Rhode, Ulrich von Wilamowitz-Moellendorff and Richard Wagner]) (Hildesheim: Olms, 1989).

Hesse, Hermann, 'Zarathustra's Return. A Word to German Youth', in *If the War Goes On. Reflections on War and Politics*, trans. Ralph Mannheim (New York: Farrar, Straus and Giroux, 1971).

Hinton, Thomas R., *Nietzsche in German Politics and Society 1890-1918* (Manchester University Press, 1983).

Spengler, Oswald, *The Decline of the West*, trans. Charles Francis Atkinson, abridged (Oxford: Oxford University Press, 1991).

Nietzsche's Aesthetic Modernity

Benjamin, Walter, *The Origin of German Tragic Drama*, trans. John Osborne (London: Verso, 2009).

Ellison, David R., *Ethics and Aesthetics in Modernist Literature* (Cambridge: Cambridge University Press, 2001).

Gooding-Williams, Robert, *Nietzsche's Dionysian Modernism* (Stanford: Stanford University Press, 2001).

Jovanovski, Thomas, *Aesthetic Transformations. Taking Nietzsche at his Word* (New York: Lang, 2008).

Young, Julian, *Nietzsche's Philosophy of Art* (Cambridge: Cambridge University Press, 1992).

Twentieth-Century Psychology and Cultural Anthropology

Adorno, Theodor Wiesengrund and Max Horkheimer, *Dialectic of Enlightenment* [1947], (San Francisco: Stanford University Press, 2002).

Assoun, Paul-Laurent, *Freud and Nietzsche* (London: Continuum, 2006).

Bishop, Paul, 'Jung and Nietzsche', in *Jung in Contexts. A Reader* (London: Routledge, 1999).

Costello, Stephen J., *The Pale Criminal. Psychoanalytical Perspectives* (London: Karnac, 2002).

Deleuze, Gilles and Félix Guattari, *Anti-Oedipus. Capitalism and Schizophrenia*, trans. Robert Hurley, Mark Seem, and Helen R. Lane (London: Continuum, 2004).

Freud, Sigmund, 'Beyond the Pleasure Principle' [1920], Standard Edition, vol. 18 (London: Hogarth, 1955).

Freud, Sigmund, 'Civilisation and Its Discontents' [1927-31] Standard Edition, vol. 21 (London: Hogarth, 1961).

Freud, Sigmund, 'The Ego and the Id' plus 'The Ego and the Super Ego' [1923], Standard Edition, vol. 19, (London: Hogarth, 1961).

Freud, Sigmund, *The Interpretation of Dreams* [1900-01], Standard Edition, vols 4 and 5 (London: Hogarth, 1975).

Jung, Carl Gustav, *Seminar on* Zarathustra (abridged and ed. L. Jarret) (Princeton: Princeton University Press, 1988).

Nebitt Oppel, Frances, *Nietzsche on Gender* (Charlottesville: University of Virginia Press, 2005).

Reich, Wilhelm, *The Function of Orgasm, Part I: The Discovery of the Orgone* (New York: Farrar, Straus and Giroux, 1973).

Strong, Tracy B., *Nietzsche and the Politics of Transfiguration* (Chicago: University of Illinois Press, 2000).

Aesthetics of Modernism

Artaud, Antonin, *The Theatre and its Double* (London: Calder, 1970).

Brecht, Bertolt, *Caucasian Chalk Circle*, trans. Ray Speakman (Oxford: Heinemann, 1994).

Burnham, Douglas and Melanie Ebdon, 'Philosophy and Literature', in *The Continuum Companion to Continental Philosophy*, ed. John Mullarkey and Beth Lord (London: Continuum, 2009).

Eliot, T. S., *The Waste Land and Other Writings* (New York: Modern Library, 2002).

Fischer-Lichte, Erika et al. (eds), 'The Own and the Foreign Orient. Schlegel, Nietzsche, Artaud, Brecht. Notes on the Process of a Reception', in *The Dramatic Touch of Difference* (Tubingen: Narr, 1990).

Frazer, James, *The Golden Bough*, 15 vols (Basingstoke: Palgrave Macmillan, 2005). Frazer himself edited an abridged one-volume version in 1922; this edition is currently available as a paperback edition (London: Penguin, 1996).

Gordon, Paul, *Tragedy after Nietzsche, Rapturous Superabundance* (Chicago: University of Illinois Press, 2000).

Lindberg, Kathryn, *Reading Pound, Reading Nietzsche. Modernism after Nietzsche* (Oxford: Oxford University Press, 1987).

McGrath, William J. *Dionysian Art and Populist Politics in Austria* (New Haven: Yale University Press, 1974), where Gustav Mahler's early contacts with Nietzsche are explored.

Rider, Jacques, *Nietzsche en France* (Paris: Presses Universitaires de France, 1999).

Styan, T. John L. *Modern Drama in Theory and Practice*; see particularly vol 2: *Symbolism, Surrealism and the Absurd* (Cambridge: Cambridge University Press, 1983).

Surette, Leon, *The Birth of Modernism. Pound, Eliot, Yeats, and the Occult* (Montreal: McGill-Queens University Press, 1994).

Nietzsche's Impact on Twentieth-Century Philosophy and Theory

Adorno, Theodor Wiesengrund, *Aesthetic Theory* (London: Routledge, 1984).

de Man, Paul, *Allegories of Reading* (Yale: Yale University Press, 1979).

Deleuze, Gilles, *Essays Critical and Clinical.* Trans. Michael A. Greco. (University of Minnesota Press, 1997).

Deleuze, Gilles, *Nietzsche and Philosophy* trans. Hugh Tomlinson (London: Continuum, 2006).

Derrida, Jacques, *Spurs: Nietzsche's Styles,* trans. Barbara Harlow (Chicago: Chicago University Press, 1991).

Ellison, David R., *Ethics and Aesthetics in Modernist Literature* (Cambridge: Cambridge University Press, 2001).

Foucault, Michel, 'Nietzsche, Genealogy, History', in *The Foucault Reader*, ed. Paul Rabinow (London: Penguin, 1991), pp. 76-100.

Foucault, Michel, *The Order of Things, An Archaeology of the Human Sciences* (London: Routledge, 2002).

Foucault, Michel, 'The Subject and Power', in *Essential Works of Foucault 1954-1984*, vol. 3 (London: Penguin, 2000), pp. 326-48.

Heidegger, Martin, *The Basic Problems of Phenomenology*. Trans. Albert Hofstadter (Bloomington: Indiana University Press, 1988).

Heidegger, Martin, *Nietzsche*, 2 vols, trans. David Farrell Krell (London: HarperCollins, 1991).

Jovanovski, Thomas, *Aesthetic Transformations. Taking Nietzsche at His Word* (New York: Lang, 2008).

Joyce, James, *Stephen Hero*; *Portrait of the Artist as a Young Man* (London: Faber, 1978), pp. 188-9.

Marcuse, *Eros and Civilisation* (Boston: Beacon, 1955), cf. especially chapter 7: 'The Aesthetic Dimension'.

Klossowski, Pierre, *Nietzsche and the Vicious Circle* (1969), trans. Daniel W. Smith (London, Athlone, 2000).

Koelb, Clayton (ed.), *Nietzsche as Postmodernist. Essays Pro and Contra* (New York: State University Press, 1990).

Pestalozzi, Karl, 'Nietzsche "An hohen Bergen"', in *Die Entstehung des Lyrischen Ich. Sudien zum Motiv der Erhebung in der Lyrik* (Berlin, de Gruyter, 1970), pp. 198-246.

Pestalozzi, Karl and Wolfram Groddeck ,'"Übermensch" und "ewige Wiederkunft". Zur Poetologie von Nietzsches *Also sprach Zarathustra*', in Monika Hofmann-Riedinger und Urs Thurnherr (eds), *Anerkennung. Eine philosophische Propädeutik. Festschrift für Annemarie Pieper* (Freiburg: Alber, 2001), pp. 200–12.

Tigges, Wim, *Moments of Moment - Aspects of the Literary Epiphany* (Amsterdam: Rodopi, 1999).

Vattimo, Gianni, *Dialogue with Nietzsche*, trans. William McCuaig (New York: Columbia University Press, 2008).

Wolin, Richard, *Walter Benjamin. An Aesthetic of Redemption* (Berkeley: University of California Press, 1994).

Index